Centre for Educational Research and Innovation (CERI)

ENVIRONMENTAL EDUCATION AT UNIVERSITY LEVEL:

TRENDS AND DATA

*Part of this report is based on the results
of a Workshop on Environmental Education at University level,
which was organised in TOURS (France)
from 4th to 8th April, 1971
by CERI in collaboration with
the Centre d'Études Supérieures de l'Aménagement
of the University of TOURS
and the French Authorities.*

ORGANISATION FOR ECONOMIC CO-OPERATION AND DEVELOPMENT

1973

001849

The Organisation for Economic Co-operation and Development (OECD), which was set up under a Convention signed in Paris on 14th December, 1960, provides that the OECD shall promote policies designed:

— to achieve the highest sustainable economic growth and employment and a rising standard of living in Member countries, while maintaining financial stability, and thus to contribute to the development of the world economy;
— to contribute to sound economic expansion in Member as well as non-member countries in the process of economic development;
— to contribute to the expansion of world trade on a multilateral, non-discriminatory basis in accordance with international obligations.

The Members of OECD are: Australia, Austria, Belgium, Canada, Denmark, Finland, France, the Federal Republic of Germany, Greece, Iceland, Ireland, Italy, Japan, Luxembourg, the Netherlands, New Zealand, Norway, Portugal, Spain, Sweden, Switzerland, Turkey, the United Kingdom and the United States.

The Centre for Educational Research and Innovation was created in June 1968 by the Council of the Organisation for Economic Co-operation and Development for an initial period of three years, with the help of grants from the Ford Foundation and the Royal Dutch Shell Group of Companies. In May 1971, the Council decided that the Centre should continue its work for a period of five years as from 1st January, 1972.

The main objectives of the Centre are as follows:

— to promote and support the development of research activities in education and undertake such research activities where appropriate;
— to promote and support pilot experiments with a view to introducing and testing innovations in the educational system;
— to promote the development of co-operation between Member countries in the field of educational research and innovation.

The Centre functions within the Organisation for Economic Co-operation and Development in accordance with the decisions of the Council of the Organisation, under the authority of the Secretary-General. It is supervised by a Governing Board composed of one national expert in its field of competence from each of the countries participating in its programme of work.

*
* *

PREFACE

There is an irreversible trend in all modern countries towards closer relationships between education and the community. This reflects the reality that education today affects many of the stages of the individual's life, and is a keystone of the capacity of societies to progress. What more natural, therefore, than that the emergence of the environment as a public issue of the highest importance should be reflected in the rapid and widespread emergence of environmental programmes in education ? Both the schools and the universities in the OECD countries are rapidly being drawn into the vortex of the environment as a social and political problem.

But the very spontaniety and rapidity of the response has brought its own problems. The young people who are attracted to the environment as a field to which to devote themselves, in terms of their education and careers, are gambling their future on society's ability to create the new educational and career structures that will enable them to express their will to defend and develop the natural and man-made environment.

The report which follows would suggest that there are a sufficient number of pioneers in the educational field to hold out the hope that young people can at least find an educational outlet. But this in itself will be frustrating - and even dangerous - if professional and career structures do not also adapt. Here the picture is less encouraging, for all the signs are that the only royal road into the environment is through the existing professions of engineer, scientist, architect, economist, and so on. We are thus faced with the question whether the rigidity of professional career structures will stifle the natural and constructive flow of young people into environmental studies - or whether on the contrary social problems such as the environment, the new knowledge and educational programmes needed to deal with them, and the relevant professions and careers can be brought into a new and more dynamic relationship.

3

In sum : will the universities be dynamic enough to create programmes which effectively bridge theory and practice, and thereby involve the professions ? Will the professions accept the reality that new social problems and the rapidly changing knowledge and techniques call for more open professional systems ?

The following Report opens up these questions and gives a picture of the educational movement now gaining momentum. A deeper probe by CERI is now proceeding and will be reported in 1974.

J.R. Gass
Director,
Centre for Educational
Research and Innovation

CONTENTS

Part One

Part Two

Appendices

ADDRESSES GIVEN AT THE CLOSING SESSION

OF THE WORKSHOP OF TOURS ON

ENVIRONMENTAL EDUCATION AT UNIVERSITY LEVEL

8th April, 1971

ADDRESS BY MR. ROBERT POUJADE, MINISTER DELEGATED TO THE PRIME MINISTER, IN CHARGE OF THE CONSERVATION OF NATURE AND ENVIRONMENT

Mr. Chairman, Ladies and Gentlemen,

To have been invited to address you at the close of your Seminar is a somewhat frightening honour. That it is an honour is unquestionable since the quality of the work that Professors Labeyrie and Weidner have just summarised is conclusive proof, if such were needed, of the competence and vision of the meeting I am privileged to attend today. But it is a frightening one in that, following in the steps of your Rapporteurs, it is I who must draw the conclusions of your meeting, although there must be many who are better qualified to do this. Yet I decided to accept your invitation, first because it came from an organisation, the OECD, whose careful and excellent work on the environment had already attracted my attention. Furthermore, there were good reasons, as you will agree, for the topic of this meeting to appeal to a Minister of the Environment who, as you earlier pointed out, has devoted several years of his life to education - not, it is true, to environmental education, but were we not told a moment ago that "in omnibus omnia" and that education today ought to be pluridisciplinary? Another reason for coming, if I may say so in front of my friend Royer without making him blush, is that Tours is a city in which university and local authority alike are concerned about the environment. It is a city where both the seeds of ideas are sown and trees are planted.

I have listened most attentively to the recommendations addressed to governments, and hence to me, and I have noted them very carefully. I realise that this is not a reassuring thing to say, since what people usually mean by it is that they hope to hear nothing further about the subject and certainly have no intention of mentioning it to anyone. I can however assure you to the contrary; I fully intend to raise these matters with

11

my colleagues, particularly with my opposite number at the
Ministry of Education.

I have been highly impressed by each of these recommendations and if I fail to revert to them later in detail it is because
I believe they require thorough study by our Governments.

Instead of drawing conclusions, which would certainly be
presumptuous on my part, perhaps I may be allowed to offer a
few thoughts prompted by the educational questions you have
been discussing in this Seminar. I should like to take a perhaps
broader and less technical approach, if only to avoid intruding
on the preserves of my colleague, the Minister of Education,
and attempt to see how citizens can be trained to acquire an
awareness of environmental matters. Three aspects are invol -
ved : arousing public opinion, training specialists, and training
generalists or co-ordinators. On the first point, that of making
our citizens aware of the problems, we are all agreed of course,
that information on the protection of nature and the environment
must be widely disseminated. This strikes me as all the more
necessary because these problems are very much in the news ;
but the mere fact that a problem happens to be the fashion does
not mean that it is properly understood. I would say that the
opposite is often true. This means that, while a great many people
are discussing the problem, a great many people are discussing
it wrongly. Furthermore, those who know nothing about it are
the most garrulous. This is a fact of everyday observation, but
it has become especially obvious in recent months.

The objective, I believe, is clear to us all ; to quote the
President of the Republic, it is to inculcate " a kind of environmental morality requiring everyone to obey a few elementary
rules", and in the kind of world we live in you will agree that
this would be no small achievement. In providing information,
it seems to me that first priority should be given to the young.
Reading, films, exercises in observation should be used from
the earliest years at school to acquaint the child with ecology.
I must acknowledge that primary teachers, especially in France,
have long since taken steps on their own in this direction, and
I have already had occasion to commend them for it. The men
and women who teach in our primary schools have certainly
accomplished a great deal in driving home the bare yet essential
principles of environmental science to small children, often
through their own personal efforts.

In France several steps in this direction have been taken
under the "100 measures" adopted by the Government a few
months ago. The holding of "sea lessons" and "green lessons"

to enable children to learn about the marine and rural environment other than for recreational purposes is currently being considered. In the same context it has been decided to set up nature-study centres, relying chiefly on the regional natural parks and in co-operation with open-air museums that have already been created. In these the great problems of nature can be presented to young people in graphic and constructive terms. The first of such centres is now being set up in Aquitaine.

Lastly, there are plans for designing and distributing aids such as manuals, posters, films and slides for teachers in primary schools, and a series of educational charts on the concept of ecological balance designed by the Museum of Natural History and the Ministry of Agriculture is in the course of production.
There is, of course, more to be done, and the papers read at this Seminar contain suggestions that deserve careful study, especially Professor Mislin's idea of educational paths.

What can be expected from these activities? First, a number of good habits. While people are apt to smile at the French public being asked not to leave litter on the beaches or in the woods. they forget that this is a real problem, both in our own country and elsewhere. Even if children were to hesitate before dropping the plastic wrapping from their sandwiches, it would be a considerable improvement. In general terms, I believe it is a good thing to teach youth what can serve the adult. If natural history were conceived as some dry string of words, it would have disappeared from the curriculum for good; if general geography is taught at secondary level as a mass of unrelated detail, the child will remember nothing. Taught properly, however, the natural sciences and geography can serve as an introduction to the basic disciplines that bear on the protection of nature and the environment, and in particular to ecology, with its concern for the relationships and resources essential to life. If this purpose is to be met, however, these subjects must be related among themselves. As has been rightly pointed out, the biologist or the natural scientist cannot be allowed to disregard what the geographer does, nor should the geographer to be unaware of some of the life sciences. To me this seems a crucial point; I fail to see how ecology can be taught without bringing in other specialisms. I also believe that ecological training of this kind has even more to be said for it because, at a time when idleness is apt to lead to agressiveness and ignorance to rebellion, learning to respect life and the conditions of life might help young people to learn about such truly

13

European values as an understanding of liberty and the dignity of man. I raise this because there was some mention just now of education in civics. It also seems reasonable to expect that an early introduction to these complex phenomena, which some prophets of doom are fond of painting in an apocalyptic light, will promote the broad approach that interdisciplinarity, an essential component of higher education, requires.

Before tackling the question of university-level training, it seems to me desirable to define the problem properly. As Professor Labeyrie has said, man is now in a position to endanger the biosphere's renewal cycle through the remote and unforeseen side-effects of some of the things he has done as "home faber". This means that conventional forms of training must be broadened by, for example, including knowledge of these side-effects in the courses for engineers.

Earlier today the idea of environmental engineering was raised, with the comment that men more specifically oriented towards the environmental disciplines were needed. Two days ago I had occasion to make this very point to some French agriculturists, but forestry specialists and mining engineers also will increasingly be required to be ecologists, just as town planners will be.

There was a reference during today's discussion to the facilities made available to medicine. It is certainly true that man is highly reluctant to accept personal disaster while, unfortunately, putting up more easily with disasters affecting the whole race. Perhaps he knows less about them. If concern for our collective destiny were as deeply felt as concern about personal destiny, environmental education might already be more widespread. You have been quite right, in my view, to urge for a change in the training conventionally given to agronomists, oceanographers, hydrologists, and the like, so that it can stress those ecological concepts from which an understanding of the biosphere as a functional unit can be derived. This is clearly the crucial consideration. Towards this end, experiments under way in various French universities are of the greatest value and I may remind you that decisions have been taken, again within the framework of our "100 measures", to go on promoting the disciplines used in town and country planning and for environmental work, and to provide for complementary teaching in the grandes ecoles. I should say that we are still at the planning stage in all this but I hope to see some concrete progress before long. You all know, however, that a working party has been convened under the chairmanship of Mr. Viot - Professor at the Institut des Sciences Politiques

14

comprising teachers who are carrying out pratical experiments of exceptional interest, an event I am happy to report in the presence of Professor Labeyrie and those who will be concerned in it. I shall be receiving an interim report from this working party in June. Particular importance is being attached to interdisciplinarity, for as you have quite rightly re-emphasized, it is dangerous for research to be egocentric. I was saying just a moment ago how paradoxical egocentricity is in ecological matters; such ecologists may be said to resemble those queer animals found in narrow bogs they cannot get out of.

The working party under Mr. Viot is also dealing with training for the environmental professions and I sense that their work on this will give us a clearer view of the problem. The intention is that such training should be designed to make certain types of graduate aware of the need to act in the light of ecological factors, or interrelationship phenomena. This is particularly important in the economic sphere, where the recycling of natural resources is now a criterion for action. You will be aware of how much this is necessary in the case of water, for example. A point raised here today was how these courses should be organised. It is difficult to comment on this, especially in view of the fairly significant differences in the way universities are structured. Perhaps I might offer a warning against the unconsidered proliferation of courses in a difficult subject. I believe that we must reinforce whatever is sound and establish nothing of a shaky nature - nothing could be worse than to allow premature, clumsy or ill-considered moves to prejudice the steps that are essential, since the survival of man and of civilization is here at stake. Environmental studies must be pressed home where they belong. It is impossible to imagine an agronomist who lacks a thorough knowledge of environmental problems, and I would say that a civil engineer without such knowledge is quite as unthinkable. Unfortunately, as you will realise, there is a gap between what should be and what actually exists, since there are still civil engineers whose training in environmental disciplines is admittedly slender. Such a state of affairs can no longer be tolerated or even contemplated.

Finally, it is advisable that the work of specialists trained in the different disciplines should be combined. This raises the question of how to train generalists or co-ordinators. It is clear that the various techniques must be made to serve an overall policy for the protection of nature and the environment. The campaign against damage to nature should be led by individuals who have received a training that enables them to take

15

account of conflicting interests. A man whose environmental training has been superficial or circumscribed may cause irreparable havoc in an area with which he is unfamiliar. In the same way, we have found that, when environmental considerations were ignored in the interests of productivity, or greater quantity, the quality of life and even productivity itself has been endangered, as in the consolidation of small agricultural holdings.

Some arbitration is needed between the industrialist, rightly concerned with profitability and production costs (how could he be otherwise?) and the biologist or geographer whose concern is to preserve the natural environment. I cannot suddenly close down the paper industry in France, if I may take that example, since you all need paper, gentlemen, if only to write papers about the environment. What one can do is to impose a minimum of discipline, and I would go so far as to say a maximum, upon the environmentalists and paper manufacturers. This is where arbitration comes in. It is a question of defining what is possible or practicable. This task seems to me to belong by definition to the State or to public authorities whether national, regional or local. These have a new task; namely to redefine the public interest in a complex sphere. What needs to be done in practice is to enable the State's body of civil servants to complete their training by extending it into the ecological disciplines.

Ladies and Gentlemen, I have spoken at great length without really saying very much. I should like to conclude, since time is short, by remarking that the environment is a hazy matter only for those who fail to realise how much knowledge, how many disciplines and what careful research its study requires. If we are to avoid a great many miscalculations and mistakes, we must train increasing numbers of specialists and disseminate information about the environment in a form that ordinary people can understand. The environment is neither a fashion nor a passing fad; it is only such in the eyes of those who pay little heed to the processes of growth in industrial societies. Nor should the environment be an object of fear or panic. Its protection demands both ethical standards and what Pascal called "the science of external things" which "cannot console us for our ethical ignorance in times of affliction, but ignorance of the science of external things sometimes leads us to a time of affliction". In short, I suggest quite simply that there are few spheres in which conscience is so greatly in need of enlightenment from science.

ADDRESS BY MR. GERALD ELDIN
DEPUTY SECRETARY-GENERAL OF OECD

Mr. Minister, Mr. Chairman, Ladies and Gentlemen :

I am happy, Mr. Minister, to welcome you on behalf of
Mr. van Lennep , Secretary-General of OECD, to this
Workshop on Environmental Education which we have organised
with the help of the Centre d'Etudes Supérieures d'Aménagement,
University of Tours, and which leading French and foreign
specialists are attending.

We are greatly honoured that you should be with us today,
and deeply appreciate this mark of your interest. May I add,
Mr. Minister, that we are not altogether surprised, since,
you are here in a dual capacity - as the government authority
responsible for the protection of nature and the environment
and as an academic unceasingly concerned with educational
problems.

It so happens that environmental problems are also an
OECD concern, not only from this twofold aspect but for several other reasons also. Through its Environment Committee
the Organisation is engaged in preparing a programme of work
which, while it places major emphasis on the economic side,
also deals with the scientific, administrative and legal aspects
of environmental policy.

We are quite aware that, unless more knowledge is gained
of the scientific and ecological groundwork and long-term
forecasts are attempted, government action in this field might
well succeed in only scratching the surface and perhaps yield
no results at all. But as an Organisation whose concern is
economic co-operation between governments we are perhaps
more responsive than others to the economic and financial
implications of environmental policies at national and international level. For these reasons the aim we hope to achieve
through our work is to propose a number of positive and constructive solutions to OECD Member governments. These are
to be based on an interdisciplinary, integrated analysis of environmental problems regarded as a unit, while the wide variety

of goals will be taken into account, including, of course, improvement of the environment, but also such others as industrial growth, full employment and the development of international trade. None of these objectives have become any less important, and you yourself, Mr. Minister, recently stated that they do not necessarily conflict with the first. We believe this socio-economic dimension to be a leading one, and if I may be allowed to make one wish regarding the outcome of this workshop, it is that in teaching the environmental disciplines such a dimension will not be forgotten.

In another branch of its activity, through its Centre for Educational Research and Innovation the OECD has gained some measure of reputation in the field of education. It was quite natural, if not inevitable, that CERI should become interested in environmental education as a typical instance requiring use of the interdisciplinary concept and where the need for training co-ordinating staff calls for new forms of teaching.

By making use of previous experiments conducted in various parts of the world to lay the foundations of environmental education (and that of Tours should be mentioned here), this workshop seems to me to promise much for the future. The public now realises the dangers that threaten the environment, and for this we must indeed be grateful. But it is no longer enough to sow the seeds of ideas ; we must take a longer-term view and teach people how to become the managers of nature and planners of space that the world needs. I congratulate the University of Tours for the timely and boldly innovative steps it has taken in this connection. The fact that Touraine, the garden of France, whose masterful management of the natural surroundings and harmonious architecture are a living illustration of the values we are trying to protect, should have been chosen as the site for these discussions seems not to be the result of pure chance but a symbolic act.

In thanking you, Mr. Minister, for having come this afternoon to share in our work and for thus demonstrating the value the French Government attaches to this meeting, may I also welcome the presence of the Ambassador Valéry, Head of the French Delegation to OECD, of Mr. Royer, Deputy Mayor of Tours, whom I must warmly thank, and may I greet all others who have contributed to the proceedings?

May I close, Mr. Chairman, Ladies and Gentlemen, by wishing you a most successful and productive working session and hoping that this will result in international co-operation in a new field.

ADDRESS BY AMBASSADOR FRANCOIS VALERY,
HEAD OF THE FRENCH PERMANENT DELEGATION
TO THE OECD

Mr. Minister, Mr. Chairman, Ladies and Gentlemen.

First, I should like to greet the participants in this Workshop, the Delegates from abroad, the governmental, administrative and university authorities, the Prefect, the Deputy-Mayor, Rector Antoine, all who are attending this meeting or have contributed to its organisation.

Secondly, I should like to say how pleased I am that Mr. Robert Poujade has kindly agreed to attend this closing session.

Mr. Poujade has the truly formidable responsibility of being the first "Minister of the Environment" to be appointed in France The creation of this Ministry and the fact that it has been entrusted to a politician of his calibre, a man known to be not lacking in dynamism, are evidence of the Government's intention to give the problem of the environment its proper place among the issues of major concern.

Not having followed the discussions at this workshop, I shall not touch upon their subject matter. But, following up Mr. G. Eldin's remarks, I think it will be more useful and certainly easier for me to stress the role of international cooperation and, in particular, that of OECD, as it is understood in France.

International cooperation must not and cannot be a substitute for national action, since the problem is first identified and requires decisions in specific national contexts. Such cooperation is, however, the essential complement to national measures. The fact that the problem in question, though not new, has created a new awareness, offers an opportunity which we must grasp and for once try to concert our actions before they create situations both nationally irreversible and internationally incompatible.

19

International cooperation develops in different contexts which may give rise to duplication in some cases but which is normal : there is the world context, because all countries are involved, irrespective of their political ideologies, social structures, or even level of development; there is the European context, of course, for how could a Europe aware of its geographical, historical and cultural identity and, moreover, in quest of unity, fail to make every endeavour to harmonise environment policies? And, furthermore, in so far as the Six are concerned, is this not to some extent a necessary course owing to the very existence of the Common Market ?

I shall enlarge somewhat upon the role of the OECD, because it is the sponsor of this workshop and its role is perhaps somewhat less well known.

The OECD groups together the industrialised countries with a market economy which, as pointed out by the President of the Republic during his recent visit to Headquarters of the Organisation, are at once similar as regards levels of living, industrial and technological potential, economic and political outlooks, and interdependent because they have followed the same road together for 25 years - despite differences and difficulties - at first in order to restore and then to maintain fundamental economic and monetary equilibrium.

There has been a twofold effect: first, as Europeans, Americans and Japanese, for better or for worse at the summit of industrial civilisation, with much to learn from each other, co-operation can save us time, effort and money ; secondly, the decisions that each individual country may be constrained to take cannot fail to affect all the others, hence the need for concertation.

It is therefore natural - as acknowledged by governments, including our own, in agreeing to grant the OECD a privileged role - that this Organisation, whose activities revolve around the concept of economic growth, should find it advisable to consider not only the quantitative aspect of growth but also its qualitative aspect.

These two aspects are fundamentally related, and any attempt to stress the contradiction between them would be to ignore reality. What the OECD is looking for is in fact the basis of a synthesis, by determining criteria to enable governments to take nationally justified decisions concerning resource allocation or legislation, but which do not lead to prejudicial distortions at international level.

20

It is precisely on account of and in accordance with its objectives that the OECD has been confronted with the problem of the environment, on the one hand, and that of educational innovation on the other, since both are linked to economic growth.

Education would seem to have a dual role in connection with the environment : first, to foster basic and applied research, train managerial staff and introduce environmental viewpoints into the teaching of various disciplines; secondly, to educate public opinion and channel its emotive reactions to the problem so as to prevent a negative response; for the choices will be so difficult and their evaluation so painful that nothing worthwhile will be accomplished without enlightened opinion among these various social groups.

I should like to venture one last suggestion ; taking our stand - like this workshop - at the meeting place between the educational and environmental fields, is it not possible to define a new culture which, while continuing to have reference to traditional values, would be oriented more towards the future : a kind of new alliance between nature which has made man, and man who gives thought and shape to nature?

ADDRESS BY MR JAMES R. GASS
DEPUTY DIRECTOR GENERAL OF SCIENTIFIC AFFAIRS, DIRECTOR OF THE CENTRE FOR EDUCATIONAL RESEARCH AND INNOVATION OF OECD

Mr. Minister, Mr. Chairman, Ladies and Gentlemen

I do not want to reiterate the votes of thanks expressed by everyone here, but I should like, as Director of the Centre for Educational Research and Innovation, to associate myself with them, and to mention particularly the valuable practical assitance afforded us by the French Government.

My colleagues who arranged this workshop have asked me to present the objectives at the end of it. This is a little like eating the hors d'oeuvre at the end of a meal. As a resident of France for some ten years now, I refuse to fall into such a trap!

From all I have heard I apprehend that we are looking for a new type of progress which, as first Mr. Eldin and then Mr. Valéry said, seeks to reconcile the quantitative and qualitative aspects of growth. This is easier said than done. I think we are all agreed that we cannot opt for blind uncontrolled economic and technical progress, which might be summed up in the formula : Gross National Products equals Gross National Pollution; but neither can we opt for a natural beauty that is at the same time unproductive. As usual, our problem is to compromise and to find the middle way between the two alternatives facing civilisation. Unfortunately, this choice is a very difficult one; firstly, because it is in our nature to be dependent on our environment - we have only to look at a living cell under the microscope to see how dependent it is on what surrounds it. Secondly, because when people reach a level at which their physical needs are adequately satisfied, they develop another powerful need, namely to be independent of that same environment. There you have our dilemma.

23

This dilemma is also encountered in education. On the one hand specialisation, which has been and doubtless will remain a powerful instrument of our technical progress, is the very basis of our educational system. This specialisation is blind to the consequences of the progress it generates. During the events of May 1968 there was an expression which seemed to me to reflect this idea; it was the term, coined, I think, by German students, of "Fachidiot" - a person who knows all the facts but has no idea how to deal with the problems. On the other hand, the separation of theory and practice, which goes right to the roots of our educational systems, creates a feeling of frustration, at least in some students.

There is no easy solution to these problems, but one thing seems to me an established certainty, and that is that the university, like all other institutions, cannot remain oblivious to this challenge. For it is, so to speak, the principal promoter and guardian of knowledge - that knowledge which is at the same time the genius of material progress and our "sorcerer's apprentice ". The university is therefore faced with the necessity to introduce changes and innovations which will relate the power of knowledge to the problems surrounding us.

I was anxious to be here today, Mr. Minister, because round this table are academics who are trying to do something. Universities of the environment are represented, as are also environmental departments or experiments in more traditional universities... I should like to emphasize that in all our countries this issue provokes action as well as thought, and those at this meeting have tried to exchange the results of such action.

Thus, this workshop agreed this morning on a number of recommendations. I shall not venture to present them to you, as this will be the duty of the participants, but I should just like to mention a number of issues that might perhaps provide the elements of a reply to the questions I have raised.

The first is that all countries have forms of pluridisciplinary higher education designed to give young people a certain training that will turn them into the elite of the nation. Conceptions differ in many countries. On the European continent a key subject is law, in the Anglo-Saxon countries - especially England - it is classics, and in America, social science. Why not a degree in environment which would have an equivalent value? That is one question I ask ...

Secondly, professional qualifications have always developed as nations progress ; they are not gifts either of nature or of

24

God; they have emerged at a particular moment in history. I might perhaps say - but I hesitate as I am not French - that the Napoleonic era is the source of a number of professions and "grandes écoles" that you see today. Why should these environmental problems not generate new qualifications? Why not environment engineers? For engineers have always been pluridisciplinary, in the sense that they studied a number of problems that could only be solved with the help of a number of disciplines.

I shall not venture to ask why there should not be a "grande école" for environment; that would perhaps be going too far. But the first question seems to be a reasonable one.

Thirdly, why should the university not undertake pilot exper-iments in environmental problems? Medicine has always been regarded as a discipline practised in a community - the medi-cal schools have their hospitals. Why should the other branches of knowledge not have experimental areas for practical appli-cations?

And fourthly, if there were such pilot experiments in the environmental field, why should students not participate in them? It seems to me that in this way we should have real educational innovations, namely a link-up between knowledge, learning, action and life, and we should at the same time manage to relate two separate aspects of our educational systems, research and teaching.

You see, Mr. Chairman, instead of offering guidelines and objectives, I have simply raised further problems.

FINAL RECOMMENDATIONS OF THE WORKSHOP

OF TOURS ON ENVIRONMENTAL EDUCATION

AT UNIVERSITY LEVEL

INTRODUCTION

Faced with the increasing and serious problems which pollution and deterioration of the quality of life pose to the survival of humanity, it has now become urgent for man to understand and improve his own environment and his role in it. The explosion of technology and the growth of industrialisation (coupled with the increasing number of people becoming concentrated in urban areas) are slowly and so far irreversibly transforming not only the biological but also the psychological and social conditions in which humanity is living and is to evolve. The consequences of this serious deterioration of the human and natural environment, both rural and urban, cannot yet be predicted. During recent years, the need for a thorough understanding of these problems has been growing ; but so far there habe been very few efforts to make knowledge available to students or to the public in this vital field of science.

During a workshop 4th to 8th April 1971, in Tours (France), delegates and experts from OECD countries analysed the serious need and urgency of establishing and developing new teaching programmes at university level in environmental science. The conclusions they reached include the following recommendations for universities, governments and international organisations.

RECOMMENDATIONS FOR UNIVERSITIES

Universities should undertake environmental education at all levels, and for all categories of people whether they are students or not.

Within their normal curricula and courses, all universities should highlight the relation and contribution of each discipline and profession to the urgent problems of the environment. Some students should be encouraged to specialise in this aspect of their discipline or profession.

A number of universities in each country should develop general courses in environmental education, such as a one-year ecological course that would attract students from a variety of backgrounds and interests.

One or more universities in each country should focus on man and his environment as their special discipline, perhaps in the short term through existing departments or faculties. Normally, however, this will require the creation of new institutions or organisational structures based on new conceptions of learning to meet these needs. In such cases, emphasis should be placed on a wide range of environmental problems and the contribution of transdisciplinary, interdisciplinary, disciplinary, and professional concepts and knowledge. Some students should be encouraged to concentrate on the ecological and cultural aspects of environmental quality throughout their university experience.

Environmental education should normally be based on the following four components :

- basic disciplines;
- integrating themes leading to interdisciplinarity;
- relevant problems;
- practical, real-life, local projects.

Such education will require contributions from existing subjects or disciplines and from people with a broader training

31

in environmental science. It will involve the establishment of dialogue and understanding between those specialised in the physical, chemical, biological, medical and technical aspects of environment, and those from the socio-economic, political and cultural aspects of environment. Interdisciplinary teams, sometimes with broadly trained co-ordinators, ecologists, and people trained in managerial sciences, must co-operate both in teaching and research. This also implies a continuing need for the training of people in the more specialised environmental disciplines, e.g. limnology, or soil science.

For problem-oriented learning, such as environmental education, universities need to broaden their pedagogical techniques. More emphasis must be placed on learning than on teaching. A close partnership, or colleagueship, should characterise the relation of professor and student. The over-reliance on the lecture method should give way progressively to substantial use of discussion, laboratory work, field work and observation, case studies, simulation models and participation in projects.

Since the problem-solving and community-action abilities of students should be enhanced by environmental education, students should be permitted and encouraged to take the initiative in their own education through independent study and in other ways. In this area, professors should assume the role of advisers rather than directors of study, and should be readily accessible to the students outside the classroom.

Environmental education should also be oriented towards the needs of local or regional communities. In this way a totally new concept of the university can arise, influencing and being influenced by the community in its teaching, project work, research, and the employment of its graduates. Accordingly universities should develop close working relations with regional and local governmental and non-governmental groups. Knowledge generated by the university may have implications for local and central government decisions and these decisions may in turn influence further development of university programmes.

The introduction of widespread environmental education is urgent. Emphasis should be placed on the training of school teachers, on providing courses for the general public as well as whole university populations and on refresher courses for the professions.

RECOMMENDATIONS FOR GOVERNMENTS

The recommendations of the workshop are of such scope and importance that they cannot be fully achieved without the co-operation of national governments and their dependent bodies. Therefore the workshop calls upon each government to support its recommendations, through action appropriate to itself, notably in facilitating regulations and allocating resources. Particular attention is drawn to the following points :

Environment education is not a single course or a single group of courses, nor is it a single speciality. In their environmental education policies, governments are urged to support me measures to train university teachers to meet the needs expressed in paragraphs 2, 3 and 4 of the Recommendations for Universities.

Manpower planning by governments should take into account the need for those with general environmental training and different kinds of environmental specialists with complementary abilities. For example, generalists would be able to perform an important role in smaller districts or communities that cannot support a team of specialists.

As a matter of urgency, the workshop recommends the training and retraining of teachers for all aspects of environmental education so as to ensure rapid development of appropriate courses at elementary, secondary, and adult education levels and the provision of information for all citizens.

Governments are requested to provide the resources to set up research and documentation centres, and to facilitate collaboration between universities in different countries with a view to tackling specific environmental problems that transcend national boundaries.

Environmental problems increase in significance in the developing countries as their social and economic conditions advance. Some of these problems might be avoided if the experience of developed countries could be properly incorporated in their national development plans. Governments are asked to facilitate research on the impact of development on the environment and make their information and facilities available to the emergent countries. Governments of OECD Member countries are also asked to take all necessary steps to assure that environmental impact considerations are included in the planning and implementation of all development projects for which they provide technical or financial assistance to the developing countries

RECOMMENDATIONS FOR INTERNATIONAL CO-OPERATION

Environmental studies in such universities are recent innovations and interest remains high in introducing them in other universities in a number of OECD Member countries. At this early formative stage, there is much to be gained by maintaining close communication between programmes in the various universities so that the experiences of each can be shared by all. It is recommended that CERI and other appropriate international bodies facilitate and co-ordinate the development of these relationships by :

a) convening from time to time meetings of persons chiefly responsible for implementing environmental education programmes in order that common problems may be discussed and experience exchanged. Such meetings might well be held in universities with strong programmes in this subject.

b) establishing, as necessary, small ad hoc working groups to assess the ways in which certain subjects and pedagogical methods can be best incorporated into programmes of environmental study;

c) establishing a small study and advisory group to keep under review the whole field of university environmental education;

d) maintaining and circulating (i) up-to-date information on these programmes of study, and (ii) the teaching materials employed, for the use of universities in Member countries;

e) making known to universities that have environmental studies programmes the needs for trained personnel as are identified through the deliberations of various groups under the aegis of OECD,

f) helping to encourage the mobility and exchange of teachers and students among universities in different countries with the purpose of promoting environmental education.

It is further recommended that the importance attached by this workshop to the development of environmental education at university level be brought to the attention of the United Nations

35

as it prepares for the 1972 Conference on Human Environment and of other interested international organisations.

CONCLUSION

The importance of an urgent expansion of education at all levels in environmental science has to be emphasized continuously. Without a thorough understanding of man and his environment, the biological, ecological, social and economic changes on earth cannot be controlled. A high quality of life for all is a major objective for humanity. A knowledge, through education, or man and his environment would make its own contribution to the attainment of this goal.

AN APPROACH TO THE TRAINING OF FUTURE ENVIRONMENTALISTS
By Pierre DUGUET,
CERI

I. GENERAL ORIENTATION OF WORK WITH REGARD TO CURRICULA AND TEACHING METHODS IN HIGHER EDUCATION

The Centre for Educational Research and Innovation began to investigate the interdisciplinarity concept and its application to education and research late in 1969. All innovations in curricula and teaching methods that are intimately associated with institutional structures and depend on the functions assigned to higher education should be capable of general application, and interdisciplinarity seemed to be the key to this.

Initial work on this subject culminated in a Seminar held in Nice in September 1970. The basic papers and an account of this seminar's proceedings were published in 1972 (1).

The objectives of the seminar were :

a) First,
- to clarify the concepts of pluridisciplinarity, interdisciplinarity and even transdisciplinarity ;

- to analyse the role of pluridisciplinarity and interdisciplinarity, and assess their respective places in a university meeting the needs of modern society;
- to take a close look at the cases for pluridisciplinary and interdisciplinary training:
- to study the means for achieving such objectives.

---

1) Interdisciplinarity : Problems of Teaching and Research in Universities, OECD/CERI, 1972, 321 pp.

b) Secondly,
- to encourage comparison between existing programmes in various Member countries and their wider adoption;
- to provide for the collection, classification and publication of data on interdisciplinarity;
- to define the character of subsequent meetings to study interdisciplinary topics,
- to assess the advantages and shortcomings of overall reforms or pilot projects;
- to suggest new university models;
- to produce reports on interdisciplinarity and on problems raised by the concept.

The findings of the seminar are reported in three parts in the CERI publication - one data-oriented, one thought-oriented and one action-oriented. Thus Part I, entitled "Opinions and Facts", presents information collected during an extensive survey of interdisciplinary activities in teaching and research in universities. Part II : "Terminology and Concepts" deals with disciplinarity and interdisciplinarity in relation to the growth of scientific knowledge and the requirements of industrial society. In Part III:"Problems and Solutions",a study is made of the institutional structures, curricula, teaching methods and teacher-training programmes that can best promote the practice of interdisciplinarity.

As a first step it was necessary to agree on terms and their meanings. For this purpose the Secretariat had proposed a terminology which was redefined at the seminar as follows :

Discipline   : A specific body of teachable knowledge with its own background of concepts, procedures and methods.

Multidisciplinary : Juxtaposition of various disciplines, sometimes with no apparent connection between them, e. g. music + mathematics + history.

Pluridisciplinary : Juxtaposition of disciplines assumed to be more or less related, e. g. in science, mathematics + physics; in the "classical humanities", French + Latin + Greek.

Interdisciplinary : An adjective describing the interaction between two or more different disciplines. This interaction may range from simple communication of ideas to the mutual integration or organising concepts, methodology,procedures,

epistemology, terminology, data and the organisation of research and education over a
fairly wide field. An interdisciplinary group
consists of people trained in different fields
of knowledge (disciplines), each with its own
concepts, methods, body of knowledge and
language, organised for a common attack on
a common problem, there being continuous
intercommunication between them.

Transdisciplinary :Establishing a common system of axioms for
a set of disciplines (e. g. anthropology considered as "the science of man and his accomplishments", following Linton's definition).

As can be seen, this terminology is already quite sophisti-
cated. The difference as between "pluridisciplinary" (a mere
juxtaposition of disciplines) and "interdisciplinary" (interaction among disciplines) will especially be noted. Moreover, to
avoid any possible misunderstanding, it should be explained
that these adjectives can apply either to curriculum content or
to institutional structures. A university is thus a multi-or pluridisciplinary institution if it is capable of offering a considerable range of subjects so long as the leading disciplines are at
least represented. But while a pluridisciplinary organisation in
a university is a prerequisite, it is not in itself sufficient for
developing interdisciplinary content. No such process can occur
simply by changing an institutional structure.

But why, indeed, should interdisciplinarity be introduced
into higher education? The answer to this lies in what it has to
offer to a number of the established functions of the university -
especially the following five.

General Education

a) The first requirement here is to enable students to find
out what their aptitudes are and to give them better guidance in deciding at an early stage on their future role
in society;

b) It is necessary that students should "learn how to learn"
before they begin to acquire some special type of knowledge. This is best done by mastering the techniques and
methodologies that are common to a set of disciplines;

c) Lastly and more generally, it is important that students
should be able to understand and evaluate the welter of

information with which they are constantly bombarded if they are to see a place for themselves in today's world.

Vocational Training

a) In most cases the practice of a profession now requires the co-ordinated use of several basic disciplines;

b) Moreover, when it is recognised that anyone nowadays stands a good chance of changing his profession more than once during his lifetime (particularly because of shifts in the job market), comprehensive vocational training seems altogether essential.

The Training of Research Workers and Research

a) The preparation of students for research work by their undertaking research themselves involves teaching them how to analyse situations, broadly state the problems, define common concepts, the real meaning of the scientific approach and how to identify the limits of their own conceptual system. Such training of research staff must inevitably school them in the fruitful practice of exchanges with colleagues in other disciplines;

b) Nowadays advance in research depends no less on the collaboration of disciplines than on the constructive comparison of methods. Such collaboration calls for a methodology all its own, one that must be worked out and taught. This necessitates the prior construction of a model classifying the sciences and showing their proper inter-relationships.

Continuing Education

Students must be trained in such a way that, after graduating, they can continue their "education" in the years to come. Continuing education therefore becomes both an outcome and an extension of general and vocational training in three aspects of adult life, in particular :

a) professional retraining

b) participation in the social and political life of the community

c) personal fulfilment in a leisure culture.

a) The course offered must prepare students for interdisciplinary research through use of an adequate methodology;

b) Research work in turn must provide the teaching programmes with the tools and concepts that constitute an interdisciplinary methodology;

c) The conclusion is that teacher training at every educational level must be guided by interdisciplinarity so that future teachers may more readily develop new attitudes and encourage these in others.

* * *

Among other matters deserving comment in the report of the Nice Seminar, analysis of the questionnaires on university teaching and research activities showed very clearly the wide divergence between traditional universities and those practising interdisciplinarity. The differences are specified in the accompanying table (1) which, although much simplified, fairly reflects the opinions of students and teachers engaged in interdisciplinary experiments :

Guy Michaud, University of Paris X (2), says that interdisciplinarity is regarded by many as "an answer to a three-pronged protest" : against "fragmentary learning" crushed between a multitude of specialities in which each person shuts himself up as though he were running away from true knowledge (wouldn't that be rather the illusion of learning?); against the growing rift between an increasingly compartmentalised university and society, which is "real life" regarded as a complex and indivisible whole, but at the same time against that society itself insofar as it confines the individual to a narrow repetitive function and alienates him by preventing him from fully exploiting his potential abilities and aspirations; lastly, against conformity and "accepted ideas". The result is that many regard interdisciplinarity as something that connotes rather strong opposition and, hence, as basically challenging the state of learning as well as society and man himself.

1) Op. cit. , page 56.
2) Op. cit. , page 282.

	Traditional University	Interdisciplinary University
Teaching	Academic abstract	Imaginative concrete
With the aim of transmitting	Knowledge old knowledge	Know-how rejuvenated knowledge
By applying the method of	repetition	Discovery
And emphasizing	Content	Structure
Teaching based on	Passive acceptance of definitive academic sub-dividing of knowledge	Continuous critical and epistemological reflection
The uni···ity is	Stuck in "splendid isolation"	Overcomes the gulf between university and society, knowledge and reality
It imposes	A purely hierarchical system and a stultifying curriculum	Restructuration based on how the institution works as a whole
And favours	Isolation and competition	Team activities and research

In his contribution, Guy Berger, University of Paris VIII, concludes by saying that (1) : "The presence of interdisciplinarity no longer appears to be a mere readjustment or improvement of traditional divisions in science, or better adaptation of the university to social function. It is becoming a whole battery of questions about the goals and functions of the university, and about the status of knowledge rather than about how it is divided up. Once again we find we are confronting a world-wide approach to the reality of universities. This approach can certainly carry on the scientific movement, fits a large number of its requirements, calls for tight theoretical thinking, and above all, shows that the university system is tackling more day-to-day and commonplace, less well defined issues concerning the relationship between man and the world, with knowledge, with others, and with himself".

---

1) Op. cit., page 47.

We are indeed fully aware that interdisciplinarity is no magic word that will cause the conflicts that lie in the higher education system's links with society to melt away. As J.R. Gass says in the preface to the publication (1) : "Interdisciplinarity is not a panacea for change in the universities, but it is a vantage point from which a good deal of critical and healthy reflection on the inner workings of the university can be stimulated".

II. ENVIRONMENTAL EDUCATION AND THE TOURS WORKSHOP

1. A general model for post-secondary educational development and its application to the environment

The analysis and clarification of concepts, construction of models, development of strategies and study of ways and means are, of course, essential preliminaries, but it is no less vital to try to implement the findings. To this end test areas had to be considered that would be broad enough for interdisciplinarity to be studied from every aspect. They had, therefore, to include not only curriculum content and teaching methods but the structure of institutions, the objectives of courses provided and their links with society.

At the Nice Seminar two fields of inherently interdisciplinary character were chosen : Environment and Health. Both were considered to be sufficiently broad for the various functions of interdisciplinarity to be analysed; at the same time they were subjects of particular concern to the governments of Member countries. The two groups that studied these fields laid down guidelines only for future work (2).

In both fields a number of common objectives could be defined :

—

1) Op. cit., page 10.
2) The publication reporting on the Nice Seminar describes in some detail, however, the work of two universities in the chapter "Experiences through Examples". One is the University of Wisconsin-Green Bay (United States) that concentrates on environment, and the other Haceteppe University (Turkey), concentrating on health.

- the need to train specialists with an exact, sector- wide grasp of certain problems, yet with a fairly broad knowledge of their particular field and, above all, speaking a common language;

- the need to train generalists who can co-ordinate the work of specialists and understand the interactions that give cohesion to the system being studied;

- the need to guide students towards one or the other of these two kinds of training in the light of their individual tastes and aptitudes.

These objectives made evident a number of considerations regarding curricula and teaching methods :

- the need to provide a common type of basic training for future specialists and generalists;

- the need to organise instruction from an interdisciplinary rather than a pluridisciplinary standpoint;

- the need to use active teaching methods and provide for ample practical work in "real" situations.

The final implication of this interdisciplinary approach was that institutional structures would have to be planned in such a way that the stated objectives could be achieved and the concepts proposed for the organisation of curricula and teaching methods could be applied. This called, in particular, for the following steps :

- setting up an institute, school, faculty or university teaching the basic disciplines in the selected field and where courses would start in the first cycle of study;

- providing for the "departure" of students at any level into working life and for the "entry" of people who had hitherto been working outside;

- replacing monodisciplinary units by an interdisciplinary structural organisation;

- developing links between the institution and local or regional communities.

As will already be apparent, the design of the study model underlying the concept is this : a broad interdisciplinary base

(i. e. a core curriculum or initial phase of joint study (1) which narrows down to allow for specialisation and then widens out again at interdisciplinary research level. At this latter level, for all practical purposes, each special course retains its autonomous character.

The common core during the beginning phase should

i) enable students attracted by what is offered in a particular field to make an informed choice of long-or short-cycle studies according to their tastes and aptitudes. This will avoid premature selection, which so far can only have been based on criteria of theoretical learning;

ii) provide real equality of opportunity by mixing the various categories of student preparing for occupations in the selected field. Without such intervention socio-cultural background alone would predispose the more fortunate to choose the more-highly regarded long-cycle course and the others the less-highly regarded short-cycle course of training;

iii) enable all those who will be working in the same team to acquire a common language and an overall perception of problems relating to the selected field. This will prevent the sort of conditioning produced by the study of one major discipline alone.

We should not hide the fact, however, that this concept of a broad core curriculum at the beginning of post-secondary education is still widely debated. Many people think the student should first acquire "precision" of thought in a single "discipline" and only become exposed to the other disciplines in his field of study when he gets to the third cycle. Although the many reasons just adduced argue in favour of starting with a wide base of study, confirmation of its preferability will have to wait until the students from institutions using this approach have graduated and their qualities can be compared with those of graduates who were first taught a single discipline.

---

1) "Core curriculum" and "initial phase of joint study" do not mean that all courses are common to all students. Most are common because all students need them, but the remainder are optional courses especially useful for orienting students or for those who already have a definite idea as to their future profession.

45

Admittedly, it is easier to train students in a single discipline at the start because neither the curricula, teaching methods nor institutional structures need be called into question. It is quite otherwise, however, when an attempt is made to set up a core curriculum for in no case can this be done merely by "juxtaposing" the many disciplines involved in the field selected.

If it were to be, jacks-of-all-trades would result, with extremely superficial knowledge and quite incapable of understanding the links between these various disciplines.

An environmental core curriculum cannot therefore be an aggregate of bits and pieces taken from the traditional disciplines. The fields that must be developed are units whose internal relationships must be designed. Another "mental outlook" must be engendered with no place for narrow specialisation or a facile encyclopaedic attitude. Through this new mental approach reality must be freshly apprehended by analysing natural systems ; but as Professor Labeyrie in his paper page 64 rightly points out :

"It is not enough to define a common or central theme in order to impart a comprehensive, centripetal quality to a subject. Many factors thus combine in ensuring permanence of the systems; human intervention can take many forms and many of the problems refer to approaches adopted by traditional disciplines. The teaching of environmental problems can thus very easily lead to a seemingly artificial juxtaposition of disparate items".

For this reason unifying themes must be sought, to reconcile the object of environmental studies and the large number of factors involved in them.

"When, and only when, these unifying themes are defined will it be possible to deal with fields covering a large number of disciplines. The danger inherent in any juxtaposition of disciplines marked by different concepts and methods can in this way be avoided. Through the use of common unifying themes, items of knowledge associated with the traditional disciplines cannot be grouped merely by merging areas taken from these several disciplines. What must be done is to recast the curriculum content obtained from various sources by examining each case in detail so as not only to select what should be kept and what should be rejected, but also to decide how the items selected should be reconstructed and thus be capable of integration.

46

The difficulty in proceeding with this kind of selective operation for integration purposes is that specialists tend to regard everything in their own field as fundamental. They show a marked reluctance to lop off any considerable part of structures which they are more inclined to build up than tear down... "

All students should undertake this comprehensive type of training in their first year at the university. This is because the longer a student has to wait before he is introduced to a universal approach by being taught to analyse natural systems the harder it will be to correct his habit of apprehending phenomena in isolation. And only by determining the precise place of each component within the systems can the sort of motivation be generated that will match the intellectual resources needed for analytical studies in depth.

But such "unifying themes" must first be found and applied. Certain experiments point to major ecological concepts, such as the recycling of elements and the transfer of energy and matter, as alone capable of allowing knowledge to be really integrated, since these forces are themselves responsible for cohesion in the natural system. This, then, is a leading subject for interdisciplinary research the results of which could promptly serve as the basis for organising and re-organising the courses given during the first cycle.

To sum up, the work done on interdisciplinary education and research in connection with the Nice Seminar enabled a number of concepts to be clarified and a very general model of curriculum development to be constructed. The chief feature of this is a common core, as concerns syllabuses and teaching methods; for the beginning phase. This model should be used in fields that are inherently interdisciplinary, for example the environment.

2. The Tours Workshop

A. Objectives of the Workshop

a) The first objective of this Workshop was to bring together teachers directly concerned with education on environmental management problems for the following purposes :

  i) To define the various aims of such education - for example :

   - to educate the environmental specialists of tomorrow (e. g. urban planners, pollution experts);

- to teach the environmental generalist of tomorrow so that he understands the role of the specialists while himself possessing an overall view of the field that enables him to take action in comparatively straight-forward cases (1) ;
- to enable adults to understand environmental issues ;
- to train researchers and develop links between environmental teaching and research.

ii) To specify the content of courses and compare teaching methods, especially at undergraduate level.

iii) To examine structures that are best suited for implementing the desired objectives and for these special curricula - as it might be a separate University of Environment, an Institute of Environment within a university or an Institute of Environment outside a university.

b) The second objective of the Workshop was :

i) To make recommendations to national and international authorities for the promotion and development of environmental education.

ii) To determine and propose co-ordinated international action with respect to specific matters - for example, the preparation of curricula, exchanges of students and teachers and the like.

B. Organisation of the Workshop

The workshop was programmed to handle three major subjects, namely, the goals of environmental education, its implications for curricula and teaching methods, and its effects on institutional structures. This approach was considered to be the most logical for a new field of teaching and research that had scarcely yet become "institutionalised". Nevertheless, all three subjects were recognised as interdependent and the temporary expedient of discussing them separately was adopted solely for reasons of efficacy. The intention was to agree on objectives promptly, if only in general and hence to a somewhat indefinite extent, so that productive discussions might ensue without delay over preliminaries.

The first day was accordingly devoted to these objectives. Professors LABEYRIE (France), WEIDNER (United States), FRANCIS (Canada), CLAYTON (United Kingdom), MISLIN

---

1) Similar to general practitioners in the health field.

(Germany), RØNNING (Norway), NEWBOULD (United Kingdom), BOISOT (France) read in turn the working papers they had been asked to produce, commented on their colleagues' documents and jointly worked out what they felt to be the main objectives of environmental education.

Professor BOURLIERE (France), who took the chair, summarised the principal objectives of environmental education as seen by the study group as follows :

- to amplify the training of the three traditional categories of environmental specialists (soil scientists, foresters, oceanographers, etc; engineers and town planners; doctors and health specialists);
- to train new environmental specialists (landscape architects and illuminating engineers, medical ecologists specialising in various types of environmental effects on man, physico-chemists to study "fallout" from industrial complexes etc.);
- to train "generalists" capable of co-ordinating the work of specialists and of bringing their own analytical judgement to bear on given problems;
- to provide environmental instruction for school children and also for the general public, particularly through courses on ecology.

As a result of this consensus on objectives (1), the three working groups were able, on the second and third days, to deal with curricula, teaching methods and institutional structures. As was to be expected, it proved difficult not to challenge certain objectives - for example the training of co-ordinating staff, whose role was contested by some of the participants.

The reports of the three working groups are printed in full in the Appendix 1 and the reader will see there the diversity of objectives selected. Nevertheless, it proved possible to work out an agreement on the three subjects at the plenary sessions.

---

1) There were, however, fundamental differences of opinion between participants who centred environmental problems on man and those who focused on nature. The first group regarded socio-economic or psychosocial problems as fundamental. The second gave priority to the interrelation of the life sciences, the interdependence of their component factors, ecosystems and the balance of nature. Fortunately, certain participants pointed out that such an opposition between man and nature was dangerous.

held on the last day, as a result of which a number of recommendations to foster international co-operation were formulated for
the attention of governments and universities.

C. Publication of the Workshop findings

While the quality of the papers presented for consideration
at the Tours Workshop and the professional experience of the
participants who brought it to so constructive a conclusion well
justify a published report of the proceedings, those who are not
as yet persuaded to a single approach to the problems of environmental education may feel that such content, by itself, would
offer a onesided view only of this whole matter. For this reason
it has been decided to include in the present volume reviews
that have been carried out in the OECD Secretariat on the Teaching of Environmental Science in a number of centres not represented at Tours. The body of the book, therefore, is in two parts :

Part One of the book consists of the basic documents discussed
at the workshop and a detailed analysis of the experiments
in environmental education on which papers were read. A
common feature of these experiments is that all the courses
are offered immediately upon university entry. The Universities concerned are Waterloo (Canada), Green-Bay (United
States), Paris VII (France), Tours (France), East Anglia
(United Kingdom), Ulster (United Kingdom).

Part Two of the book consists of three studies of environmental courses given in OECD countries at various levels and
standards :

- the first study, based on a questionnaire reproduced in
  the Annex of Chapter 1, analyses such courses in the OECD
  countries other than the United States and Australia (1);
- the second study analyses courses in the United States on
  the basis of diverse data (2) ;
- the third study compares a number of environment courses
  in selected universities in the United States.

In short, therefore, Part One attempts to stimulate reflection and discussion of the approach adopted by the experiments

---

1) At that date Australia was not a Member of the OECD
2) There was no time to send the questionnaire to all post-
   secondary institutions in the United States.

50

described at the workshop while Part Two contains general information on the state of environmental education in Member countries (1). This, admittedly, is incomplete and in some cases will no longer be applicable by the date of publication.

III. CONTINUATION OF THE WORK ON ENVIRONMENTAL EDUCATION

Research can reasonably be undertaken to ascertain if new structures of post-secondary education, exclusively oriented towards the study of an inter-disciplinary theme or problem-based on a broad core curriculum, would meet known needs or constraints as well as solve certain problems in higher education. A possible break-down of the research area is this :

i) Meeting known needs or constraints :

- a centripetal, interdisciplinary development of knowledge consistent with the search for axiomatic rules common to various groups of disciplines;
- needs of society and for its future development;
- aspirations of citizens for an education geared to the realities of professional, economic, social and cultural life.

ii) Solving certain problems of higher education :

- integration in the same structure of existing institutions offering short and long cycles of post-secondary education, or development of a single cycle of studies in newly created institutions offering outlets to working life at all levels:

- replacement of selection (warranted in traditional compartmentalised disciplines corresponding to separate streaming) by guidance at all levels towards an ordered set of courses, whatever the criterion (epistemological and/or vocational) used to group them;

- educational costs can thus be reduced and the frustration drop-outs avoided;

---

1) We should like to point out that this information dates from 1971.

- promotion of effective continuing education within a similar (but broader) professional field;
- promotion of recurrent education insofar as professional
practice is a matter of close concern in the new structures. The links between post-secondary institutions and
employers will be easier to establish if there is consistent provision of such facilities in particular fields. It
will also make it easier to switch from one vocational
stream to another.

We have already indicated the merits of the core curriculum,
or initial phase of joint study, organised for all students in a
particular field. What should its content be? The answer seems
that it should be split up between theoretical subjects and practical and vocational studies if it is to comply with the concept of
the course.

The theoretical training should consist of :

i) <u>instrumental disciplines</u> :
Acquisition of "tools" (correct use of a foreign language,
statistical techniques, etc.) and methods (methodology of
experimentation, operational research, etc.);

ii) <u>transdisciplinary disciplines</u> :
Provided that these at first apparently conflicting terms
are accepted, such subjects would be logic, systems analysis, information theory, etc.

iii) <u>basic disciplines</u> in the chosen field insofar as they contribute to the study of a problem (integrated teaching). But
they must be approached from an interdisciplinary standpoint.

<u>Practical training</u> should mainly be provided in a professio-
nal context over extensive periods and preferably be remunera-
ted. This will call for the closest consultation at all levels between employers and the university, especially as concerns the
planning and sequence of study courses.

All other forms of practical training (e.g. in the laboratory)
based on advanced teaching methods, simulation games, the use
of stringent experimental techniques and so on, will retain their
present importance.

One difficult problem still remaining is that of linking up
practical instruction with theoretical training and determining
their relationship with each other. When and how should practical

instruction precede theoretical training? How can the training acquired during outside attachments or in regular employment be correctly assessed?

* * *

Universities or other institutions provide environmental courses as soon as the student is admitted ans will be the test-ing ground for answers to some of these problems ; at present it would be utopian to attempt to consider them all. Projects in the near future are likely, therefore, to confine themselves to some of the following;

i) Interdisciplinary organisations of the subject matter of education and appropriate teaching methods. How are the disciplines to be integrated? What problems will they create for the teaching body, the student body, employers and institutional structures?

ii) The organisation of practical training in the institutional and professional context. What are the problems of estab-lishing the close links needed between the various com-munities and the institutions? How are theoretical and practical training to be correctly linked up?

iii) Switching of students from short to long cycles and vice versa for students failing in their first choice. The possi-bilities of readmission to an institution for people who have since entered working life.

iv) The retraining of environmental experts, the specific train-ing of decision-makers in the environment sector, the education of the ordinary citizen and the training of tea-chers at all levels, i. e. primary, secondary and higher.

v) Lastly, it would be particularly expedient to use this new field of environment for trying out the recurrent education scheme which offers the best prospects for innovation in higher education with respect to its links with society (1).

* * *

With our thanks to all who contributed to the organisation of this workshop in Tours and the preparation of the present publication the OECD Secretariat would venture the opinion that this analysis of environmental education has proved particular-ly useful to the development of the universities everywhere.

---

1) See the roneod document : Clarifying Report on Recurrent Education CERI/CD(72)22 , OECD 1972.

The necessary curriculum reform involved in this education, the teaching methods proposed and the institutional structures and links with the community which are planned represent a most promising point of departure and a rewarding field of action.

It is also a welcome development when the problems of higher education and those of the community converge and when the solutions adopted for education can thus contribute to solving the problems of society.

But how can it be otherwise when genuine innovations are made in the educational system?

Part One

CONSIDERATIONS OF THE PROBLEMS RAISED BY
ENVIRONMENTAL EDUCATION AND DESCRIPTION
OF EXPERIMENTS PRESENTED AT THE
WORKSHOP OF TOURS

Chapter I

OBJECTIVES, CURRICULA, TEACHING METHODS
INSTITUTIONAL STRUCTURES

OBJECTIVES, CONTENT AND ORGANISATION OF RESOURCE-DEVELOPMENT AND RESOURCE-MANAGEMENT EDUCATION

By V. LABEYRIE, Director of the Centre d'Etudes
Supérieures de l'Aménagement, University of Tours, France

I. OBJECTIVES

1. The body of knowledge has so increased in recent years
that the number of research workers now active is greater than
the total for all such people who ever lived before. This increase
in the population storming the frontiers of knowledge has
been accompanied by a proliferation of areas of study while the
splitting-up of the traditional scientific disciplines has generated an abundance of new specialisms.

2. The time lag between the analysis of a scientific phenomenon and its application is being substantially reduced. The
links tying science to technology and fundamental research to
practical applications are becoming constantly closer.

3. These two factors are characteristic of our times and
amply justify the term "scientific and technological revolution".

4. One of the first results has been the creation of a capacity for human action and a power for man to influence the natural
environment that was scarcely conceivable less than a century
ago.

Man's responsibility grows as a function of his capacity for
action. He is now able, not only to re-fashion our planet, but
to interfere with the normal accomplishment of life cycles.

5. Meanwhile, increased knowledge calls for training in increasingly specific sectors. Specialisation is the order of the day.

For these reasons, specialists are finding it increasingly harder to keep abreast of developments in other areas of knowledge. They are growing farther and farther apart from one another, and have difficulty even in settling upon a common language.

They are also increasingly faced with the problem of locating, and hence integrating, their own particular activity along the frontiers of new knowledge.

6. Owing to the growing capacity for action in science and technology, the spin-off from human activity is often felt in areas far remote from those originally intended. Meanwhile, the force of such action gives greater scope to the effects which extend over space and over time.

These facts make it even more dangerous to define economic objectives in terms of sectorial and short-term returns.

A misunderstanding of these same facts leads to degradation of the environment, and causes the beneficial nature of science and technology to be challenged by large segments of opinion. The result has been to saddle research scientists with the responsibility for negative phenomena affecting the social and economic structure.

7. Already, the lag in knowledge of the externalities or side effects of technological applications is slowing down the practical use of scientific and technical innovations. In years to come this delay can paralyse technological development. Use is made of the argument to advocate a needed pause in promoting fundamental research and a slower pace for scientific investment.

It is thus essential to broaden at once the scope of traditional education which should now aim towards an understanding of the side effects of human activities the pattern for which has already firmly been set.

8. An ever more vital necessity is that human activities should be co-ordinated and planned. The trend towards specialization is an obstacle to such co-ordination, for which a minimum common vocabulary is needed. Co-ordination is essential for developing, organising and managing the human environment.

Since it is impossible to arrest the trend towards specialization, a more general type of education must be provided alongside specialized training, such that a basic knowledge of the concepts and methodology relating to the specialisms concerned can be combined with training of a more comprehensive sort, a co-ordinating link between different types of specialist can be forged, and the various actions thus be harmonized. Scientific bases for decision-making by political authorities, whether regional, national or international , would accordingly be provided.

The training given these co-ordinating agents must not be of an encyclopaedic kind, it should bring out the fundamental features in the whole area of scope for human action.

9. The increasing weight exerted by man's actions over space and over time calls for a general appraisal of how the planet as a whole is affected.

Meanwhile, the formulation of ecological concepts is promoting knowledge of the functional unity of the biosphere. This has led to the notion of an open ecosystem, whose internal links and interactions determine its degree of permanence.

The constraints imposed by the very existence of life on earth, by the enduring quality of ecosystems and by man's own physiological and sociological needs mark the boundaries, at the present stage of human development, of his capacity for action For example, the earth's thermal and energy balance determines the types of energy source needed for economic development that can be tapped.

The permanence of the biosphere and of ecosystems bears witness to the fundamental importance of such processes as the transfer of energy within and among systems at different levels, the recycling of basic materials and elements, and the fragile, flexible nature of equilibrium phenomena.

During the present revolutionary scientific and technological phase, disregard for the economic laws of the biosphere and of ecosystems, as well as of specific human needs, can endanger man's very existence.

Humanity should act in compliance with ecological criteria because it is now entering a new era dominated by ecological concepts. Economic activity, owing to the present intensive use of basic materials, must rely on ecological models for recycling the elements.

10. The ecological standpoint should serve as the basis for training the co-ordinating personnel essentially needed for harmonizing human activities in an industrialised society. Only ecology, as an overall concept of the biosphere's economy, can provide a comprehensive basis for educating such generalists, who are an indispensable counterpart of specialist staff. Only if co-ordinating personnel are trained along ecological lines can they acquire a global outlook and hence the ability to combine the fragmented analysis of the specialist and harmonize their approaches. Only on such a basis can the education be planned for people capable of preparing and implementing decisions made by the political authority.

The ecological approach must not merely consist in training co-ordinating staff to help develop and manage the human environment. It must also determine the orientation of training that traditionally deals with the environment and specific natural processes and of new kinds of training evoked by the current development of knowledge.

Traditional training, such as for agronomy, town planning, forestry, landscaping, oceanography and hydrology, must be altogether redesigned ecological concepts providing the basis for binding the different fields of study together.

Man's physical and mental balance requires the training of doctors with a sound knowledge of human ecology, in other words they should have studied the physical and social environment as affecting man's physiological functions and mental equilibrium. These medical ecologists should be responsible for managing man's health.

The functional unity of the biosphere and the notion of the ecosystem have acquired such importance that they cannot afford to be ignored even by those who stop short of higher education. Furthermore, the ecological concept of systems enables otherwise disparate notions regarding geography, the natural sciences, economics and sociology to be combined. Hence the unifying nature of an ecological approach can serve to reduce the encyclopaedic, disjointed character of secondary education.

The teaching of ecology must not be introduced at this level as a complement to some traditional subject . Rather must it be a preliminary as well as ultimate requisite in the teaching of traditionally separate subjects. There is an urgent need to train teachers able to provide this type of education.

At the same time, in training the different corps of specialists whose activities will to some small extent alter the human environment in an industrial society, the basic principles of energy transfer regulating the environment and the constraints imposed by human nature itself can no longer be ignored.

Environmental physicochemists must be trained who are capable of supplying each industrial complex with the expertise needed to prevent undesired side effects.

11. Two complementary objectives should therefore be sought. First, to provide new types of training that, on account of their comprehensive nature, will play an essential role in promoting the development, organisation and management of the countryside as well as man's safety and education. Secondly, to impart ecological concepts to the various kinds of specialist.

Although the second task can perhaps be accomplished by injection of the basic components into already well-established curricula, only by means of utterly new courses with an ecological bias can the first objective be attained.

Only a type of education that defines man's area of action and integrates his activities with any and all constraints imposed - first by his environment and secondly by his own requirements - can form a basis for humanising industrial society and furthering its subsequent development.

II. METHODS

1. The training of co-ordinating personnel able to apprehend the consequences of human action and interference requires an outlook to which specialization and an encyclopaedic, exhaustive mode of approach are inimical.

Only rarely can such a comprehensive type of training be grafted on some earlier oriented university curriculum. Since it is a new way of apprehending reality, it is bound to conflict with the approach used in traditional forms of education.

A comprehensive education of this kind, whose aim differs from that of traditional teaching and which is designed to pave the way towards the integration of information later acquired, should begin in the first year of university study.

The longer the student has to wait before he is introduced to a universal approach by analysing natural systems, the harder he will find it to correct the habit of apprehending phenomena in isolation. Only by determining the precise place of each component within the systems will it be possible to generate the sort of motivation that matches the intellectual resources needed for analytical studies in depth.

Since profitable study implies an understanding of the importance and value of the subject being taught, it is high time to discard curricula that appear to be imposed arbitrarily because their significance does not become evident until after university graduation and entry into working life. It is therefore essential that at the very outset the systems to be studied should be so described as to prepare the student for subsequent analytical work.

2. It is not enough to define a common or central theme in order to impart a comprehensive, centripetal quality to a subject. Any approach that fails to do more than describe the systems involved is superficial, and the result of teaching is negative. While education of this sort may perhaps shape men with open minds, they will acquire very limited knowledge.

Many factors combine in ensuring the permanence of the systems; human intervention can take many forms, and many of the problems refer to approaches adopted by traditional disciplines. The teaching of environmental problems can thus very easily lead to a seemingly artificial juxtaposition of disparate items. Lacking the teacher's experience and not having shared in preparing the curricula, the student is incapable of grasping links between subjects. He quite naturally tends to rank the subjects by the degree of their attraction, or even by their importance as a requirement for obtaining a degree.

The search for unifying themes is thus imposed by the objective of environmental studies and by the large number of factors involved.

To the extent that these unifying themes are defined, it will then and only then be possible to deal with fields covering a large number of disciplines. The danger inherent in the juxtaposition of disciplines marked by different concepts and methods can in this way be avoided.

3. Through the use of common unifying themes, knowledge associated with traditional disciplines cannot be grouped by merging areas taken from these several disciplines. What is needed is to recast the curriculum content derived from various sources by examining each case in detail and then, not only selecting what should be kept and what should be rejected, but deciding how the items thus selected should be reconstructed so as to be capable of integration.

The difficulty in proceeding with this kind of selective operation for integration purposes is that specialists tend to regard everything in their own field as fundamental. They show a marked reluctance to lop off a good part of structures. As a rule they prefer to build them up rather than tear them down. Often they are even unwilling to eliminate terms from the scientific vocabulary that only make their field of knowledge more unwieldy and artificially more difficult of access.

The selection of teachers for this new curriculum is therefore of capital importance, and the success of the undertaking depends upon it. It calls for a corps of volunteers, scientists re-grouped from all types of universities and institutions.

Since such ecological concepts as the transfer of energy and matter, open systems and the recycling of elements are to serve as unifying principles upon which analytical study in greater depth can be based, ecologists who have gone beyond an exclusively naturalistic view of problems can act as the co-ordinating force within the teaching body.

The organisational complexity of such a type of education, part of which must necessarily deal with ecological systems and part with analysis, requires a high degree of cohesion among the group of teachers responsible for integrating the various components. No such cohesion can be obtained unless all take part in choosing in detail the content for each subject.

By means of frequent seminars in which all the participants review the situation and analyse the curriculum as it unfolds, any weaknesses and conflicts can be corrected during the course of the academic year. This implies that the teachers should all be in one place, a practice incompatible with that of repeatedly summoning staff from other universities and institutions.

Although it is essential that the teaching body should be a coherent, adequately established group, another requisite is

that people directly involved in developing, managing or protecting natural resources, the human environment and man's physical and mental health, should come to explain concrete problems and discuss them with the students.

The tests designed to assess the students' knowledge, and
to ascertain their aptitude to progress further in the course,
must be of a comprehensive nature. A student must be able to
demonstrate his ability to integrate the analytical components
supplied to him separately into the course. Tests of this sort
must indicate his aptitude for processing information and written
material. The subjects of these tests should be drawn up jointly
by the different teachers, and all should examine the students'
answers together.

Such a practice conflicts with traditional university methods
whether in France or in other countries ; neither does it mean
that secondary school teaching methods should be introduced
into the university in the form of a so-called "continuous" procedure of control consisting of partial tests given throughout the
academic year.

The work of integration should be prepared throughout the
year in the form of practical work, and by means of individual
and group projects by the students, especially following field
study and training courses.

The organisation of field studies and training courses calls
for great flexibility in the weekly timetable. Studies and courses
of this kind will not attain their real values unless organised
jointly by the teaching staff.

4. To the extent that the ecological foundations and traditional
sources supplying the components basically required for understanding the phenomena relevant to the development, for under-
ment and preservation of the human environment will already
have been determined, the student cannot be left completely
free to choose his curriculum content.

Thus the basic knowledge to be acquired will be imposed
on the student, although he should be afforded the opportunity
of increasing discrimination as the curriculum unfolds, to
adjust it to the field in which he ultimately proposes to work.

In theory, the first two university years may thus be thought
of as marking the acquisiton of , first, a certain number of basic,

compulsory credits of and, second, an additional number of credits freely chosen from among the fields corresponding to some compulsory subject.

The choice of subjects taken in ensuing years will thus be based on the student's preferred orientation during the first two.

5. The experience of the Centre d'Etudes Supérieures d'Aménagement at Tours has so far been limited to the first two university years. Despite all its efforts, integration of the different subjects still remains incomplete. The main difficulty is the small size of the local teaching body. Another is the staff's reluctance to integrate teaching, that is, to engage in mutual criticism, and jointly prepare demonstrations and field excursions as a group. Some, in line with French university tradition, jealously tend to protect their own specialism.

Only a part of the curriculum could effectively be integrated over a period of time. Changes have had to be made in the teaching body because some were unprepared to accept and engage in any integrated education, whether in the matter of lectures, practical work or examinations.

These inadequacies call for re-organisation whenever any negative aspects are noted, thus implying considerable freedom in planning curricula and university structures. While the 1969 "Loi d'orientation" gave the universities greater freedom, tradition and ministerial restrictions still limit the capacity to make adjustments.

Already this form of education has received student support, as reflected by the massive participation in elections to university bodies (which is exceptional in France) and by constant participation in discussions regarding the future and growth of the Centre.

III. CURRICULA

1. The curricula are difficult to organise owing to the combination of such different approaches as the functional study of ecological systems and analysis of their component parts. French universities have no experience in this and the various teachers can hence do no more than adopt a theoretical approach.

The preparation of curricula can only be undertaken by a working group composed not only of ecologists, geographers and sociologists trained to study natural systems, but also of open-minded specialists, ranging from the statistician, computer scientist and physicist to the doctor, psychologist, economist, town-planning expert.

2. The curricula should consist of two complementary parts, each occupying one of the two-year successive periods of university education. The second period may lead either to an extra year of study (the total period corresponding to the time of training for an engineering degree) or to a third level of preparation, that for research and university teaching.

The first level (two years) would be devoted especially to acquainting the student with the problems and teaching him the fundamentals.

The second level would consist of the elective subjects corresponding to the different areas where human activity impinges on the environment.

3. The critical period, that determining the value of the system, is the first-level curriculum. On just how well students are introduced to environmental problems and the value of concepts is imparted will hinge their ability to study some particular area of knowledge in depth and to correlate any matter later learned with the general problems of modern civilisation.

The first level would be entirely directed towards an understanding of the key mechanisms controlling natural phenomena, the constraints imposed on man's actions, and an initiation into the mathematical and graphical processing of subject matter.

The Centre d'Etudes Supérieures d'Aménagement at Tours (C. E. S. A.) started by teaching at first level by grouping the various subjects under four headings. Environmental factors are thus divided between the physical, biological and human environments, while under the fourth heading come technical subjects (statistics, information processing, the science of signs and symbols, cartography and a foreign language).

Experience shows that this sort of division limits integration, and that ecological aspects have the appearance of being too closely linked with the biological environment. Therefore as from October 1971, more extensive integration will cover four fields : constraints imposed by natural factors; those imposed by human activities; operation of the biosphere and of ecosystems; and the processing of information.

The study of constraints will consist in analysing the parameters that characterise man's immediate environment. This analytical kind of teaching will be coupled with a course on the functional processes of the biosphere and of ecosystems. The two subjects will be taught simultaneously, but at first more time will be devoted to the study of constraints imposed by the environment than by human activities. The opposite will be true during the second year.

In information processing and in the foreign-language course, materials and documents resulting from the study of constraints and the functional processes of ecosystems will be used.

4. The CESA 's weekly teaching load will average some 25 hours. Group work conducted by teachers will enable typical ecosystems and problems of urban and rural management to be studied.

Owing to the shortage of premises and to the commitments of many teachers in other faculties, the timetable at the CESA is far too rigid. One inconsistency is to allot the same amount of time to all practical classes, whatever the objective of the course.

During the first two years, the average weekly timetable breaks down as follows :

- Functional processes of the biosphere, ecosystems
  and economic regions .... 5 hours
- Study of basic constraints imposed by the
  natural environment .... 8 hours
- Study of constraints due to human activities ... 7 hours
- Mathematical and graphical processing of
  information, languages .... 5 hours

Owing to material difficulties, it has not been possible to provide for elective credits in the curriculum corresponding to the particular field the student later proposes to pursue. There additional credits are only available under the headings "constraints imposed by the natural environment" or "by human activities". A student who inclines towards the option "organisation and management of parks and reserves" is certain to need a greater amount of basic knowledge on plant physiology and animal physiology and ethology than one who proposes to take up "urban management". It has thus been necessary to envisage such elective credits in terms of the different choices available. A student will not, however, be compelled to select his major subject during the first two years.

Upon completing the first two years a "Diplôme universitaire d'études mésologiques" (University diploma of environmental studies) is awarded. A guidance committee will decide whether or not the student is capable of handling CESA 's theoretical studies during the next two years. If not, depending on his performance during the first two, be will be counselled to enter a short course of a technical nature, allowing him to train as a technologist in one year.

As organised at present, the CESA is in no position itself to provide this type of technical training. The French university structure is moreover such that technologists are supposed to be trained in special establishments, the Instituts Universitaires de Technologie (IUT), which are entirely independent of the university faculties and admit students directly from secondary education. In view of this arbitrary division, the CESA has had to negotiate agreements with different IUT's so that, after their first two years, certain students might be directly admitted into the second year at these establishments.

5. The third year of study at the CESA continues to offer a core curriculum. Two themes are covered :

- Man's effect on the environment (problems of physical planning and pollution).
- The effect of the environment on man (human ecology).

A study of man's effects on the environment must not only include such problems as long-term forecasting, economic planning, management and legislation, but also basic techniques of hydraulic, civil communications and transport engineering, as well as methods of pollution control. A programme of this sort needs the close co-operation of engineers, economists, computer scientists, lawyers, sociologists and ecologists.

A study of the environment's effects on man must deal with the physiological and social consequences of environmental changes resulting from economic activity and man's way of life. The subjects taught cover hygiene, epidemiology, and human physio-ecology and psycho-socio-ecology.

The average weekly load has been reduced to half that of the first two years, with the students devoting much of their time to visiting plant, to investigations, reading and to learning to work as a team when undertaking case studies.

6. The fourth year is arranged in the form of elective subjects corresponding to the main types of environment.

These are :

- Urban management.
- Rural management.
- Management of mountain areas.
- Management of Mediterranean areas.
- Management of tropical areas.
- Management of reserved, scenic and parkland areas.

These different elective subjects are not taught in the same university. The universities dealing with such subjects are however chosen according to their location and the teaching staff able to provide such courses.

Such an elective subject as "coastal management" thus requires the student to study the constraints imposed by tidal action, silting and the productivity of estuaries, corrosion by salt, wind action, the economic activities of ports, fishing, tourism, and the sociological problems raised by the prolonged absence of fishermen, the cosmopolitan nature of trading ports, the seasonal influx of holidaymakers, etc., and can only rationally be taught by a university situated in a coastal area.

The main deciding factor in choosing the universities where the different elective subjects should be taught is geographical. Since the subject is elective, the number of students will be but a fraction of the original number. In these circumstances, the same university could well teach some particular elective subject to students who earlier attended other universities.

It would be desirable for groups of countries to organise jointly allocation of the subjects between the various universities. For instance it would seem that the "management of mountain areas" might logically be taught in a Swiss or Austrian university.

7. The curriculum of the first two years drawn up by the CESA as a basis for training co-ordinating personnel for the

71

planning and management teams, could be used (by increasing the study of certain constraints while limiting that of others) as a common core for a whole set of courses corresponding to the different approaches to environmental phenomena.

For example, by increasing the amount of time used for analysing constraints due to the nature of physical environmental factors and studying methods of mathematical analysis, and reducing the time devoted to such constraints as those imposed by the nature of living things and certain activities of man, it should be possible to use the structure of this first two-year period to devise a curriculum culminating in the training of environmental physicochemists.

Similar action can be taken to shift the relative importance of various components making up the first two years of study, thus enabling preparation for such other professions as public-health ecology, teaching and so on.

IV. STRUCTURES

1. University structures should be examined in terms of objectives, teaching methods and curriculum content. This excludes the reverse working approach of adapting courses to existing university structures.

The objectives, methods and syllabuses of courses dealing with environmental management and allied problems vastly differ from those of traditional university subjects. Traditional structures can therefore interfere with the organising of effective instruction. It is hence a question of adapting structures to the type of teaching, and of seeing, in the light of experience with the older structures, how the latter should be modified to meet objectives.

2. Such courses should therefore be undertaken in new universities whose faculties no longer follow traditional divisions of knowledge but are geared to the proposed educational curricula.

By organising faculties or the "educational research units" (according to the new French nomenclature of "Unités d'Enseignements et de Recherches", or UER) in line with the curricula, consistency of location, teachers and fields of interest can be achieved. This is a fundamental requirement for achieving unity and consistency of thought.

The fact that each curriculum will be taught on adjacent premises will allow the students to keep in constant touch with the teachers, have access to diversified documentation and be physically present where research in the areas concerned is being conducted.

3. Since each curriculum will necessarily consist of items of information coming from very different sources, all such teaching staff and the special facilities required for pratical work must be available on the spot.

In considering each specific curriculum, it is evident that there will be limits on the extent to which specialised staff and the workshops fitted out for teaching particular techniques can be used. Since a large number of subjects is involved, an appreciable number of teachers and classrooms will be involved.

Hence, one curriculum alone does not warrant being assigned a large number of specially trained teachers and narrowly specialised installations. Such an investment in premises, equipment and manpower resources would be economically unjustified. To obtain the premises, funds and staff required for teaching of this sort, structures must be found to justify the investments.

As each of the curricula is designed for training different types of generalist dealing with the environment and will all but in varying amounts make use of components from the same specialised fields, grouping them in a single university will warrant the creation of posts and the building of special premises not earmarked for any single curriculum. The quality of infrastructure and of teaching staff can thus be improved by housing several curricula in the same university.

In France, during recent years, different courses on environmental problems have been set up in the universities. Most are of graduate level, while others are in juxtaposition to traditional courses. Additionally, many plans have been proposed by universities.

Some of these courses have had but a fleeting existence, and in all serious difficulties have been encountered since no university has had the necessary stock of teachers or adequate laboratories and equipment. The reason for failure is that the courses are scattered among too many different universities.

Regrouping in the universities designed for this purpose is the only way to prevent energy and resources from being wasted, and avoid the discredit which in the long run any large number of abortive attempts or short-lived experiments is bound to attract.

It is unthinkable that government authorities should be left to assess the value of any such steps in terms of their ability to survive, and that financial help should depend on how well material difficulties can be overcome. In the environmental field, the chances of conducting any lasting experiment can but be inversely proportional to the gap between them and the objectives, methods and curricula of traditional systems of education. To rely on any so-called "natural selection" in this context must unfailingly lead to the elimination of those experiments most closely suited to the problems. Such a selection, therefore, has a negative effect.

The most desirable system is a limited number of universities combining a set of curricula dealing with these problems and enjoying considerable educational freedom.

Courses of a technical nature should be organised by these universities to provide guidance for students at the end of the first two years to enable them to train at different levels. This implies that the Institutes of Technology (the French IUT's) should not be designed as entities separate from the universities.

4. An obstacle to improving the content and form of courses is one often raised, namely the restrictions put on the granting of a national diploma. Usually official recognition is subject to ministerial decrees carefully specifying the curriculum content, the grading system and the nature of examinations. Such a petty type of regimentation, which is already bad enough in traditional fields in view of the rapid evolution of knowledge, is hardly to be throught of in a field where everything is in a state of flux.

In view of the rapidly changing nature of the objectives and content of environmental teaching, there is no point in setting up all curricula at once in the new environmental universities. It is preferable to begin with a few in which the content and methods will have been best defined and then set up new ones gradually.

This gradual process will enable use to be made of the experience acquired in organising the first two years of study and lead to the recognition of a common core for the whole environmental university system. It will then be possible to combine the compulsory credits of the common core with additional credits for each specific curriculum.

Administrative problems and structural inadequacies can no longer be allowed to jeopardise the establishment of types of education that the growth of knowledge and man's technological attainments now make essential.

Section 2

ENVIRONMENTAL EDUCATION : IMPLICATIONS FOR INSTITUTIONAL STRUCTURE

By Edward W. WEIDNER, Chancellor of the University
of Wisconsin - Green Bay, USA

The structure of colleges and universities throughout the
world is invariably based upon a philosophy of education and,
more importantly, a philosophy of life whether explicit or not.
So, too, with environmental education. Environmental education
involves fundamental values and ethics, and it calls for a philosophy of personal responsibility and involvement in this world.
The university structure appropriate for it must reflect these
facts.

Man has worshipped in the house of many religions. Invariably these religions have identified peace and love as cardinal
virtues. Certainly this is true of the three great religions that
came out of West Asia - Christian, Judaic and Moslem. It is
likewise true of the great religions that have come out of South
Asia - Hinduism and Buddhism. There is no doubt that peace
and love are, indeed, cardinal virtues for all of mankind. Still,
there is great difficulty in ascertaining the conditions sufficient
for their attainment. The cardinal virtues are obviously inter-
related. It probably impossible to have one without the other.
Today, it is impossible to have either or both without another
condition : environmental quality. There no longer can be true
peace, there no longer can be true love, without a substantial
measure of environmental quality. It may be preferable to think
of environmental quality as a cardinal virtue along with peace
and love, the three being fundamentally and integrally related.
Today a man cannot possibly violate the tenets of environmental
quality with impunity and claim in any rightful manner to be vir-
tuous. More positively, he is morally compelled to take action
to assure environmental quality for the future, even for generations yet unborn.

Environmental education flows from such value premises. Its basic elements are related to the ethical imperatives of environmental quality.

ELEMENTS OF ENVIRONMENTAL EDUCATION

1. A Problem Focus.

Environmental education is problem-focused education, as contrasted to education focused on the idea of the well-rounded renaissance man. For the last five hundred years education around the world has been based upon the idea that each human being should be educated in as many subjects as possible. Centuries ago it was possible for a student to cover exhaustively many if not most areas of knowledge during a few years of higher education. But as the 19th century and the 20th century came along, it was obvious that the explosion of knowledge prohibited such a goal from being realized. Therefore the approach to exhausting knowledge in different fields was replaced by the idea of sampling knowledge in many fields. The major educational concepts of higher education in the United States for the last hundred years have been based upon this sampling idea. The liberal education tradition has been deeply influenced by the well-rounded renaissance man idea. More explicitly, the liberal arts major, in which a student selects courses from many different fields, is rather explicitly based on such a concept. The liberal arts major was particularly promoted during the 1930s. Twenty years later, the general education movement had its zenith in the United States. Here the aim was to make available samples of knowledge from many different fields. Students sometimes could pick and choose among them, but frequently they were on a required basis. Almost all universities in the United States have distribution requirements, under which a student is compelled to select courses from a number of different groups of disciplines. Another typical requirement is that of various tool subjects, such as mathematics and foreign languages. Again, the justification for these requirements is that every educated person should have knowledge and skills of this kind.

As knowledge exploded ever more rapidly, the necessity of specialization became more and more recognized. Majors and professional degrees were developed in all types of disciplines and all types of professions. However, the well-rounded renaissance man idea on which higher education was based had nothing to say about the relationship of one profession or one discipline

78

to another. Presumably each of them were laws unto themselves. Thus it has come to pass that each discipline and profession has developed substantial barriers around it, becoming like a kingdom unto itself.

The well-rounded renaissance man idea in higher education has resulted fundamentally in an education for gentlemen and ladies. It is something for the upper middle class and upper class. It is passive in terms of society, and backward looking in terms of concern.

In contrast, problem-oriented education is fundamentally involved with the instrumental abilities of students in relation to problem solving in the years ahead. Problem-oriented education is based on the assumption that the first priority of society and of education is to insure the future for generations yet to come. Education has a vital role in contributing to this worthy objective.

Thus problem-focused education is fundamentally theme-related. It is concerned with the major problems confronting a society and the entire world today, and in the future. One example of such a problem is environmental quality. There are many other examples, such as human conflict and cooperation, human rights, and empathy, understanding and love.

Problem-focused education approaches the liberal arts and sciences and general education with a set of values that rejects the validity of <u>random</u> sampling of knowledge. Not only does it provide a set of criteria on the basis of which knowledge can be sampled, but it has much to say about the relationship of one specialized discipline or profession to another. All disciplines and all professions become related, one to another, in their approach to a particular problem. They are instrumentally related to problem identification and problem solution.

In brief, problem-oriented education is education for all classes, all races, and based upon the brotherhood of man and a sense of responsibility for the future of mankind flowing from such brotherhood.

2. Future Time Orientation .

Environmental education, in common with other problem-focused education, requires a future time orientation. A shortcoming of our colleges and universities is that their time dimension has essentially been that of the past tense. If environmental education is to be embraced, the time dimension must be changed into the future tense, with a good measure of the present tense, also.

Youg people have been demanding more relevant education.
They have not always been able to define the term relevance
precisely, but it is apparent that they point to the urgent problems facing the world, and they point to the present, and especially to the future, rather than to the past.

There are two issues here. First, there are many persons
in higher education who suggest that what a scholar does is his
own business, and not the business of society. They insist that
students should return to the library, and sample the stored
knowledge. Universities should continue to do what they have
been doing for centuries, it is said. The defect of this approach
is that it overlooks the value judgment underlying the accumula-
tion of knowledge and wisdom. What books in the library should
one select for reading and study? What problems should a scholar consider? What is significant to the life and learning of student and professor? And what measure of social responsibility
should an institution of higher education exhibit? The search for
all knowledge is based upon a value judgment, stated or unstated.
It is no criticism of problem-focused, environmental education
that the knowledge it organizes is based upon a value judgment.
All knowledge is. In fact, the explicit nature of this value judgment is an advantage. The precondition for existence lies in the
securing of the cardinal virtues of peace, love, and environmental quality. From all points of view these are the urgent priorities. It is of great moment upon what a student, a professor,
and a university focus.

A second issue in the future time orientation of environmental education lies in the enjoyment of things of value. It is said,
and properly so, that a painting by a master, a symphony by
Beethoven, or a sonnet by Shakespeare is a thing of beauty.
Beauty is one of the underlying values of life. Therefore, goes
the argument, a future time orientation to a university is incon-
sistent with the main purpose of life.

Beauty is an important value. But it is important to distin-
guish between the kind of beauty traditionally associated with
the upper class, and the lack of beauty so frequently associated
with the mass of people. The urgent imperative is that all mankind proceed to a new level of beauty, and the full enjoyment of
life. Education should take the leadership in such a struggle,
rather than just being the principal custodian of the culture of
courts and kings. We need to assure the future and the quality
of life for everyone, before the values associated with the few
can have their proper place in the scheme of things.

Changing the time orientation in learning does not mean that history, the humanities and the fine arts are ignored. However, it does require a new approach to history and the humanities, just as it requires a new approach to other subjects. History must be studied not alone, and not primarily, from the antiquarian point of view, but from a future time orientation. Similarly, philosophy and the great books must be studied not primarily from a past orientation, but from a now and future orientation. All subjects, including history, literature, philosophy, and the fine arts are related to environmental education. But they are related to environmental education only to the extent that the subject is oriented to the future.   —

Of course the values of the fine arts and the values of the humanities are good in and of themselves, whether or not they have any relationship to the present or the future. Still, it is not true that such values are the primary role of education today or in the future. The great majority of men and women are oriented in other ways. The fine arts and the humanities can be future time-oriented in a very meaningful fashion. Not to do so restricts these fundamental and exciting areas of knowledge to a few persons of the upper class, and removes them from the mainstream of human action and thought.

3. Transdisciplinarity and Interdisciplinarity.

An environmental education approach to higher education means a problem oriented approach. Problems are by their very nature interdisciplinary and even transdisciplinary. Thus all parts of the university need to be called upon to contribute to environmental education. Every discipline, every subject matter, and every profession is an important contributor.

Transdepartmental and transdisciplinary efforts are imperative for all aspects of environmental education. For example, the biophysical aspects of the environment cannot be considered without going far beyond the biological and physical sciences; the humanities and the social sciences have much to contribute. Similarly in regard to the social environment; the biological and physical sciences and the humanities again must contribute heavily . The environmental problem of human identity together with the environmental problem of human adaptability are wide-ranging problems, to which disciplines from all areas are relevant. Regardless of the facet of the environment to be considered, a transdisciplinary, multi-subject multi-professional problem is at hand. We cannot solve our biophysical environmental problems with just the physical or biological sciences. We cannot solve our social environmental problems with just the behavioral sciences. The environmental ethic is not the monopoly of the philosophers. Our universities must reflect these facts.

In launching environmental education, universities must provide for the cooperation of disciplines and professions in regard to matters of environmental quality. Such a process can be considered interdisciplinary. They must go further. They must provide for the welding of traditional disciplines and professions together in a genuine transdisciplinary approach and program. Both efforts are required, not just one.

4. Education for Both Employment and Citizenship.

Environmental education is education for both future employment and future citizenship. Under traditional education theory and practice citizenship education was viewed as basically different from education that was job oriented. Thus in the last few decades those concerned with social problems put forth a theory of citizenship education which was largely based upon the idea of the well-rounded renaissance man and a sampling of knowledge. If students sampled many different areas of knowledge, they would presumably be more effective citizens. Of course, this assumption was never proved. As the movement for citizenship education developed, it came to be thought of as a movement that contrasted with specialized education or specialized majors and professions. It was heavily involved in liberal education, the liberal arts major, and general education. In the United States, at the height of its flowering in the 1950s and 60s, citizenship education brought some unusual courses into the curriculum of colleges and universities. American studies, international studies, and courses in effective communication, interpersonal relations, and family living were among the items introduced under the rationale of citizenship education. Since citizenship education was thought to be different from education for future employment, there was no impact on the disciplines or professions as a result of this movement.

In the middle of the 1960s, as a few institutions for the first time considered a problem focus, and more specifically an environmental education approach, it became apparent that it would be necessary to develop an alternative model. A new definition of citizenship education was necessary. After all, most citizens spend a large proportion of their lives working in their chosen professions, disciplines, or subject matter fields. If environmental education was to be restricted to the avocational area, it would a superficial additive to education. In addition, it would

82

not affect much of the core of life's activity.

True citizenship education needs to be related to the future positions that persons will hold on an employment basis, as well as to the roles that each person will play as a citizen quite removed from his occupation. In fact, if the focus be on environmental quality, it is obvious that every discipline and every profession is important, as well as most non-vocational activities that persons perform from time to time. Problem-focused environmental education thus provides a way of relating one discipline to another, one profession to another, and the specialized disciplines and professions, as a whole, to liberal education and general education. It provides a framework within which the biologists can cooperate with the artists, the sociologists can cooperate with the chemists, and the political scientists can interchange with those in business administration or teacher education. And all can cooperate with all concerned citizens.

In summary, environmental education is essentially transdisciplinary and inter-professional. It is basically related to all professions, all disciplines, and all subject matter fields. It makes each of these disciplines and each of these fields come alive. It assists each student and each professor in relating a discipline or profession to others in regard to a major problem of the world, namely, environmental quality. It meets the test of relevance and social applicability, at the same time it is integrally related to the world of knowledge, and to future employment.

5. Community Action.

The values associated with environmental quality argue for the impelling need for community action in support of environmental quality. Therefore, environmental education is of necessity associated with the community action approach to education, focused on environmental problems. Such an approach obviously is consistent with a number of the basic ideas of John Dewey. While there are a number of supporters of John Dewey in education, education has really not extended the "to do" idea outside the confines of the classroom. Higher education has not concerned itself with community action to any great extent. Had we done so, our students would not be telling us that higher education is irrelevant. It is time we receive their message.

A community action approach to higher education does not mean that the role of the university is direct community action. Rather, the role of the university is to teach students how to take effective community action in matters related to the environment now and in the future. In addition, its role is to relate creatively to the community, or to a series of communities, assisting them as requested in carrying out appropriate environmental action. Thus universities need to be concerned with improving the skills of students in regard to decision mak- ing, problem solving, and community action. Skills in these areas are undoubtedly far more important than skills in some of the traditional tool subject areas. Yet most universities do not even have a course in the techniques of cooperative commu- nity action. The entire curriculum is simply not instrumentally oriented.

The case for environmental education rests upon the values associated with environmental quality. The role of the universi- ty is not to indoctrinate but to focus attention on, and considera- tion of, the values of environmental quality and associated and competing values. The role of the university is not to take direct action itself, but to prepare its students to be capable of taking such action in the future. The role of the university is not to direct community change in regard to environmental quality, but to consult and work with communities on an invitational basis in regard to such objectives, lending its special resources and expertise.

Environmental education involves consideration of an environ- mental ethic, environmental awareness, technical knowledge, and plans for effective community undertakings. The goal of the well-rounded renaissance man is a value-laden goal. The goal of an environmentally oriented and instrumentally equipped man is no more and no less value-laden.

6. Experiential Education.

Environmental education must, of necessity be experiential education in large degree. In no other way can a student -- or professor -- gain insight, knowledge, and experience. Students cannot receive a complete education in the classroom or in the library and laboratory.

Therefore an environmental education-community action approach requires a university-community relationship of a kind different from that found in the great majority of campuses around the world. What is necessary is a kind of cooperation with the immediate community that permits student and profes- sor to be associated with the community in environmental quali- ty undertakings. This is a two-way process. There must be the basis for students and professors going off campus and ob- serving, studying, and working directly in the fiels or with community groups. There also must be a basis for lay citizens to come to the campus and participate with students and professors in courses and other university affairs.

It is often suggested that a university that focuses on man and his environment will get into some kind of trouble with its nearby community. Those who are concerned about this matter frequently assume a simplistic devil-angel theory of environmental deterioration, with a few polluters being the devils and the many citizens being the angels. This is a tragically incorrect reading of the environmental crisis. Everyone is a polluter. Everyone encourages pollution by others. Everyone has a responsibility to see that governmental controls and policies are established that will minimize pollution by everyone, the heavy polluters and the somewhat lighter polluters alike.

Of course forceful governmental and community action must be taken to end major pollution and ensure environmental quality. But educational institutions must be themselves. They must examine all kinds of strategies for environmental quality, and determine which seem to be most effective under what circumstances. In relating to communities, universities as institutions are confined to observational, consultative, and cooperative approaches. Experiential education is impossible on any other basis.

7. Comparisons of Space.

Environmental education requires a firm consideration of the space dimension in education. In much of higher education we follow the vignette or cafeteria approach to space or geographic distance. A student is free to pick or choose subjects that may relate to something close at hand, or something far away. What the student learns about one geographical area is not necessarily what he learns about another geographical area. Universities in the United States have separated American studies and international studies in this very manner. American studies programs select their focus. Separately, international studies programs select theirs. Thus junior study abroad programs have brought thousands of American students to Europe, Mexico, and elsewhere. However, they often represent little more than an exotic and unique experience. They usually do not represent a part of an overall academic plan for students. The observations made abroad are not backed up by observations close at home.

Environmental education requires a systematic comparative approach to space. It begins at home. In fact, it begins on the

85

university campus itself, spreading to the home and the community beyond the boundaries of the university. A student and a professor should not leave their university and larger communities unless they have locked at them in regard to the same problems that they intend to explore in some distant community. Otherwise, the basis of comparison is not at hand, and in particular the student and the professor cannot appreciate the kinds of pressures and community relations that are involved in environmental problems.

8. The Communiversity.

An environmental education-community action approach requires a university to engage in a melding of the teaching, research, and community outreach functions. At many of the universities in the United States undergraduate teaching is quite separate from basic research and graduate teaching. Each of these, in turn, is rather separate from community outreach or extension functions. Environmental education sees each of these three activities as integrally related. In fact, in environmental education it is often difficult to discover if a given activity of a professor relates to teaching, applied research, or community implementation. The three are often very closely intertwined. Of course, if the three are going to be integrally related professors must be attracted who are happy with this kind of approach. A professor who wants to isolate himself in his laboratory, quite removed from any social application of what he is undertaking, is not one who is likely to make a substantial contribution to environmental education. Similarly, an extension professor who is removed from applied research in teaching will have a very limited role and impact. The teacher who does not go outside the classroom or the library will likewise have limited results to show.

What is needed is a professor who sees the entire society as his classroom, and understands the close connection between teaching, applied research, and community action. Communiversity projects are projects that involve teaching, applied research and community implementation. They must be numerous enough so that all themes, all transdisciplinary efforts, and all disciplinary and professional areas at a university can have their classroom, laboratory, and studio efforts supplemented with opportunities for participant observation in live community undertakings. And these community undertakings should include some close at hand and others that are in communities with contrasting cultures. That is the meaning of the community action, experiential education, comparisons of space, and communiversity elements of environmental education.

9. Close Student-Professor Relationships.

An environmental education approach to higher education requires a close student-professor relationship. A whole undergraduate generation has been turned off just on this one point. Professors are seldom around; the teaching assistant may be, now and then, but not the professor. Professors pride themselves on the extent to which they do not teach undergraduates. The overwhelming focus of the classroom is a teacher-student relationship, with the student taking notes and largely in a passive role. It is not possible to have an effective problem-solving approach on environmental topics under such circumstances.

Environmental education places the emphasis on problem solving, and problem solving requires collaboration of many persons. The professor becomes the number one learner as both the professor and student explore ways in which community action can be secured in regard to a variety of environmental problems. Every community is different, every problem has some distinctive aspects. Therefore, each community and each environmental problem has a different group of concerned people that must be melded together if proper community action is to be secured. Professors have substantial opportunities to assume the role of number one learners when so much of the learning involves application and the exploration of problems that have not yet been fully identified, let alone fully solved.

The professor may be the authority in regard to the abstract portion of a subject matter. He may be the authority within the confines of a classroom lecture. He is the number one learner as professor and student consider community problems of an urgent and emergent nature.

10. Student Initiative Education.

An environmental education approach to higher education requires student initiative education. Environmental education is fundamentally problem oriented. Problems such as those of the environment cannot be identified, understood, or moved closer to solution by routine lectures engendering passivity and rote learning. Nor is a detailed syllabus, teaching outline, or list of readings adequate. What is needed, fundamentally, is to develop the capacity of young persons to solve complex problems. In addition to subject matter content, this requires some experience by the learners in taking the initiative. Community problem solving requires initiative by the many, not just by the few. If students are to be effective in later life as community leaders or even as intelligent community followers, they must have some experience in taking the initiative relative to the urgent requirements of society.

It is not an easy matter to go from a traditionally structured curriculum or course to a flexible and open curriculum or course. Students do not automatically know how to take initiative in their own learning. Universities must therefore develop learning modules that help teach the student how to take such initiative. A number of courses a student selects during his years in higher education must use this approach if much lasting impact is to be obtained. In other words, student initiative education cannot come about just by immersion ; it must come about by planned development of a student's capabilities.

STRUCTURAL IMPLICATIONS - THE UNIVERSITY OF WISCONSIN-GREEN BAY

The ten elements of an environmental education approach to higher education have widespread implications for the structure of colleges and universities. First of all, they require a university to focus its activities on the problem of environmental quality. The University of Wisconsin-Green Bay has adopted man and his environment as a focus for all the activities of the university. Thus all academic efforts, whether transdisciplinary, interdisciplinary, disciplinary, or professional have a common focus. This focus was recommended by the Chancellor, after consultation with a series of advisory groups, to the President and Board of Regents, and other supervisory bodies in late 1966 and early 1967. It was officially approved as the focus of the academic plan of the University of Wisconsin-Green Bay on a preliminary basis in March 1967, and on a final basis in March 1968. The plan was implemented in the fall of 1969, when UWGB, a new university, opened its doors.

Transdisciplinarity. Within the official focus of the University of Wisconsin-Green Bay, the university is divided into four theme colleges. Each of these colleges is authorized to study a particular set of environmental problems. One college is devoted to the biophysical environment, another to the social environment, a third to human adaptability to different environmental conditions, and a fourth to human identity and the attempt to change environmental conditions. Each college is further subdivided in two or three concentrations. There are eleven

concentrations all told, each concerned with a specific transdisciplinary environmental problem area. Transdisciplinary
and interdisciplinary courses at the University of Wisconsin-
Green Bay are college or concentration courses, and only transdisciplinary and interdisciplinary courses are found at the concentration and college levels. The aim is to have each concentration offer about a dozen transdisciplinary courses at the undergraduate level. In the future, graduate work will add to this
number.

In addition to transdisciplinary, problem-oriented courses,
it is, of course, necessary to offer disciplinary and professional
courses. Thus courses in biology, chemistry, sociology, economics, literature, art, music, and mathematics as well as
courses in teacher education, business and public administration, social work, and other areas are an important part of a
university. In fact, the normal university is organized around
such courses, with disciplinary and professional departments
or schools. However, at the University of Wisconsin-Green Bay,
disciplinary courses are grouped together in organizational units
called options. Professional courses are grouped in still other
organizational units. Thus a full range of transdisciplinary,
interdisciplinary, disciplinary, and professional courses is
available to students. All transdisciplinary and interdisciplinary
courses are focused on the environmental theme. Disciplinary
and professional courses are of two kinds : basic or general
courses that are not particularly environment-related, and
environment-related courses. UWGB seeks to be adequate in
the number of basic or general courses in disciplines and professions, but it aims at unusual depth in regard to environment-
related courses in these same disciplines and professions.

The content and thrust of all courses, whether transdisciplinary, interdisciplinary, disciplinary, or professional is crucial
to a university focused on the theme of man and his environment.
Every effort is made to assure a high number of future time-
oriented courses. There is no difficulty in regard to such an
orientation as far as transdisciplinary and interdisciplinary
courses are concerned. Indeed, the reason such courses have
been created at UWGB is to fulfill a need for this kind of course.
In the disciplinary and professional area, the difficulty is somewhat greater. In order to minimize the difficulty, effective planning prior to course approval is necessary. As courses are
developed, active supervision by the Dean of the Colleges, the
Concentration Chairmen, and the elected faculty divisional committees (which have the approval function over all courses) is
required, plus the marshalling of financial resources in an appropriate manner by the Chairmen, Dean, Vice Chancellor
and Chancellor.

The University of Wisconsin - Green Bay encountered orientation problems in regard to traditional disciplinary and professional fields. The greatest difficulties initially occurred in some of the professional courses of study and in the humanities and fine arts. Today, two years later, there is probably more creativity relative to the focus on man and his environment in the humanities, fine arts, and professional courses of study than in the biological, physical, and behavioral sciences. This dramatic change is the result of intensive faculty committee work and leadership at faculty, dean, and administrative levels.

While citizenship education is melded with employment education at UWGB, special concern for the former is evidenced through college-wide courses and university-wide courses called the liberal education seminars. These courses are transdisciplinary, and they focus attention upon environmental awareness, environmental values in a world of conflicting values, environmental problems in the upper Great Lakes region of the United States, and an examination comparatively of similar environmental problems in different cultures. Students are required to enroll in the liberal education seminars each of the four undergraduate years.

A student selects one of the concentrations. He has the additional option of choosing one of the disciplines and/or one of the professions. In other words, a student must choose an environmental problem area, or concentration, but it is up to him whether he chooses a disciplinary and/or a professional area of study in addition. If he makes the second choice as well as the first choice, his program provides for specially relating the discipline or profession to the environmental problem represented in the concentration.

It is in this manner that the University of Wisconsin-Green Bay has tried to make citizenship education compatible with employment education, and to make transdisciplinary education compatible with disciplinary and professional education. There is little purpose in developing an undergraduate transdisciplinary program if a student cannot continue his education in a graduate or professional school, or if a student cannot use the knowledge gained to obtain employment after he leaves the university. Yet a transdisciplinary, problem-oriented approach can actually improve disciplinary and professional education. The program of the University of Wisconsin-Green Bay is predicated on the belief that students making the second choice, that is, making a choice of emphasizing a discipline and/or a profession in addition to concentrating on an environmental problem, will increase their understanding, motivation, and retention concerning the discipline or profession far more than those students who take a conventional course of studies at another university. UWGB seeks to make the profession or discipline "come alive" through relating it to other disciplines and professions, and relating the whole to environmental problems of the present and the future in a transdisciplinary setting.

Experiential Education. The University of Wisconsin-Green Bay has also developed special structural aspects of the university in regard to community action, experiential education, comparison of space, and the communiversity. One of the unusual features is the liberal education seminars at the sophomore and junior years. They are under the general supervision of the Dean of the Colleges, who is the principal academic officer at UWGB. During the sophomore year a student is exposed to environmental problems in the Upper Great Lakes region of the United States, and during his junior year he is exposed to similar problems in another cultural setting. There is a chairman or coordinator of each year's work.

However, students and professors cannot successfully go into communities either near or far without some substantial advance preparation, and, in particular, without some substantial community cooperation and participation. This has been provided in a number of different ways. First of all, the university makes extensive use of community advisory committess. This stems from the first days of UWGB in the fall of 1966, when local citizens were asked to volunteer to help the new Chancellor plan and develop the university. Six committees were established that year. Gradually the number of committees has expanded, so at the present time there are more than fifteen with more than two hundred members. A general university advisory committee serves as a monitoring body for the entire advisory committee system and relates directly to the Chancellor. Each of the four theme colleges has its own citizen's advisory committee. There are two professional advisory committees -- one in the area of business and public administration, and another in the area of teacher training. Most advisory committees meet three or four times a year. They have agenda and minutes, and there is substantial follow-through on their suggestions. In January 1970 the university appointed a new staff member, one of whose chief responsibilities has been to provide staff services to citizen advisory committee chairmen. Shortly thereafter, UWGB initiated a newsletter called The UWGB Community Voice to help all committee members keep up to date on the concerns and accomplishments of the individual committees.

Another way of relating to the community has been the appointment of a number of community lecturers. Currently, approximately fifty lay citizens serve in such a capacity each semester. They bring their experience and insights into the classroom, often combining with a professor to form a panel. Typically, they help plan the course with the professor, and have responsibility for one or more sessions during the semester. They serve without pay, but UWGB is considering formalizing their status through grouping them into committees or panels on a continuing basis.

A third way of relating to the community so that the town-gown relationship is close and mutually supporting lies in the development of communiversity projects. In the short course of its existence, UWGB has engaged in fifteen or twenty communiversity projects of some substantial nature. One of the largest of these involves a lake that has some problems of water quality. A combination of university resources, assistance from the national government, and support from the county government has permitted an intensive study of the lake, aiming toward community action to eliminate the difficulties. Undergraduate students receive credit for working on the project, and in courses from several disciplines, professors use the lake and the data collected about it as illustrative material. It is truly a cooperative effort, with people trained in political science, law, economics, sociology, chemistry, biology, oceanography and other fields participating. It is an example of many students profiting from an applied research and community outreach project. A single communiversity project may enhance the value of many kinds of courses -- the liberal education seminars, concentration courses, independent study, and discipline or professional courses.

The University of Wisconsin-Green Bay is also actively considering the establishment of formal field stations or observation points. Of course, the communities closest to Green Bay serve this role already. The effort is to develop such opportunities at some distance from the campus, and under markedly different cultural conditions.

The community action-communiversity approach requires an academic structure in which research and community outreach activities are intimately intertwined with the teaching function. Such is the case at UWGB. There is no separate extension service, nor is there a separate research organization. Teaching, research, and community outreach (or extension) are all the responsibility of the Dean of the Colleges, and the supporting staff and professors of the colleges. Merit increases and promotions, as well as the general status and tenure of faculty members, are determined with all three criteria in mind, plus a fourth : the creativity evidenced in developing the institution along the lines of environmental education. It is only natural that an institution committed to environmental education should emphasize transdisciplinary applied research rather than disciplinary basic research. UWGB is more aptly characterized by the meld of teaching, applied research, and community outreach.

Student Initiative Education. Close student-professor relationships and student initiative education have implications for the structure of a university, as well. Both permeate the spirit as well as the structure of the University of Wisconsin-Green Bay. Students are voting members of virtually all the faculty committees. This means that they are able to contribute to the formulation of University policies. There is a special Chancellor's Student Advisory Committee, and there is an advisory committee for each of the theme colleges and for two of the professional fields. Shortly, student advisory committees for each concentration will be established. Students participate in the hiring of professors and staff through interviewing prospective faculty members and passing their recommendations on to the concentrations and the administration. Their role is advisory, not determinative. Several aspects of the UWGB academic plan have been adopted as a result of student suggestions.

Close student-professor relationships depend in part upon favorable physical arrangements. Through the design of university buildings, UWGB has tried to foster such relationships, particularly emphasizing informal physical spaces in which small groups of students and faculty members can be accommodated. There is much encouragement through official channels for professors to relate to students outside of the classrom, and even in their homes.

In regard to student-initiative education, the experience of the University of Wisconsin-Green Bay during the first year of its new curriculum pointed to the desirability of assisting students in learning how to take initiative in their education. Thus certain learning modules have been developed with this objective in mind, and some of these will be introduced for the first time in the fall of 1971. A few have already been introduced. Student initiative education is also reflected in curriculum choices. If a student does not like any one of the concentrations, or the supplementary opportunities to specialize, he may propose his own concentration. A number of students take advantage of this opportunity. In addition, all honors students are exempt from

93

all course and curricular requirements.

Faculty Organization. One of the advantages that has been
enjoyed by the University of Wisconsin-Green Bay has been that
it is a new institution, and could start from the very beginning
in attracting faculty members to its ranks. In fact, the preliminary academic plan was developed prior to the hiring of faculty members. Consequently, the academic plan has been a guide
and a stimulus to all those who have considered an academic
appointment at the university. Those who were interested applied,
and those who were not interested went elsewhere. This has resulted in a faculty that is fundamentally sympathetic to the academic plan. In the three years of planning, 1966-69, and in the
two years of operation that have followed, never once has the
academic plan been questioned in any fundamental way by faculty members. Instead, faculty members exude a spirit of creativity and even excitement in contributing to a problem oriented
transdisciplinary academic plan.

Unlike their colleagues at most other universities, the faculty members of the University of Wisconsin-Green Bay are organized according to transdisciplinary, environmental-problem
units called concentrations. These are the only units that can
hire a faculty member. In other words, the basic appointment
of each professor at the University of Wisconsin-Green Bay is
an appointment in a transdisciplinary concentration. In turn, it
is the eleven concentrations that are given budget and personnel
authority, and the power to plan and propose new courses. A
professor need have no attachment at UWGB other than to his
concentration. Each concentration is headed by a chairman,
who reports directly to the Dean of the Colleges. The Dean,
together with his immediate staff and the concentration chairmen constitute the Concentration Council, an important policy
body in regard to academic matters. Disciplines and professions do not have representation on the Concentration Council.

Faculty members may also decide to associate themselves
with an option committee (or, in other words, a disciplinary
committee). Most choose to do so. However, the option committees do not have budget or personnel authority, and are more
or less service units. The chairman of each option committee
reports to a single officer called the Associate Dean of the
Colleges, and hence these chairmen do not have the important
visibility or policy role of the Concentration Chairmen. Nor are
they organized within the framework of one of the four theme
colleges.

The organizational structure, procedures, and rules of the
University of Wisconsin-Green Bay support a problem focus on

man and his environment, transdisciplinarity, experiential education, student initiative education, and their corollary elements. However, one of the difficulties a professor faces is that much of his professional future depends upon how he is viewed nationally and even internationally in regard to his specialty. Under conditions in the United States, a professor's future is often dependent upon moving from one institution to another several times during his career. With a limited number of institutions adopting a problem focus such as environmental education, a professor can find himself penalized in some respects for being associated with such a program. Professors at the University of Wisconsin-Green Bay openly discuss this problem. Their general feeling is that they came to the University of Wisconsin-Green Bay to do the kinds of things that uniquely can be done at the institution, and thus they are willing to run the risk of sacrificing some mobility for the gains in participating in a creative enterprise. Whether this spirit will carry over in the long run, only the future can tell. However, there has been an unusually low turnover in staff members during the first five years.

Advanced Levels of Study. The University of Wisconsin-Green Bay has had the opportunity of developing a four-year undergraduate program, together with appropriate applied research and community outreach. In a series of planning sessions, it has considered the applicability of its program to the graduate and post-graduate levels. As the opportunity to offer graduate work comes along, the University of Wisconsin-Green Bay intends to follow the same general lines at the graduate level that it has followed already at the undergraduate level. Under such a program, the university would offer a limited number of masters of arts and doctoral degrees.

Quite aside from the possibilities of graduate work at UWGB, it is evident that an environmental education approach is applicable to a broad range of graduate professional fields, such as architecture, engineering, law, medecine, business administration, and education. One or more graduate schools in these fields have evidenced interest in the program at the University of Wisconsin-Green Bay.

In the last year, the first post-doctoral fellows have come to UWGB on their own initiative, in order to study the kind of program that is being created, to participate in it, and to deepen their experience. Additional fellows are expected next year, and each year thereafter. An active program of advanced seminars and institutes has brought many persons to Green Bay at the post-doctoral level. There is special interest on the part of such persons to see if an environmental education approach is appropriate to their particular situation and field of study.

STRUCTURAL INNOVATIONS : SOME OTHER EXAMPLES

There are a number of institutions that have experimented with structural innovations in regard to transdisciplinarity and a problem focus. In some cases they have focused on environmental quality. Those institutions that have been able to intro-- duce structural innovations on an institution-wide basis have in general enjoyed a greater degree of accomplishment than those that have sought to innovate in a more restrictive manner.

The University of California-Santa Cruz is organized fundamentally on the basis of residential colleges. Currently, there are six in all. Approximately 500 students make up each residential college. Some of these colleges emphasize traditional areas of knowledge, such as the humanities, social sciences, and natural sciences. Others strike out in a problem direction, such as a college that focuses on emerging societies and cultures.

College courses at UCSC are heavily interdisciplinary, and some are even transdisciplinary. Disciplinary courses are handled through a Board of Studies, and usually a professor teaches both within a college and within the disciplinary programs of the Board of Studies. A senior academic administrative officer reports to the chancellor in regard to the program of the Board of Studies, and another senior efficer reports to the chancellor in regard to the program of the several colleges. It has been difficult for the University of California-Santa Cruz to keep a proper balance between the disciplinary programs on the one side, and the college programs on the other. In particular, the weight of the disciplinary programs has been heavy.

As is the case at the University of Wisconsin-Green Bay, the University of California-Santa Cruz has found that the development of a new transdisciplinary or interdisciplinary course is a substantial intellectual undertaking, and is carried out successfully only after a long period of time, and with many resources being made available. In the UCSC case, the courses supervised by the Board of Studies have been developed much more quickly. And professors have felt that their rewards, at least outside the university, would be more substantial if they focused in traditional disciplinary areas.

Another example of structural innovation has occurred at Eisenhower College which is located in Seneca Falls, New York. It has organized faculty under divisions rather than departments, in order to facilitate interdisciplinarity. Quite a large number of relatively new colleges and universities have adopted this pattern. At Eisenhower College, the philosophy of education requires that each discipline be concerned not with its own focus, but with the possibility of presenting data and methodology which can serve as material on which students can draw to construct concepts. Proliferation of disciplinary courses is strictly limited, and a number of interdisciplinary courses , such as in world studies, are emphasized. Being a new institution, Eisenhower College has had the advantage of recruiting a small faculty that is sympathetic to the objectives of the institution.

In most of the colleges or universities that have followed the divisional pattern of organization, the disciplines have rather naturally asserted their primacy in relatively short order. The only difference between the divisional form of organization and a departmental form of organization is that it may encourage interdisciplinary work within each division. For example, it may encourage interdisciplinary work among the humanities in one division, among the behavioral sciences in a second division, among the physical sciences in a third division, and among the biological sciences in a fourth division.

In a typical departmentally organized university, the difficulty in developing interdisciplinary programs lies in the fact that the departments control the basic appointments to the faculty. In other words, there is no unit within the university that is transdisciplinary or even interdisciplinary, and which can appoint professors. Instead, any transdisciplinary or interdisciplinary program must rely upon one of the regular disciplinary departments for appointment of each of its members to professorial posts. Recently, this has hampered the development of an environmental studies institute at the University of Wisconsin-Madison. The departments objected strongly to the suggestion that an interdisciplinary institute be formed with the power of appointing its own faculty. The idea was vetoed, and the primacy of the departments confirmed.

On the other hand, within a number of the professional schools in the United States, considerable experimentation with transdisciplinarity and with an environmental focus has occurred successfully. Professional schools have the power of appointment of their own academic staff. One such promising experiment is being carried out at the University of Wisconsin-Milwaukee, in regard to its newly established School of Architecture. Its focus is a broad concept of architecture and environment, with special emphasis on the urban environment. Staff members from a wide range of disciplines have been recruited, and a transdisciplinary and interdisciplinary curriculum is basic to the program.

Thus it would seem that unless there is a self-contained school, college, or university, which devotes itself to a transdisciplinary and interdisciplinary focus on man and his environment, the chances for substantial innovation and departure from traditional professional and disciplinary concerns is severely limited. Without such self-containment it is possible to develop many interdisciplinary programs, with representatives from the various disciplines and professions, but these programs remain largely at the mercy of the component departments, and lack adequate freedom for substantial innovation.

CONCLUSION

We are living in a time when national and world-wide priorities are being questioned and reordered. Inevitably, higher education is a part of such questioning and reordering. Central to national and world-wide priorities are human survival and survival at a humane level.

Universities are being asked to orient themselves to the future of mankind. This is a reasonable and justifiable request. It requires the universities to give up their heavy preoccupation with the past on a disciplinary basis, and look to the future with a problem focus and on a transdisciplinary basis. Environmental education is a part of this sobering and exciting challenge.

Section 3

ENVIRONMENTAL SCIENCES AT THE UNIVERSITY OF EAST ANGLIA

By KEITH M. CLAYTON, Dean of the School of
Environmental Sciences at the University of East Anglia,
United Kingdom

The range of the environmental sciences can hardly be less than the range of the sciences themselves. In addition it is difficult to study the science of the environment in isolation without paying some attention to the socio-political aspects of decision-making about the environment, the economics of industrial societies and so on. Yet an approach over such a broad front adds up to much more than one person can study, whatever the length of course. There results a need to identify from within the full range of environmental studies, a series of areas, or programmes, of study that are coherent enough to be the basis of a degree course, and yet broad enough to provide a realistic introduction to complexities of an environmental situation There are many such areas, and it is to be hoped that they will develop within the context of the particular opportunities of different universities. The pattern described here was adopted at the initiation of the School of Environmental Sciences at the University of East Anglia in 1968, and different structures already exist in the United Kingdom at Lancaster and the New University of Ulster (coleraine). As at virtually all English universities, the course for the Bachelor's degree lasts three years.

Although the School of Environmental Sciences was initiated de novo, a number of constraints guided the approach that was adopted, and these should first be identified. The new University of East Anglia was planned as a series of broad interdisciplinary units called Schools. Each of these was broader in scope than the traditional English department; indeed most Schools cover the academic spread of at least two departments. Thus

99

there is a School of English and American Studies covering the language, literature and history of England or America, and a School of Mathematics and Physics in which all students taking one of these subjects must also do courses in the other. Alongside the course pattern of an American Liberal Arts College this is a very modest spread of requirements, but in the context of the traditional English specialist Honours degree it does represent innovation. It is true that at most (although not at all) universities, subsidiary subjects are taken alongside the departmental specialism. But it is novel to establish a teaching unit that integrates within it a range of subjects leading to an Honours degree. From its earliest days the University was aware that environmental sciences represented a sensible use of the scope for integration offered by the School, and it planned to introduce this new School once the initial group of Schools has grown to a viable size.

The idea of a School of Environmental Sciences was developed within the University, largely by academics with a hazy idea of the scope and nature of the subject. The actual name seems to have been contributed by Sir Solly Zuckerman, who was a member of the Academic Planning Working Party. It was regarded as a Science School, and from the description of the range of subjects when the first post was advertised, was seen as a study of the physics of the environment with an interdisciplinary wing provided by some vaguely geographical studies, notably land use. Interviews for the Dean of this new School were held in 1966, and a wide group of people, including many geologists and geophysicists and at least one geographer gave their views on the scope and nature of a School of Environmental Sciences. As but one of the participants I am badly placed to report on the result, but it seems clear that the University was offered a wide range of ideas on the scope and approach of its proposed School. Certainly the interviews pinpointed some of the difficulties in the University's sketch of the School; in particular the problem that while it sought a respectably scientific approach, this posed problems for both the recruitment of undergraduates and placing of the graduates. This problem is exacerbated in Britain by the traditionally introspective nature of geology, which has found expression in small departments, with a tradition that their graduates should take up a professional career in geology. With an initial intake of 50 undergraduates and a designed output of 100 graduates a year, the new School could not operate within that ethos.

The resolution of these problems occupied the University in internal debate for some time, and it was a year later that, following a second interview or discussion, I was appointed the first Dean. At the same time, my Professorial colleague, Brian Funnell, was appointed. He is a marine geologist and is to be the second Dean from August 1971 for three years. The academic pattern I had put forward involved teaching such subjects as geophysics , hard rock geology, oceanography, meteorology and geomorphology that had always figured in the University's shopping list. But it extended the range of subjects beyond even land use to include economic geography and urban geography and planning. There were three reasons for this. In the first place whatever the attraction to students of a course in environmental sciences, their potential employers are likely to be much more conservative. It is necessary, if we are to place 100 graduates a year in employment, that some of them should be able to enter such traditional outlets as the teaching of geography in school. This may be accomplished if their course covers the whole systematic field of geography, but would not be possible if only physical geography were included. Secondly, these particular areas of geography are intellectually the most active at present. Here is the best of the innovation, with model building, statistical processing of numerical data and the common use of computers. Physical geography has not lagged too far behind because of its contact with these fields in geography departments, but there are certainly areas of geology where these innovations need to be adopted. Finally, these subjects bring Man and his works into the School, giving point and purpose to the study of the environmental sciences.

The adoption of this range, then, from geophysics to economic geography and planning seemed to solve some of the problems of this School. It is a wide scope, including most of the traditional departments of geology and geography, together with geophysics, oceanography and rather more soil science and meteorology than would be found in many geography departments. The wide spread has to be offset by some trimming of the scope of the traditional fields. Fortunately the cuts were obvious enough : regional geography, currently under something of a cloud, and what I like to call the "regional geography" of geology, stratigraphy and palaeontology.

One other fundamental decision remains to be discussed. The selection of this particular interpretation of the environmental sciences involved a decision virtually to exclude biology. There may also have been a feeling that chemistry would not play an important role, but as a significant technique in several fields (oceanography, soil science, rock chemistry and so on) it has come to take up an important position as a research technique in the School. A major factor in the decision to exclude biology was undoubtedly the existence of a large and flourishing

School of Biological Sciences. This is an integrated School of cell biology including much biophysics and biochemistry. Ecology is of minor importance within the School of Biological Sciences. Nonetheless, there seemed no reason to draw too close to their sphere of interest in the early stages of development. The advantages of that decision have proved to be greater than I would have guessed. I am happy that others should use ecology as their road to the understanding of the environment. But I am clear that it is not a road I seek to follow at present. The ecologist is still studying small sub-systems in isolation, and neither he nor anyone else can relate the limited understanding he has achieved to the different scale problems of the world. It is even unlikely that the cause and effect relationships established at the scale of ecological research apply to the world as a whole. Certainly elsewhere in the environmental sciences a change of scale causes a change in the status of variables from dependent to independent or vice versa. The other problem with ecology (apart from its present status as a semi-religious cult - an aspect the academic may ignore) is that it has been unable to come to terms with what Kates has called the human climax. For a School of Environmental Sciences which has included man in its curriculum this is an unhelpful approach.

The wide range of our teaching means that a broad survey course is appropriate for the first two terms. This has several advantages. Much of what we teach in the options is new to our students and we can hardly expect them to select intelligently if they are not given some idea of what Hydrology or Geophysics or Tropical Resources and Development is all about. Conversely, it is dangerous to ask students to choose courses (and here I include any choice between subsidiary subjects) in the first week of their university career. A further advantage is that little if any of the Preliminary course has been covered in the sixth form, so that we avoid some of the problems of overlap. At the same time it allows us to be very vague about appropriate subjects for admission - we ask for Mathematics at '0' level and one science (which may be geography) among the 'A' levels, but that is all we list - and we practise what we preach. This means that the course fulfils another important role, offering a conversion towards science for the sixth form Arts student.

The Preliminary course introduces the student to the complexities of any attempt to handle the environment scientifically. We do not at this stage teach particular laboratory techniques, but we do need to introduce Arts students and physicists alike to the practical problems of measurement and experimentation in environmental science, whether in the laboratory or in the field. A danger is that the students will equate scientific achievement with the successful performance of a laboratory exercise - if that is where the only skill lies we might as well teach them to cook. It takes a good deal of time to establish the importance of experimental design and to demonstrate the real role of intellect in tackling an experimental or observational problem. The final element in the Preliminary course is numerical - a brief course in calculus and mechanics for the large group without 'A' level maths, and a more important and time-consuming course on statistics. The statistics course is central to our teaching and we could not envisage a course in Environmental Sciences without it. It has proved to have a second role that is most welcome; success in statistics is unrelated to the achievement of 'A' level mathematics and seems poorly correlated with numerical ability. This is not surprising, for it is concerned as much with concepts as numbers, and we make the numbers as painless as possible by investing in rather expensive but fool-proof electronic calculators for class use. Statistics plays a role as a leveller-down and integrator that is of some importance.

After the first two terms we offer some thirteen options as set out in Table 1, and students take three in each of the 2nd and 3rd years of teaching. A little more flexibility is offered by allowing one option to be dropped in favour of a course in another School (Computing science or Mathematics) or a strongly applied course taught within the School.

We also require a project of about 10,000 words. The number of options has been limited, and if we are to add new topics they should be organised within the existing number, otherwise students will cover an inadequate range of topics. Additionally, while not seeking to avoid traditional subject fields, we have seen the options as a further chance to stress interdisciplinary areas. Thus there is no option on geomorphology as such and Surface Processes links part of geomorphology with sedimentology. Quaternary Studies and Tropical Resources and Development are similarly interdisciplinary, as of course is Oceanography. Choice within these options is free (subject to time-table restraints in any one year) for we have not felt able or willing to indicate any ideal or unsatisfactory combination. A contributing influence here is a need to give students as free a choice as possible for the more highly motivated they are the better the work they are likely to do.

Table 1

In the two years Honours Programme, students take six of these options, or they may substitute one course from the

103

following : Computing, Mathematics, Environmental Planning

Applied earth science
Ecology and palaeobiology
Economic geography and locational analysis
Geophysics and earth structure
Hydrology and fluvial geomorphology
Meteorology and climatology
Oceanography
Quaternary studies
Rock chemistry
Soil science
Surface processes
Tropical resources and development
Urban and regional planning

One practical advantage of a laboratory-based subject is the constraint on course proliferation imposed by the availability of laboratories. Indeed we have recently sought to reduce the number of options we offer in an attempt to simplify our own timetable. The solution has been to reduce the number of options by one by some recombination within Hydrology, Quaternary Studies, Surface Processes and Applied Earth Science, and by offering Tropical Resources and Development as a Second-year version of the Third year applied option, Environmental Planning and Pollution. This is a thoroughly conservative, not to say timid, adjustment, although it does indicate a satisfaction with something close to our initial pattern. A more radical proposal sought to divide up that part of the environmental sciences we teach into eight units, few of which could be as closely tied to the terminology used elsewhere as our present courses. It found few adherents, and similar proposals put forward when we first designed our programme were not favoured. I find this an interesting problem, for in some ways it would seem appropriate to establish new, integrated courses as part of the integration appropriate to this field. In a modest way we have tried to do this, by keeping oceanography a single unit, by our course in Surface Processes which combines part of geomorphology with sedimentology. But more radical grouping has been resisted. The reason is not the absence of textbooks - in common with most British universities we find none that suit our needs whatever the course. It seems to lie in the need we all have to retain our external links with those fields of teaching and research to which we belong. Those fields contribute in their different ways to what we know as the Environmental Sciences. Attempts are being made to describe new systems that link these fields, but in my view the environmental sciences are likely to remain a federation of subjects for a long time to come.

One particular adjustment we have made to the broad scope and federal nature of the environmental sciences deserves further comment. As may already be apparent, our option courses are taught to second and third (final) year students together. This precludes any hierarchy of courses in the School, other than the basic distinction between the compulsory course of the Preliminary programme and the Options. This is not to say that all students taking each Option course do so at the same level. Even where the enrolment comes from a single year we are used to differing levels of performance by students of varying intelligence and motivation. It is no great step to extend that to include the varying range of experience of second and third year students. Nor is the mix, in seminars particularly, any disadvantage, indeed it improves the level of discussion and helps the second-year student to mature more quickly. But there is more to it than this. The aim of an education in the environmental sciences is clearly not that the student should know more and more about less and less. Certainly competence is required in the subjects of his choice and a level of attainment there that will give him confidence and bring him respect. But the real challenge of the environmental sciences is to achieve a spread of knowledge and an ability to relate the approaches of different disciplines to problems which arise. It is not easy to avoid the sort of survey course that would be appropriate enough (if a little dull) for a general degree. It may be that our device of options available to second and third years alike has advantages in this respect.

This then is a School teaching some (and by no means all) of the environmental sciences. In a recent article, Professor Hare has doubted whether geography as such could fit into such a scheme - he thought that if it had anything to contribute it would be through its separate specializations. I think this is so, geography as a co-ordinating, integrating subject has no special role to play here. Yet its real concern with man is a fundamental contribution that gives part of the distinctiveness of the School at East Anglia. Further - we have no departments within the School and will, I hope, manage to do without them for a long time. If allegiance to geography or geology can be left to those in a more appropriate environment in other institutions, we can concentrate on our various separate but inter-related contributions as environmental scientists. And it avoids that non-question, is an oceanographer or a soil scientist a geologist or a geographer. We find that very few of our students think of themselves as geographers or geologists; they are environmental scientists.

The methodology or philosophy of a new course of study of a new department, of a new subject, can be established in two principal ways. It may be adopted as an intellectual concept from the moment the new activity is conceived, the methodological position dictating the choice of content, the way in which it is arranged and dominating the selection of teaching staff. Alternatively it may establish itself more gradually from the sum of the many minor practical decisions taken as the course and the department take shape. Later on, looking back, it may be possible to see that the philosophy was already implicit in what, at the time, were viewed as straightforward, practical decisions. But its role was probably ill-perceived, perhaps little more than a subconscious influence, and it never played the dominant part. At East Anglia our evolution has followed the second course, and if we have a methodological position it has come from our pragmatic solutions to the practical problems of attempting to establish a large and successful department. With a very few general exceptions we have not taken a stand on any matters of principle before designing a course as the instrument of our policy.

As Hare says, it is simultaneously praiseworthy and dangerous to found a new academic venture in response to social demand. We seem to be successful, but we must watch our step. So far few have called us academically dishonest, whatever they may have felt. A few have wondered at our rate of growth and at our obvious appeal to students. Yet we have the foundations for more than short-term success; a strong and keen staff, strong student applications, sizeable funds for research equipment, technical staff to utilise it, adequate space and assured growth in the next quinquennium. It is an encouraging basis on which to face the remaining years of rapid growth.

Section 4

THE TEACHING OF ENVIRONMENTAL STUDIES AT UNIVERSITY LEVEL

By P.J. NEWBOULD. The New University
of Ulster, United Kingdom

I. THE OBJECTIVES OF UNIVERSITY EDUCATION IN ENVIRONMENTAL SCIENCE

Education is the process of learning to live. The world we
live in is changing and it is generally agreed that there is at
present an environmental crisis. The components of this are
the human population, increasing not only in numbers but also
in expectations and therefore per caput demands, and finite
world resources. The results include shortage of resources,
pollution of environment, destruction of wildlife and natural
beauty, and among the human population, anger, stress and vio-
lence. At a superficial and immediate level, legislation can
mediate and reduce pollution and to some extent conserve natural ecosystems. Social welfare can reduce the stress and vio-
lence. In the long run a basic reappraisal of the man-environment relationship is required. This can only take place as part
of an educational revolution in which the man-environment
relationship (human ecology, if the term has not been debased)
becomes the central theme of all education - learning to live in
a human society in its environment without destroying either.

I see four main roles for the universities :

i) In training school teachers and others concerned with the
training of school teachers who will have to carry the
main burden of the new environmental education.

ii) In the education of the most influential sections of the population whether they be doctors, lawyers, politicians,
engineers, business men, scientists, technologists. They

107

will form the vocal element of the general public who can participate effectively and knowledgeably in legislation and planning. Planners claim that they welcome public participation; it is a vital component of democracy. But it will not work unless the public are appropriately educated to understand the issues.

iii) In the professional training of the so-called landlinked professions - farming, forestry, landscape architecture, planning, civil engineering, traffic engineering, architecture, recreation management, social-administration. The planning and management of resources including land is now so complex that it can only flourish as a team activity. The essential here is that the members of the team have sufficient common vocabulary and concepts to converse with one another.

iv) In the training of ecologists and environmental scientists who will have responsibility for research and management activities directly related related to the environment.

II. THE SCOPE OF ENVIRONMENTAL EDUCATION

In fulfilling these objectives the first problem is to attempt to define the scope, curriculum or syllabus of environmental studies or environmental science. This can become excessively diffuse and some strong unifying theme or themes are required. Three themes, not necessarily mutually exclusive, are discussed here - energy because every interaction of organism and environment is an energy transfer, every important environmental system an energy system; systems analysis (Van Dyne 1970) because the general principles used to describe systems by logically defining their elements, states and relationships, provide in themselves a strong enough discipline to unify environmental studies ; finally the man- environment relationship, starting with human biology, physiology and behaviour and extending out to the physical, biological and social environment.

1. Energy as a unifying theme

The single, most essential requirement of all living things is energy. Energy is the ability to work. Without energy no work is done and all life processes would stop. Growth, cell enlargement, cell division, breathing, pumping of blood, translocation, chemical reactions and all other processes require energy. If the environment is to influence an organism it must do so by energy transfer between the organism and the environment. If not by energy transfer, then by what other process? There is no other process than energy transfer. All interactions can be reduced to an energy basis . (Gates 1968).

Far and away the largest energy input to the world is solar radiation. The study of its impact on the earth's atmosphere is meteorology. The circulation of air masses and the evaporation and reprecipitation of water are driven by solar energy. The energy of wave, wind and current alters the coast-line, building or eroding cliffs, shingle beaches, sand-dunes or salt-marshes. The erosion and deposition of mineral matter by river systems is another geomorphological energy system. The whole moulding of the landscape is therefore carried out by quantifiable energy systems. Man's manipulation of natural hydrology, by the felling of mountain forests or the draining of lowland swamps may be his most important overall modification of environment.

A third major energy system, quantitatively smaller but qualitatively more important, is the energy fixed as organic matter by photosynthesis, the ecosystem energy, providing for the maintenance, growth and reproduction of all living organisms in the world including man. This perhaps accounts for 0.1 per cent of the solar energy income of the world. Over certain past geological epochs, notably the Carboniferous, some small part of this energy income accumulated in swamps as undecomposed organic matter and is now being used up very rapidly in the form of coal, oil and natural gas.

This in a sense leads into a fourth global energy system, man's harnessing or manipulation of energy resources. Man on average uses nine times as much energy to create and alter his environment as he uses in the form of food to maintain himself- one can say each man has nine energy slaves. In the United States to whose standard of living other countries aspire, each man has more than fifty energy slaves. These are used in manufacture, communication, transport, domestic electricity, administration - all the fabric of civilisation. It would be interesting to see how the fifty energy slaves are allocated to different purposes since ultimately we may have to reduce the total.

To illustrate the value of the energy approach to environmental studies I will give three examples. An example of man's manipulation of environment is provided by the following figure, a summary of British agriculture and its contribution in feeding the British population. Each of the energy transfers shown in the diagram deserves a chapter to itself but here I simply present it to illustrate the potential of the energy approach.

British agriculture, annual energy transfer

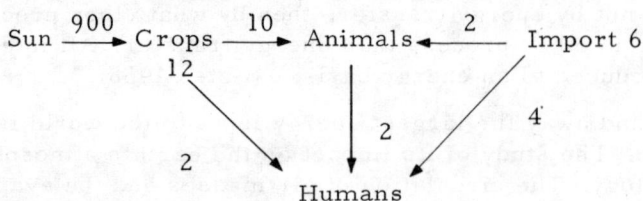

$$\text{Sun} \xrightarrow{\;900\;} \text{Crops} \xrightarrow{\;10\;} \text{Animals} \xleftarrow{\;2\;} \text{Import 6}$$

Crops: 12 → Humans (2), 2 down to Humans

Animals → Humans (2)

Import → Humans (4)

Humans

Units 10^3 MW.

Secondly, on a global scale, let us examine one example of
the interaction of global energy systems, the proposition that
the present heat balance of the earth is a fortuitous balance be_
tween the heating effect of more CO_2 in the atmosphere and the
cooling effect of more dust. Atmosphere CO_2 has increased
from about 280 p. p. m. one hundred years ago to 318 p. p. m.
now and is currently increasing about 0. 7 p. p. m. per year
(Johnson 1970). This increase is attributable to the use of fossil
fuels, the use and chemical alteration of limestone and the clea-
rance of forest to create grass or arable land with a lower total
organic biomass. The proportion of the change attributable to
these three causes is uncertain. Also there is about sixty times
as much CO_2 in the oceans as in the atmosphere and it is not
certain how long an increase in atmospheric CO_2 will take to
equilibrate.

The increase in atmospheric CO_2 is postulated as having
two main effects. One is to cause a small increase in rates of
photosynthesis. This is not likely to be large enough to measure.
The second is to affect the radiation balance of the earth by absorbing more of the long wave re-radiation than of the incoming
radiation. If this were definitely shown to occur it would cause
a melting of the ice-caps and a rise in sea-level perhaps as
great as 30 or 40 metres.

Another process affecting radiation balance is the increasing
dustiness of the atmosphere (Wendland and Bryson 1970). There
is good evidence that this is happening. It seems to me inevitable that increasing energy use will anyway produce more heat,
noise and disturbance and the disturbance will produce dust.
Cities, industries and the widespread savanna burning in Africa
will all produce smoke. The increasing numbers of vapour trails
from jet aircraft create additional cloudiness. All this dust and
smoke has the potential effect of reducing the penetration of solar radiation to the earth's surface and therefore of causing cooling. The problem is the extent to which the earth's energy

balance is currently controlled by this fortuitous and precarious balance between CO_2 warming and dust cooling. I am suggesting that to study this example fully would involve the examination of a great many different energy systems and would illustrate the educational interest and potential of this approach.

The third example I want to discuss is the approach to the study of an environment by consideration of the energy balance of an organism in that environment. Gates (1965) has studied the energy balance of leaves; research into animal husbandry is now much involved with the total energy balance of the animals (see for example Blaxter, Kielanowski and Thorbek 1969).

And Waggoner (1963) made an approach to the study of human comfort in different environments via the study of the energy balance of a man. The components of the energy balance equation include a solar radiation gain and a long-wave radiation gain from surrounding objects and long-wave radiation, convection and evaporation losses. They depend upon a variety of climatic parameters as well as the clothing, activity and surface area of the man and whether he is wet or dry. However, Waggoner makes some assumptions about a standard, lightly clad man, who can be specified as either wet or dry and then examines his energy balance in a variety of micro-climates in Connecticut. I have reproduced some results in the Table below:

	Energy loss, kg cal m^{-2} hr^{-1}			
	Midday		Early evening	
	Dry man	Wet man	Dry man	Wet man
Pasture	8	139	497	1506
Apple Tree	121	336	402	1259
Clearing	-24	135	314	779
Thicket	77	137	215	460

Energy loss from a man, in different environments, in Connecticut, September 20, 1962. Data from Waggoner 1963.

A man for energy balance purpose has a surface area of about 1m^2 so the values are approximately those for a man. The pasture is an open field. The apple tree is in the pasture, it is about 5m tall with a crown 8m across and has no branches or leaves within 2 metres of the ground so that air circulates freely below it. The thicket is essentially a low woodland and the clearing, about 8m in diameter, is situated in the thicket.

In terms of human comfort the problem at mid-day would be

to lose heat without sweating. The man under the apple tree has
the benefit of shade, reducing his solar radiation gain, and
still has a reasonable loss by convection. In the thicket this
convection loss is reduced. In the pasture he has a relatively
large solar radiation gain nearly outweighing his convection
loss. In the clearing he has the worst of both worlds, a solar
radiation gain and little convection loss. The wet man loses heat
by evaporation and this reduces the difference between the pasture, clearing and thicket. In the evening we can envisage the
pasture becoming too cool for comfort.

The point I want to stress is the use of energy balance as an
integrating concept in studying the organism-environment relationship. This also introduces the principle of studying an environment at the level of its recipient; temperature measurement
often tells you only the temperature of the thermometer. Heat
flux indicates a relationship. In all the discussion of pollution,
one approach I have not seen developed to any extent is the measurement of environment at the level of the person subjected to
it. In this approach a number of fully instrumented sample men
would be walking around recording the composition of the air
they are breathing, the water they are drinking, the food they
are eating, the energy flux they are undergoing, the radioactivity and the noise levels they are subjected to. Linked to this
would be some simple measurements of physiological response,
such as pulse rate, encephalograph records, respiratory rate,
temperature, etc... Again this is central to environmental
science, to energy transfer and to the man-environment relationship and I would suggest it as a more worthwhile approach
to modern pollution and environment problems than seeking
broad correlations between environmental conditions revealed
by monitoring and human population statistics.

2. The systems approach as a unifying theme

Here I find myself on much less certain ground. The basis
of the systems approach lies in the description of all systems
in terms of elements, states and relationships (Schultz in Van
Dyne 1970). It has already been suggested that energy systems
are of crucial importance and that a variety of environmental
systems can be described in energy terms. The problem as I
see it is to determine what aspects of environmental science
are ill-served by the energy approach. As a biologist I suspect
that behavioural and genetical aspects of human and other populations come in this category. It seems likely that more than
90% of the energy flowing through an ecosystem flows through
10% of the species in that system, the commoner or more

dominant species. Difficulties of sampling and measurement and the sheer labour involved make it difficult to do justice to the other 90% of the species. Yet in many respects species diversity, i.e. genetic diversity, is an important characteristic of an ecosystem. It reflects past history and future potential; species, rare now, may have been or may become dominant. They contribute to the aesthetic diversity which is one of man's strongest reasons for nature conservation. They, rather than the common species, may serve as indicators of environmental change, of pollution or eutrophication, for example.

Similarly the systems approach originating from engineering is increasingly used in planning (Mc Loughlin 1969) which embodies man's organised manipulation of his environment, physical biological and social.

In designing environment for man, planners, landscape architects, civil engineers and others are coming to realise the crucial importance of human perception of environments. This perception may be by touch, sound, smell but most generally by sight. It represents information transfer.

It is the genetic composition of an ecosystem, even more than its stored energy and its structure which gives its continuity. Most of the information content of an ecosystem received from preceding ecosystems takes the form of genetic information. Seeds, pollen grains, eggs represent devices for the spatial and temporal transfer of genetic information in a compact form. Only man has replaced the use of genetic information to give continuity by written, spoken and learnt information. I think this is one of the most important distinctions between natural ecosystems and man-controlled ecosystems. Again it exemplifies the inadequacy of the energy approach alone.

I am not certain how far the systems approach is helpful in providing some common basis for considering these various aspects of environmental science.

3. Man and environment as a unifying theme

The third possible unifying theme would be to take man as the starting and central point and to study all environmental systems in terms of their influence upon man or vice versa. Human physiology, psychology and genetics become essential. Social psychology leads us in the direction of sociology. Many of the themes developed above such as the human environmental monitor or human perception of environment fit readily in with this theme.

113

A possible scheme for this approach is set out in Fig. 1.
This derives from a recent conference in Hertfordshire, England which was trying to produce a syllabus for environmental
studies at 'A' level (i.e. upper school, age 16-18).

4. Comparison

I have given very unequal treatment to these three approaches, related to my own background and knowledge. Much of
the basic material is common to all three approaches and it is
the conceptual frameworks, the attitudes that are different. I
can only give my personal impression of their merits The man-
environment theme is the most pragmatic and real and perhaps
therefore the best for use in schools, certainly at the more
elementary level. It is easy to follow.

At the university level I have a preference for energy systems, starting with the sun, rather than with man and working
back to man. Energy resources seem to me the most compel-
ling limitation to development. With unlimited cheap energy,
problems of food, housing, water supply, pollution and the
creation of a congenial environment are minimised.

The systems approach I find too artificial and abstract,
though clearly it is more comprehensive and all-embracing.
Essentially it is only a methodology, a way of looking at things
and as yet I am unconvinced of the value of a common methodology for totally dissimilar systems. However, linked with the
electronic computer it may prove very powerful and flexible
and I would not wish to rule it out for the future.

III. METHODS AND DIFFICULTIES IN TEACHING ENVIRON-
    MENTAL SCIENCE

The practical difficulties involved in educational reform are
formidable. There is a chicken and egg problem; if universities
are to run courses in environmental science they need (i) appli-
cants from the schools wanting to attend such courses and (ii)
employers wanting to employ the environmental science graduates. Until there are environmental science graduates employed
in relevant and senior positions, or teaching in the schools,
neither of these prerequisites will be attained. There are signs
of improvement. In Britain, for example, there is a fairly impressive set of "environmental courses" set out in Table 1 (see
page 119 . I have first-hand knowledge of only a small number of

114

these courses - in some cases actuality is less impressive than the title but most live up to their promise. I have not done a historical exercise but my impression is that comparatively few of these courses existed ten years ago. So change is occuring but I feel a far more radical upheaval of the educational system is required, something transcending the types of institution involved and their objectives and also existing subject categories. I can see how to achieve change within, say, the biology curriculum or the geography curriculum but not how to put them, subject boundaries and all, into the melting pot. How do you create an educational system which is susceptible to change? There are large vested interests seeking stability, fossilization of formal educational systems. The inertia of the educational system is immense and I imagine Britain is not unique in this. Possibly more autocratic systems may be easier to reform.

A further difficulty is that of effective integration of the different facets of environmental science. Whether one adopts the energy, systems or man and environment theme as central, no one person can fully comprehend or teach the syllabus. Team work in teaching is required just as team work in environmental planning is needed for effective implementation. Normal educational methods will be used, lectures, discussions, seminars, film etc. I want to stress one teaching method that I consider of very great importance - the multidisciplinary site study. If you can get different specialists out on the ground, discussing a real planning or management problem, differences in vocabulary, concept and outlook become much clearer. Compare, for example, university lecturers in geography, plant ecology and animal ecology conducting a day's field outing; the scale of their operation may be : geographer, km^2; plant ecologist, hectare; animal ecologist, m^2.

This difference, seldom explicitly recognised as existing, may colour their respective attitudes to field problems. Suppose the problem involves the establishment and management of a country park, perhaps 50 hectares in area. To the geographer it may be a small part of an environmental complex, to the plant ecologist a unit containing two or three main plant associations and to the animal ecologist a complex pattern of a hundred or more discreet animal habitats. To these outlooks must be added those of the economist, sociologist, planner, landscape architect, civil engineer, park superintendent. Each has his own terms of reference, text books, concepts and so on. Synthesis in conceptual terms is difficult if not impossible. But synthesis in practical terms, stood out on the site, arguing for example about management, confronted with a real tangible problem, is not only possible but helpful to all concerned. I

115

attach great importance then in environmental science to multi-disciplinary field studies concerned with real problems in a defined area approached from the standpoint of several traditional disciplines.

IV. FULFILMENT OF OBJECTIVES

I refer back to the objectives set out in section 1. The multidisciplinary field study just described above should fulfil objective (iii), broadening the education of the land-linked professions, and should become an integral part of such education. It involves administrative and academic co-operation between disciplines, a procedure for which higher education in general and universities in particular are ill-adapted. Departmentalisation and entrenchment are all too common. Institutions must seek their own solutions and this seminar, by establishing dialogue, is a step in the right direction.

Objective (iv), the training of environmental scientists, could be fulfilled by undergraduate and postgraduate courses at universities. But the all-round environmental scientist would have no time to pursue any aspect of environment in depth, would truly be a jack of all trades and master of none, unemployable except as a teacher of environmental science. I see undergraduate courses in environmental science as providing just such general education, perhaps with bias towards either lithosphere, hydrosphere, atmosphere or biosphere at different institutions. These courses could provide for objective (i), school teachers trained in environmental science. They would be followed by one year vocational courses aimed at particular facets of environmental science, from oceanography to recreation management, from conservation to water resource management. Many such postgraduate courses do exist at present in Britain and some have been listed in Table 1. Most were set up after the Robbins Report on Higher Education in a period of euphoria when it was hoped to make the first degree less specialised and divert about 30% of those graduating with a first degree to an appropriate and more vocational diploma or M. Sc. course. Government support for this policy seems now, regrettably, to be declining.

The idea of a wide range of vocational postgraduate courses requires co-ordination and co-operation between universities as well as within them and this is a delicate area, touching on the traditional autonomy of a university, now coming under increasing pressure. Rationalisation, ensuring that postgraduate courses work to defined and distinct objectives, complementing but not duplicating each other, is difficult to achieve but nonetheless essential.

Finally, objective (ii), broadening the education of all university graduates or other products of higher education, would partly be met by the improved enviromental education provided by schools in our future Utopia. But it also questions the narrowness of university education; it is unfortunately true that graduates may emerge from university with a greater depth but no more breadth of knowledge than they had on entering. Various self-conscious experiments have been tried in Britain, the first and most famous being the foundation year at Keele University. Here the first year of a four-year course is designed to ensure that science students learn some arts subjects and vice versa. There have been numerous other attempts to legislate breadth into the university system. None, I think, has been an unqualified success but the criteria of success are difficult to judge. A system like that at Keele tends to appeal and recruit those students least in need of it. An alternative and older solution is to be found in the social structure of a university, for example, the traditional Oxford or Cambridge college, enforcing a degree of mixing of disciplines at student level. We can only note the problem and add it to all the other problems that contribute to the changing pattern of higher education.

V. REFERENCES

Blaxter, K.L., Kielanowski, J. and Thorbek, G., 1969, Energy Metabolism of Farm Animals. European Association for Animal Production, Publication N° 12, Newcastle upon Tyne.

Gates, D.M., 1965, Heat transfer in plants. Sci. Amer., 213, 76-84.

Gates, D.M., 1968, Towards understanding ecosystems. Advances in Ecological Research 5, 1-35.

Hertfordshire County Council 1970, 'A' level Environmental Studies. Mimeographed report on a conference held in Hertfordshire on 23-25 October, 1970.

Johnson, F.S., 1970, The balance of atmospheric oxygen and carbon dioxide, Biol. Conservation 2, 83-9.

Mc Loughlin, J.B., 1969, Urban and Regional Planning. A systems approach, London.

Van Dyne, G.M. ed. 1969, The Ecosystem concept in natural resource management, New York and London.

Waggoner, P.E., 1963, Plants, shade and shelter, Bull. Connecticut Agric. Exp. Stn 656.

Wendland, W.M. and Bryson, R.A., 1970, Atmospheric dustiness, man and climatic change. Biol. Conservation 2, 125-8.

Table 1

UNIVERSITY COURSES WITH ENVIRONMENTAL RELEVANCE IN THE U.K.

First degree (undergraduate) courses mostly 3 (or 4) year courses for B.Sc.		Postgraduate M.Sc. or Diploma Courses, mostly 1 year duration.	
Orthodox or long-established subjects such as Biology, Geography, Geology, Town Planning, Forestry, Agriculture, Horticulture are not listed.		Conventional and professional courses as in aspects of Town and Country Planning, Landscape Architecture, Architecture, Civil Engineering, the Social Sciences, Agriculture, Horticulture or Forestry are not listed.	
Environmental science (earth science oriented)	East Anglia	Geology, Geophysics Geochemistry or economic applications thereof	Aberdeen, Birmingham, Durham, Leeds, Leicester, Newcastle, Oxford, Bedford College, Imperial College.
Environmental science Environmental science and physics. (atmosphere oriented)	Lancaster		
Environmental science (civil engineering, public health, administration oriented)	Salford	Hydrogeology Meteorology or similar	University College London, Birmingham, Imperial College, Reading, Bangor.
		Natural resource survey	Sussex
Environmental science (ecology-oriented)	Ulster	Environmental resources	Salford
Wildlife and fisheries management.		Environmental conservation	Heriot-Watt
		Environmental design	Newcastle
Resource management	Edinburgh	Environmental control and resource utilization	Strathclyde
Ecology			
		Ecology	Bangor, Aberdeen, Durham
		Conservation	University College London
Soil Science	Aberdeen	Soil science	Newcastle, Oxford Reading, Aberdeen
Oceanography	Liverpool	Oceanography and other aspects of Marine science	Southampton Bangor
Human Ecology	Ulster	Applied Hydrobiology	Chelsea
		Biology of Water Management	Aston
		Water Resource Technology	Birmingham
		Water Resource Engineering	Dundee
		Freshwater Biology	Liverpool
		Water Resources	Newcastle

Figure 1

A DIAGRAM INDICATING AN OUTLINE SCHEME FOR AN ENVIRONMENTAL STUDIES CURRICULUM

Hertfordshire County Council 1970

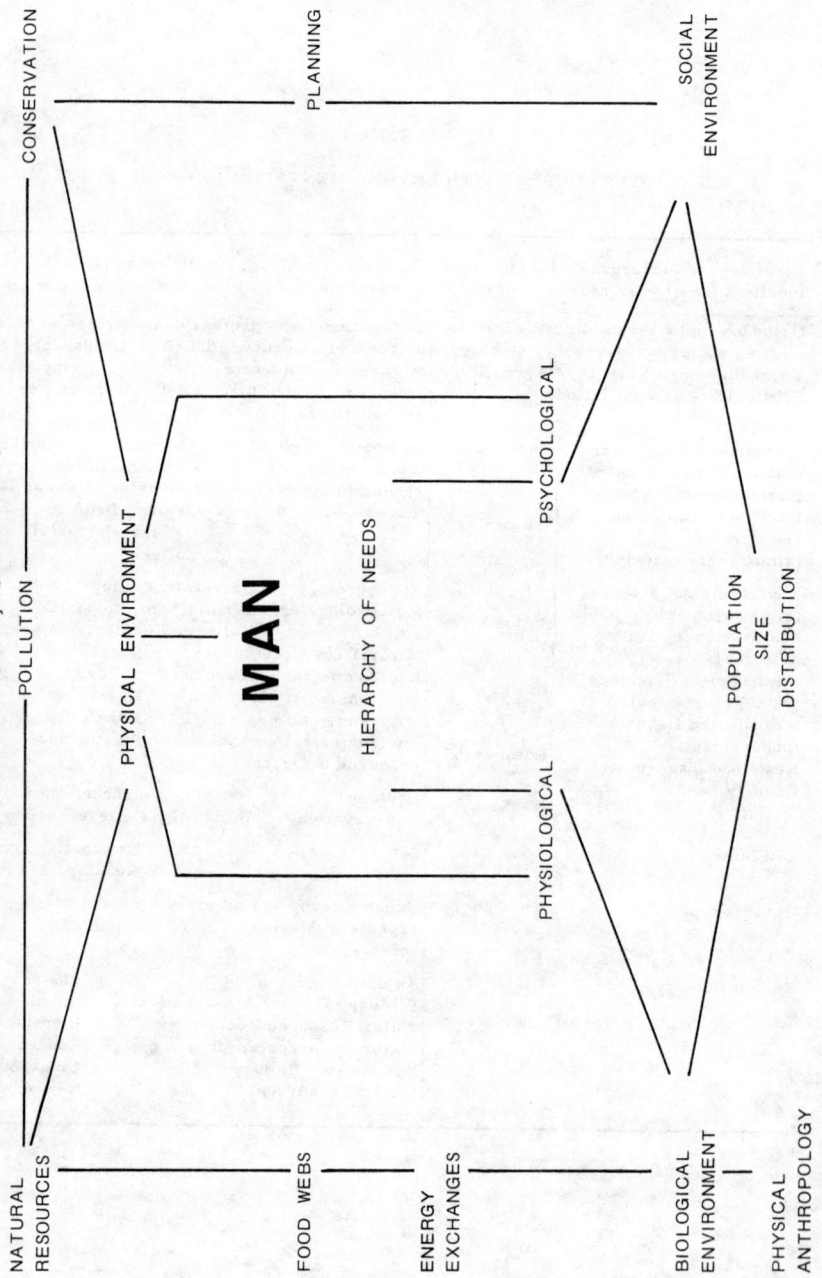

OBJECTIVES AND APPROACHES TO ENVIRONMENTAL EDUCATION : SOME FIRST REFLECTIONS FROM A BEGINNING EXPERIMENT

By George R. FRANCIS, Chairman of the Department of Man-Environment Studies, Faculty of Environmental Studies, University of Waterloo, Ontario, Canada.

INTRODUCTION

During this past academic year, I have participated in the initiation of an undergraduate environmental education programme at one of the new Canadian universities, the University of Waterloo, in Ontario. It has been a year of almost continual discussions around essentially the same questions that have been posed for this workshop. We have been made aware, sometimes abruptly, of varied views and perceptions of other academics not all of whom agree with what we are undertaking, and we have benefited from the reactions and insights of the first two groups of students who have been attracted to the experiment. Increasingly, we have also talked with persons in the community beyond the university, some of whom in due course will be potential employers for graduates from environmental studies.

I suspect that many of our preoccupations about environmental education will turn out to be similar to those of other participants in the workshop who are also involved or about to become involved in similar endeavours. Indeed, I personally find the workshop a most timely one. I will try then to highlight some of the main issues and concerns we have been facing in the expectation of receiving helpful views from the other participants, and in the hope of contributing some in return.

I will have to start with a few brief remarks about the university within which the particular environmental education programme I am basing my observations on is being developed, since some aspects of the context in which it is set may help understand both its opportunities and its limitations. I will then consider the main topics which form the basis for the workshop sessions. While there is no intention of dwelling unduly upon the particular experiment at Waterloo, on some points I can only report what we are attempting, and I would not want to generalize further.

THE UNIVERSITY OF WATERLOO AND ITS DIVISION OF ENVIRONMENTAL STUDIES

The University of Waterloo is only some 12 years old, and is one of several "instant universities" created in Canada during the past decade or so to serve the considerable need for post-secondary school educational opportunities. Institutionally, it is quite conventional with features similar to either British or United States universities which have long served as working models for the English language universities in Canada. It has five faculties, four professional schools and four Church-affiliated Colleges assembled on the same campus. The engineering and mathematics faculties are the largest of these units. The Faculties are divided into discipline-based departments which collectively cover virtually the full array of established subject areas. Enrollment is currently over 12,000 students, and steps are being taken to level off the growth in numbers to a steady state of some 15,000.

Although the university has been given a traditional struc_ ture , there has been a demonstrable willingness to experiment and innovate in its programmes of study, a characteristic which is probably related to its newness. One of its innovations was the creation of a Division of Environmental Studies in 1969. This is administratively similar to a faculty but it is meant to re-main very much open to continuous cooperation and communica-tion with the established faculties. At present this Division is composed of the School of Architecture, the School of Urban and Regional Planning, the Department of Geography and a new Department of Man-Environment Studies which was created at the same time as the Division. The two Schools award profes-sional degrees in their respective areas, and the Department of Geography does the teaching and research in the discipline which is perhaps the most appropriate for environmental studies. The fourth unit, with which I am associated, was brought into existence to serve at least four related education functions.

Its faculty was to be a pluridisciplinary team whose formal training and experience would represent much that is relevant to a broadly defined programme of environmental studies. It was hoped that this could facilitate the creation of a wide communications network within the university which in turn would enable useful mutual cooperation to develop across disciplinary and faculty boundaries. The anticipated benefits from this were two-fold : it could enable relatively close touch to be maintained with those doing significant research of interest to environmental questions, and it could also give some encouragement to the development of an environment-oriented outlook among students and faculty whose primary interests otherwise lie in some on particular discipline or profession.

The main function of this new Department of Man-Environment Studies was to be undergraduate teaching. This was to include the organization and presentation of courses of general interest open to students throughout the university, and participation in the pre-professional training of students heading into professions such as planning and architecture, which clearly have a major role to play in environmental matters. Perhaps the main responsibility seen for this department however, was to mount a new four-year "theme-oriented" university education programme justifiable in its own right. It was to focus on the broad theme of man-environment interrelationships in all their many aspects. It is this last endeavour which raises most directly the topics of interest to the workshop, and which has given rise to most of our preoccupations as it gets underway.

With these diverse expectations, the new department began its existence modestly in 1969 with the equivalent of about three full time faculty and some 20 students for its new man-environment studies programme. For the 1970-71 academic year the faculty was increased to the equivalent of ten full-time members, and 60 new students were accepted into the first year. The faculty have brought to the programme educational qualifications in fields such as anthropology, biology, communications science, economics, engineering, fine arts, geography, psychology, sociology and social work, as well as a variety of other experience in such diverse areas as the planning of education sustems, ecological research, the creative arts, international development, economic studies, and urban affairs. Most important however, they have brought interests in an array of problems and issues now said to be environmental, and an enthusiasm for working closely with others having similar kinds of interests derived from otherwise quite different backgrounds. It is from my direct participation in this group, working individually and collectively with students, and in close cooperation with faculty

123

in the other three units of the Division, that I offer some reflections on the topics which follow.

AIMS OF AN ENVIRONMENTAL EDUCATION

In trying to specify the aims of an environmental education, one is forced to take account of a number of quite large and unresolved issues pertaining both to "environment" and to university education itself. Mention will be made of some of these before venturing a suggestion of what the aims might in fact be.

First of all, the sheer size and diversity of problems now increasingly identified as environmental or as directly related to environment should be noted. A soaring world population; the awesome potential of modern technologies; worrisome concerns over the future availability of energy, food, fibre and other raw materials; the growth, congestion, decay and pollution in urban-industrial regions; the severe disparities between have and have-not countries, and have and have-not peoples within countries; quests for meaningful life styles for the future; all are among the topics of the new environmentalists. One thing they all have in common is the severe doubts they raise about the ability of contemporary institutions and conventional ways of doing things to solve problems of such magnitudes and complexity.

One of the institutions being questioned is the university itself. To discuss the aims of environmental education is to raise nagging questions about the aims of any university education, especially for those whose time is destined to span the remaining decades of the 20th century. This in turn comes at a time of persistent questioning about the role and function of universities in contemporary Western societies when it is anything but certain that university institutions as now constituted will be able to meet the challenges being put rather forcefully to them.

Environmental education can be expected to be particularly attractive for students who are challenged by the big issues facing the world. They are going to discover early the uneasiness among their elders about the very possibility of solving the complex problems of the day before these go beyond reasonable control, and with little difficulty they are likely to join their peers in questioning the conventional way of doing things in the universities. They may resist traditional studies which direct them prematurely into narrow research-oriented specialities, they are almost bound to question conventional pedagogic methods and above all they will be seeking some sense of "relevance" in what they are required to learn.

The relevance criterion is undoubtedly ambivalent, referring partly to the pressing problems of the society students are in the process of inheriting and partly to their own needs for personal self-development. Environmental education must nevertheless respond to these concerns. This should be possible if careful consideration is given to the curriculum that is established and the pedagogy that is employed. But to ignore or dismiss this expressed need is virtually to destroy the possibility of having an environmental education programme which will succeed in achieving any aims set for it.

A determination of aims will depend very much on the scope of the definition given to "environment". Since this is such an all-inclusive term, it becomes necessary to decide whether and to what extent it is to be bounded in any particular environmental education programme. Given the considerable range of things now said to be environmental, and the fact that "environment" now symbolizes so many "gut issues" for increasing numbers of the present generation, I would contend that an environmental education programme should be very wide in scope and encompass "environment" from all of its many definitions and aspects. The studies encouraged by it would range over the complex interrelations of Man with the biophysical, socio-economic and man-made physical environments in its attempts to understand better the main features of these systems within which Man operates, and this would be in no way limited by the conventional and arbitrary boundaries set by the established academic disciplines.

There is anything but unanimous agreement with this view. The opposing one is that most of the concerns now said to be "environmental" are wrong identifications of real problems, or if valid they are properly carved up and distributed for treatment within the existing compartments of knowledge and expertise. Educationally, if solutions are in fact needed, they are to be sought entirely by training more people with the same array of technical and professional expertise as already exist, with at best only minor modifications in curricula or teaching methods.

This is the view that also appears to be reflected in a certain amount of re-labelling which uses "environment" in reference to established university courses of study in, for example, engineering, architecture, biology, geography and natural resources. The need for name changes is not clear, but perhaps there are gains seen in staking academic jurisdiction on behalf of existing disciplines or professions, in pointing out some contemporary relevance for existing courses of study, or merely in the expectation that research funds are more readily forthcoming for "environment" than for other things. It is not for one moment denied that useful contributions are being made in the already existing teaching and research programmes but their particular objectives and approach may differ considerably from what is implied by the expressed need for broad perspectives and pluridisciplinarity in considering environmental problems.

However, to take an all-encompassing approach in the scope of an environmental education programme means that the aims being sought from this have to be carefully considered. They could hardly be seen in terms of providing all the requisite bodies of knowledge and the multitude of specialized skills which may be called upon to cope with problems said to be environmental. This would pose unmanageable problems of deciding what had to be included and what could be left out. Few of the existing disciplines from the sciences and arts could be readily excluded and the list of professions to be considered would be lengthy.

One is left then with the apparent dilemma that environmental education should be of the widest possible scope yet somehow selective in ways seen to be "relevant" to the various students who elect to undertake it. This can only be resolved if an environmental education is conceived more in terms of processes than contents, and in terms of widely applicable and adaptable skills rather than in specific disciplinary or professional ones. The aims may not be dissimilar from what is sought through other approaches to education. Ultimately, the aims would be to sustain a process in which students learn how to learn, find out how to find out, and carry this forward methodically and with increasing sophistication and creative self-direction long after they leave university.

The complex contemporary problems represented by those said to be environmental provide the basis for initiating this process, in that they give ample scope for developing considerable intellectual acumen and other skills which are not artificially constrained by academic disciplinary boundaries. At the same time a broad perspective can be provided from which students can decide in a much more knowing way the particular role or career relating to environment that particularly suits them. The potential roles and careers are many, ranging from critic, advocate, initiator, coordinator or manager of the process of social change and adjustment, through to the array of specialized

126

skills needed to contribute to the solving of individual problems. An environmental education per se can do no more than introduce the possibilities and provide sufficient common ground from which preparation for various careers or roles might begin through both concurrent and subsequent study.

This approach to conceiving the aims of environmental education would seem to place it well within the tradition of a liberal education, in terms of the broad perspective and generalized skills being sought. In a way this is so. But the significant distinction would be looked for in the type of curriculum and approaches to teaching. These must meet the expressed need for "relevance" in the present day world which is generating so many of the environmental problems now having to be faced. The orientation is much more towards the future than the past, and the stress is much more on processes of learning than on the acquisition of received bodies of knowledge and traditions. This hardly seems inappropriate in a world of increasing change where the "knowledge explosion" is itself a major problem rendering existing bodies of knowledge vulnerable to rapid obsolescence, and leaving the practitioners of specific professional and technical skills with increasing difficulties about how to keep up-dated. It suggests that flexibility, mobility and adaptability will be the survival skills of the future.

Reflections such as these have contributed to the rationale for the man-environment studies programme at Waterloo. However, it still leaves a number of considerations about the curriculum and pedagogic methods best suited to achieve such aims.

CURRICULUM

The kind of curriculum which would facilitate the achievement of the aims of an environmental education programme as indicated would have to be pluridisciplinary in approach, flexible in terms of the subjects which may be studies, and problem and issue oriented to provide scope for developing the kinds of skills which are deemed useful. It has to be pluridisciplinary if it is to accomodate the full range of concerns now said to be environmental, yet selective in terms of subject matter and ways of focusing on it, if it is to serve the desired educational process.

There may be merit in striving for a truly interdisciplinary approach to environmental education, although progress towards this may be long in coming. The intellectual underpinnings for interdisciplinarity may be provided best by systems theory and decision theory. The former would provide the basis for comprehensive analyses of man-environment systems, and would help to interpret environmental problems as symptoms of malfunctioning in systems. Ecologists for example have provided particularly useful concepts for examining biophysical environmental systems and the impact of Man's activities in them. Decision theory on the other hand provides a problem-solving focus for assessing and relating information from diverse sources. The curriculum should certainly include systems theory, with ecology as a particularly relevant example of it, and decision theory. However, the sheer complexity of phenomenon represented by environmental problems would seem to suggest it is premature to rely on these as the overall intellectual schema for structuring the curriculum. Rather they should be introduced in individual courses within the curriculum.

A problems and issues orientation gives considerable opportunity to meet the "relevance" test both in terms of utilizing situations accepted as being important, and to the extent they are selected by students, they will be situations of considerable interest to them. This is essentially a pedagogic device which has considerable merit in terms of effective learning if it can be skilfully used. It is also one way of selecting out from the enormous array of potential subject matter those topics or aspects which will best serve an educational process. The curriculum should however, ensure that the selection is not completely random and opportunistic, and that there is in fact a progression through time from the relatively straightforward to the relatively complex in terms of the situations used and the analyses and interpretations required of them.

Problems and issues should also be selected from the diverse orientations which are emerging as the main interpretations of what environmental studies include. Examples are : environmental perception studies and the significance these have for urban-architectural design; environmental pollution in all its many forms; the conservation and use of natural resources; or alternative futures and life styles. Each of these are bound to generate a number of specific problems and issues which can serve as topics for pluridisciplinary consideration, and collectively they can give quite a wide overview and broad perspective.

Besides encouraging intellectual skills for analyses and syntheses, a curriculum would do well to make provisions for developing communications skills utilizing means other than reports and oral presentations. Much information lies unread and unused in libraries and archives. One important role for environmentalists is to help bridge the gulf between research specialists who generate new information and ideas, and those in various institutions and organizations who use, or should use research results. This requires not only an ability to document a case, but also an ability to present it persuasively to the right audiences. Usually this is a prerequisite for effective social action. While it is probably not feasible to require each student to obtain reasonable skills in making and using films, video-tapes, radio documentaries or other audio-vidual devices, nevertheless as many provisions as possible should be made to incorporate these into the curriculum for students who have audio-visual interests and aptitudes. In the current generation, this can be a sizeable proportion of them.

The curriculum presently in use for the man-environment studies programme at Waterloo covers four years and lead to a Bachelor of Environmental Studies (B. E. S.) degree. It specifies just under one half of the courses which are required of all students. and these reflect the considerations discussed above. Virtually all of the mandatory courses are in the first and second years, so that the third and fourth year is open almost entirely to elective choices.

Generally, the intent of the required courses is to introduce the wide range of problems, subjects, and perspectives inherent in a programme of environmental studies, and to develop some elementary skills in searching out relevant information and using it methodically. The wide range of elective choices, which can consist of courses selected from anywhere in the university, permits each student to select a mix of subject and skill courses best suited to his own self-development and career needs.

It is expected, and so far this has been borne out, that by the end of the first or at least the second year, most students have a much clearer idea of the directions in which their particular interests lie with respect to environmental studies. On this basis they can make a knowledgeable and firm commitment on the way they wish to proceed.

Two broad options are open to them. The first is to obtain the qualifications of a baccalaureate degree and then proceed to a professional programme in fields such as public administration, business administration, law, planning, or secondary school teaching. The other is to combine environmental studies with some one discipline. This may be a matter of concentrating elective choices in one other department of the university,

129

or it may mean transferring to another department and selecting
environmental studies as the electives permitted by that department. This should provide them with most of the options open to
students of the discipline in question, although it should give
them particular advantage in pursuing pluridisciplinary graduate studies relating to environment. One such programme dealing
with both environmental professions and environmental sciences
has recently been established in Canada at York University, in
Toronto.

The core of the existing curriculum is a sequence of semi-
nar-workshop sessions which run throughout the four-year programme. These provide opportunities for students to work
individually and in small groups on problems they themselves
select after consultation with faculty. In the first year this becomes the occasion for students to explore situations of considerable personal interest to them, with the almost inevitable
result of discovering for themselves the major gaps in knowledge and skills. This serves as a useful guide and incentive for
directing their learning. In the second and higher years the
intent is to retain the problem focus, but require increasing
sophistication in gathering and assessing information, based
increasingly on hypotheses or theories, relating it to whatever
problems are selected and posing various means which may
lead to their solution. This is the occasion for drawing together
background knowledge and insights gained from other sources
and also for applying skills in the use of different media. One
other aspect to these sessions is that students learn to cooperate with one another in small groups. While this is seldom consistent with the individual competitiveness they experienced in
primary and secondary schools, it is consistent with the situation they find themselves in after they leave the formal education system.

Since it is not possible to "cover" all of the substantive
areas which are relevant to the full array of environmental
concerns there was a need to consider how best to introduce
students to some of the main possibilities and indicate how
these relate to environmental interests. This is being attempted
by having one series of required courses which leads into areas
otherwise covered by the social sciences, and another which
leads into areas covered by certain of the natural sciences,
especially biology and ecology. The intent of these is to introduce some of the main themes and concepts provided by disciplines and indicate the extent to which they are, or can be used to
understand environmental questions. Again, the problem and
issue approach seems to be an effective one for arousing interest in some of the contributing disciplines. Students can then

130

follow up these interests by electing other courses for more concentrated study in the appropriate departments of the university.

A third feature of the curriculum considers some of the basic skills for problem solving and communications. The former starts with a review of the main sources of information, how these may be obtained and utilized, and proceeds to considerations of structured research techniques involving experimental designs and survey research, and it includes an introduction to statistics and the use of computers. Some familiarity in using various media for communication is obtained with the assistance of an audio-visual centre at the university, courses in the fine arts and through the use of modest facilities within the Division of Environmental Studies. When doing individual or small group projects, students are encouraged to present results when appropriate, in the form of films, video-tapes or with other audio-visual techniques, and in certain cases reports can be prepared in the form of scripts or briefs suitable for public hearings on some particular issue.

These are the three areas which are required of all students in the man-environment studies programme during their first two years. Any one can be supplemented by a few elective courses which students take during the first two years, and developed further by the directions chosen for more concentrated study during the final two years. Among the electives available are some courses given by our own faculty, but for the most part such courses will be selected from other sources.

PEDAGOGIC METHODS

Dissatisfaction with traditional pedagogic methods and the kinds of faculty-student relations associated with them is a recurrent feature of the unrest in universities. As already mentioned it is reflected in the demand for "relevance", which so often expresses a plea for interactions which meet the self-development needs of students. At least in North America, dissatisfaction may be increased by the commitments many students make to social action groups which go beyond the university, and a corresponding impatience with programmes of study which do not seem in any way related to these interests or do not appear to enhance their potential effectiveness in the roles they foresee for themselves after leaving the university.

One essential response of university teachers to these

131

expectations is to reconsider carefully their approach to teaching. Diverse approaches reflect different implicit theories
of learning as well as differences in preferred styles of teaching.
This should invite closer attention to be given to relating approach to the type of learning that is being encouraged in different
situations. Similar attention should be invited to the process of
grading and assessment of students particularly to reconsider
the purpose, the means, and the effects of various assessment
systems.

If nothing else, these considerations should warn against
placing too much reliance on lecturing, and retaining the implicit traditional assumption that a valid education can only be
gained from the university's faculty and its libraries. It requires
instead much greater willingness to experiment with alternatives such as team-teaching, student selected projects, the
involvement of non-academics in the programme of studies, and
the explicit use of off-campus events and situations as opportunities for effective learning.

At this point I can only indicate some of the approaches we
are trying out at Waterloo. While we do use the conventional
lecture and discussion group format, we have also experimented with student-selected and student-directed learning situations, which sometimes go beyond the university campus and
in which faculty serve more as advisers and consultants than as
teachers in the traditional sense. This is perhaps the main innovation we have tried to introduce.

In these latter situations, the perception of the role of a
faculty member must broaden correspondingly. He must see
himself as a facilitator, and a catalyst for various learning processes and he must be prepared to organize and coordinate the
involvement of other people in the process, rather than assume
the role of sole possessor of wisdom before groups of students.
This means that much of his time will be devoted to learning
with his students by participating in some of the same situations
with them. He will be responding more to their expressed interests in questions and ideas, rather than dictating what subjects are to be "covered" and when.

This more open-ended learning process has been used for
the series of seminars-workshops which are seen as the core
of the curriculum. For first year students these are essentially explorations based on projects they themselves select to
work on in small groups. A broad theme is used to relate
these, such as environmental pollution, or population problems.
Carrying out such projects requires among other things library
research, the interviewing of people and the presentation of a

report in some form to the larger class for discussion.

For example, a group may elect to study a particular instance of water pollution. In the process they learn about some of the simpler chemical and biological indices of pollution by being guided through an exercise of taking and analyzing water samples; they will find out something about the operation of sewage and waste treatment facilities from visits and meetings with technical personnel who manage municipal treatment plants or certain polluting industries, and they will learn something of the political and administrative problems from discussions with officials in pollution control agencies, and the mayor or city councillors. The learning involved at this introductory level is essentially about the complexity of some of these problems which, if they are to be properly understood, must draw upon fields such as biology, chemistry, hydrology, sanitary engineering, economics, city planning, law, and politics.

As another example, under a theme of population problems groups of first year students investigated the availability of birth control devices and family planning services in their own communities. They soon encountered strong conservative views from members of the medical, nursing and pharmacy professions, who were found to be exercising forms of discrimination and control not always related to their professional competencies when it came to providing these legally sanctioned services. As groups reported their various encounters, discussions led rather naturally to questions about attitudes and values, the explicit and implicit power structures in communities; perceptions of roles and responsibilities of professions, and governmental policies for health and social services. In the process it was realized that understanding would be enhanced by knowing more about psychology, sociology, politics, and certain religious philosophies.

While these types of exploration projects can generate considerable interest in finding out more about the various academic fields, the problems and issues approach also seems effective for some lecture and discussion sessions. This is especially so with students who are not initially or primarily interested in the disciplines. The considerable relevance of biology for example can be demonstrated by introducing various topics in relation to environmental questions. Pollution and the abuse of drugs can provide the basis for introducing physiology; a discussion of nuclear testing may be the occasion to introduce genetics, and population problems can lead to considerations of reproductive biology or the ecology of animal populations.

133

The social sciences can be approached in a similar manner.
Concerns with poverty, particularly as it effects minority
groups, can be the basis for discussions on social class and
power; the economics of the distribution of income, and government policies for income maintenance and stability. Recent
controversies surrounding the sale of Canadian oil and natural
gas to the United States and the proposals for transporting oil
from the Arctic by tankers and pipelines easily provide the
occasion to examine questions about the role of government
in guiding the pattern of economic development and protecting
natural environments, and about alternatives to the "continen-
talization" of the Canadian economy. A number of proposals
to restructure the local government of the county in which the
University of Waterloo is situated provides a basis for examining the roles and functions of government and the approaches
to planning for future growth and change.

Individual assignments to students then develop this approach
further. Essentially they are asked to select problems and situations of interest to them, and carry out some enquiry which
necessitates locating resource materials and persons, using
these methodically to explore whatever problem was selected,
and presenting the results in an essay or some other agreed_
upon form. This offers almost unlimited possibilities for self-
directed work, but faculty must be willing to recognize that
the process being encouraged is as every bit important as the
results, and progress should be guided and monitored with this
in mind.

Two examples from among our second year students may
illustrate this. A student is a volunteer youth worker in a new
high rise apartment and low income town house community on
the outskirts of Toronto. The developers declared bankruptcy
without providing the community facilities incorporated into
their plan, and the government has called a hearing to review
the needs for such facilities and how they may best be provided.
As a course assignment this student is to gather data to give
a sociological profile of this community ; do some sample interviewing on the problem of facilities, and on the basis of this
enquiry and his own first hand experience, present a brief
at the hearings.

A major industrial development calling for a new steel mill,
an oil refinery, and a thermal power plant was announced for
a rural area on the north shore of Lake Erie. The government
has initiated planning studies to help it decide on the best pattern
for the new urban developments which will be required, and to
indicate the magnitude of new public investments needed for

134

roads, schools, water and sewerage, and so on. The area in question is in an ecological zone having several unique natural features, and some species of plants and animals not commonly found elsewhere in the province. A student particularly interested in wildlife conservation is undertaking, as a course assignment, an enquiry of naturalists, anglers and hunters, conservationists and others familiar with this area to try and determine what the unique natural features are; what the possible impact of the anticipated developments might be on them, what else needs to be known, and what can be done to preserve this natural variety. The result of this enquiry may then form a basis for a critique of the planning which is being done.

There is really no lack of "real-world" situations which can be utilized to introduce concepts, techniques and relevant background information from disciplines which normally would cover these. It does however, require access to information not always readily available in university which puts almost all of its priorities on textbooks and the major academic journals. This of course means that the faculty themselves must make a point of developing and maintaining contacts outside of the university, and academic circles.

There are other means for relating the course of studies to concerns of the non-university world. The obvious one is the involvement of non-academics in seminars and discussion groups where they are asked to share their first hand knowledge and experience with students. Almost invariably this arouses considerable interest among both students and their guests. Again, an interpretive theme which relates diverse presentations is desirable. One which we have found successful for first year students is an enquiry into how the many different organizations now expressing concerns about "environment" perceive or define the main problems. Representatives from governmental agencies, businesses, and various citizen groups were invited to share their views and participate in discussions. Essentially the same function is performed by arranging for students to attend and perhaps participate in conferences or other special meetings and report back about the proceedings.

For the more activist student, direct involvement in community actions groups can provide an effective bridge between the academic world and the "real" one. One such community group called "Pollution Probe" has chapters based in several Canadian universities where it draws heavily on students for support and faculty for advise. Through it, students become involved in the documentation of violations of pollution laws, or situations which point to the need for closer inspection and

135

more stringent regulations. They then advocate legal or other proceedings through briefs to the appropriate government authorities and publicity for their findings.

Traditional academics often scorn such groups, especially when they become controversial and even although they fall within a traditional view of the university as being a place for reasoned dissent. Although such group activities are extra-curricular, they provide the occasion for relating valid academic studies to the activist commitment of student participants. For example, through Probe activities, a student became interested in knowing more about the motivations people have for joining such groups, and this became the topic for a reading assignment in the relevant sociological and psychological literature. For another it sparked off interests in the emerging field of environmental law, and for others it led to an interest in how the successes of Probe could be applied to citizen involvement in other environmental problems.

I have stressed the means by which we have been experimenting with student initiated projects, and relating academic study to the on-going world beyond the university. This was the aspect of our programme in which we felt innovation was needed. It should be remembered however, that concurrent with these activities students are also taking courses in various academic disciplines and, increasingly, they are expected to bring these to bear on the environmental questions they elect to explore.

Obviously it is too soon to draw conclusions about the results of these attempts. There is no doubt that they are greeted quite enthusiastically by some students, who proceed to devote considerable effort and interest into problems and subjects they select. At the other extreme, there are a few that feel lost without a clearly perceived structure to relate to and definite instructions to follow. For some this is a temporary situation as they adjust from the structured education they have received up to the point of entering university, to the more self-directed approach being encouraged of them.

For the faculty on the other hand, the more open-ended educational process requires the closest of cooperation with one another in order to contribute effectively to the process. It is no longer a case of a professor dominating a situation so that what is being learned is confined to that which he himself already knows. The device of team-teaching in which several faculty may participate directly in the process, and having "stand-by" arrangements whereby students can be referred to faculty in various departments for help in certain areas, is

136

essential. This means that a considerable amount of effort should be devoted to building up an informal network of "resource persons" from throughout the university and beyond, and this is something which obviously takes time and care.

INSTITUTIONAL STRUCTURE

The type of environmental education programme I have been describing does not fit neatly into a traditional university structure. It is of necessity pluridisciplinary, so its orientation spreads horizontally across the vertical jurisdictions of established disciplines where it is liable to be resented as an unwarranted intrusion. It pays little or no attention to the boundary separating the university from the rest of the community and thereby implicitly challenges some cherished notions on both sides of the boundary about the proper role of the university. It gives a degree of latitude to students to determine the direction and nature of their own studies which in the view of some is irresponsible. It may also commit the worst of all academic sins, according to some viewpoints : it may become popular.

To the extent that its curricula and pedagogic methods are at variance with established practices, an environmental studies programme will encounter difficulties in acceptance by other than the students at an established university. I think it significant that the only really new environmental studies programmes I have been made aware of are located in quite new universities or come only with major organizational innovations in established universities. This I would be inclined to relate to structural rigidities more than the absence of individuals who would be interested in a new venture and very capable of contributing towards it.

Perhaps structure in itself is less important than the prevailing attitudes with which innovation is greeted in the larger university community. The point of basic agreement must be that universities can and should provide a wide array of alternative approaches to education, each valid for meeting different needs of students and society. It is not the case that there is one true path. While this may be grudgingly accepted among established disciplines and professions, with jurisdictions established accordingly, the test seems to come when programmes are proposed which ignore these traditional ways of organizing knowledge and expertise.

The Waterloo undertaking refered to in this paper was given the traditional garb of a department with an honours level education programme to administer. It does not have or claim its own discipline, and constantly deals with subjects that existing disciplines firmly believe are "theirs". This would provide a rich source of misunderstandings were it not for the kind of freshness and flexibility associated with a new university and a relatively young faculty. In a conventionally structured university this is really about the best that could be expected, and our task is to build up an informal network of cooperative relationships which will permit a genuinely pluridisciplinary undertaking to function from such an organizational base.

If I was given a completely free hand to prescribe an "ideal" structure for an environmental education programme in a university context, I rather imagine it would be one in which theme programmes provided the major basis for organizing curricula, and the disciplinary skills would be subsiduary components, each contributing to several theme programmes. Man-environment relations would be one of a number of thematic orientations. However, I would not want this to become a new dogma for all education. Philosophical discussions about the environment repeatedly stress the need to maintain diversity and variety in natural, social, and man-built environments. The same should hold for universities.

Chapter II

DESCRIPTION OF EXPERIMENTS IN ENVIRONMENTAL EDUCATION PRESENTED AT THE WORKSHOP OF TOURS

By Marie-José de FELICE
Department of Environment
University of Paris VII, France

DESCRIPTION OF EXPERIMENTS IN ENVIRONMENTAL EDUCATION PRESENTED AT THE WORKSHOP OF TOURS

. Preliminary remarks

. Comments

. Sheets on environmental education experiments : East
Anglia, Green Bay, Paris VII, Tours, Ulster, Waterloo.

PRELIMINARY REMARKS

During the Workshop held at Tours in April 1971 various
environmental education experiments at university level were
presented.

All these experiments had been in operation for only one,
two or exceptionally three years and in consequence it was not
possible to gauge to what extent they had been successful since
none of the courses had yet been completed.

It was, however, useful to make a general appraisal of the
situation and although the information available was of necessity incomplete, it was nevertheless a starting-point. Exchanges
of information must be continued before any comparative analysis of experiments can be usefully carried out.

The six environmental education experiments described in
the attached sheets are all being carried out in OECD Member
countries : USA, United Kingdom, Canada and France. These
are "developed" countries; they are highly urbanised and industrialised and at the present time their long university traditions
are often felt to be more of a handicap than an advantage. It
would be interesting, at a later date, to extend the analysis to
experiments being tried out in other parts of the world (such
as the "developing" countries, the USSR, etc.) to see how these
educational problems arise there, what form university activities take in this field, what teaching methods are used, etc.

1. These sheets would have given more information (thus
   enabling comparisons to be made more easily) had they

141

been accompanied by summary tables giving details of :

a) the official educational systems of each of the countries in which the experiments are being carried out;

b) parallel training facilities for managerial staff (if any) and the origin of managerial staff already engaged in industry, administration, etc. ;

c) the number of students in relation to the total population of each of the countries concerned;

d) the status of teachers, etc.

2. With the educational system thus clearly outlined, a brief description of trends in the demographic, economic and political situation of the region and the major ecological problems at present facing environmental experts would have enabled each experiment to be placed in its proper context.

3. If, as those who took part in the Tours Workshop hope, meetings between Member countries on environmental education are to be continued, documentation compiled on these lines would no doubt enable errors of interpretation to be avoided and lead to a better understanding of the motivations of the proposed education as well as the difficulties encountered in its implementation. It would thus facilitate any transpositions from country to country.

COMMENTS

For the sake of clarity, the environmental education experiments were presented in the form of sheets, with one sheet for each experiment and eight headings per sheet :

. Address of the university where the experiment is being held.
. Documentation used for the sheet.
. Motivation of the experiment in operation.
. Educational aims.
. Year in which the course (the new training section) was started.
. Framework of the experiment.
. Structure and management of the body in which the

142

experiment is being carried out.

Detailed analysis of the proposed education (certificates aimed at, duration of studies, audience, enrolments, teaching staff, syllabus, main subjects, educational principles, progress of the education, outlets for graduates).

Owing to the diversity of the documentation, it has not been possible to complete the various sheets in accordance with this pattern.

Address of the university

Although it is of interest to know where the experiments are being carried out (thus enabling any future contact to be made directly with the university), it did not seem necessary to give the name of a particular person in charge. Chancellors, Presidents Principals and Deans, whether elected or nominated, hold statutory office for only a few years consecutively.

Documentation

Although in several cases this could be supplemented after the Worshop (some documents are dated 1972), the documentation lacks consistency and is not detailed enough.

It is generally of two types : either an information brochure prepared for students or the working document prepared for the Workshop held in Tours in April 1971.

Information is therefore available mainly on :

a) the subjects taught and their sequence

b) the aims, intentions and principles as well as the personal views of the departmental heads who drew up the working documents for the Workshop.

It would be useful to study :

- the statutes of the bodies carrying out environmental education and their internal regulations;
- their balance sheets or activity reports;
- class syllabuses (integrated education) and syllabuses of field work;
- students' work;
- etc.

143

Motivation of the experiments

1. The motivation of the environmental education experiments present similar features from one university to another, although they are differently organised in different countries.

2. The main concern is to find a response to uneasiness (stress or anxiety) due to a realisation of failure on three levels:

- relationship between man and his environment;
- relationship between the universities and society;
- relationship between teachers and their students.

3. The most strongly motivated universities intend, by means of environmental education and research :

- to help to define new values (Green Bay), new behaviour (Ulster), or new life styles (Waterloo);
- to put themselves at the service of the community in endeavouring to solve the very real problems posed by the "environment crisis";
- to meet the student challenge by establishing syllabuses and teaching methods which are relevant to the modern world.

There are enormous problems, but the clearsighted resolve and rational dynamism emanating from the various documents are commensurate with them.

However, despite this apparent unanimity, further details show that three important points (not necessarily points of discord) need greater consideration.

Point 1 : Although the "environment" is the central theme of all the experiments, the term has not been previously defined and in consequence each university gives it a different content.

For some, environment refers primarily and almost exclusively to nature, natural balances and natural laws. Ecology will thus be the basis of the education provided.

For another, the environmental sciences are understood "virtually to exclude biology ... and ecology" ... the ecologist is still studying small sub-systems in isolation ... and ecology has been unable to come to terms with the human climax; ... for a school of environmental sciences this is an unhelpful approach.

The same difference in attitude is found with regard to the place of the human sciences, law and economics.

144

Although some of these attitudes can be explained by a lack of resources to achieve the objectives, others, as indicated below, are founded on firm principles.

There are still very few universities with a comprehensive conception of environment and which organise their syllabuses accordingly.

In these circumstances, it would seem necessary to try to determine when exactly a given form of education can be described as "environmental education".

Point 2 : The role of the university, the conception and objectives of its departments will differ according to whether it views environmental problems as everybody's concern or simply the concern of those who will work in this field (town planner, landscaper, engineer, administrator, co-ordinator or generalist, etc.). In each of the six experiments examined, both conceptions are present although seldom explicit, except in the case of Green-Bay and Paris VII. Here there is a problem of general university policy, which, because of its important consequences, would merit joint discussion.

Point 3 : One sometimes has the impression that rather than the formulation of new ethical values, a new religious cult is being created and the impassioned tone of certain statements seems that of the priest or apostle of a new doctrine. Will the next stage be the appearance of temples, dogma, initiates, fanatics and heretics? And is this approach to the problem not more likely to delay its solution?

Educational aims

Depending on the attitude adopted by the university (i.e. whether the environment is everybody's concern or simply limited to environmental experts) and the extent of the role which it wishes to play within the community, the education given :

1. will be limited to providing further education over one or two semesters to future environmental specialists;

2. or to train, over three or four years, environmental generalists or co-ordinators and/or environmental teachers;

3. or it will also try to make all students aware of their responsibilities towards the environment (throughout their studies whatever their future jobs may be);

4. and even beyond the university, to inform the general
   public and help it to play an active part in this area
   (in addition to the experiments described in the sheets,
   this type of education is particularly well developed in
   Norway as shown in O. Rønning's report (ref. CERI/HE/
   CP/71. 03) .

The aims of environmental education at university level are
thus very varied; ranging from being simply a supplement to
traditional university courses to the ambitious (but no doubt
necessary) attempt to provide a general core for all departments
and an extramural service available on request. In addition,
the three objectives may be pursued simultaneously within the
same university, due no doubt to the fact that most of the experiments are still in their early stages.

Year in which a new course was started

All courses are of recent creation (the earliest in autumn
1968).

Reflection and caution seem to have been the qualities pre-
siding over the establishment of such courses.

Either a group of academics working in collaboration with
non-academics formulates over two or three years plans
for a university entirely geared to environmental problems;
or, in a traditional university, the transition is made in
stages over one or two years from environmental education
offered as an unattached option, to the organisation of a
specific department, and then of an autonomous structure
to manage it (unless the structure precedes the department);
or an educational reform enables projects which have long
been held up by the rigid divisions between disciplines to
be carried out.

The opening of a specific department of environmental
education has always taken place on an experimental basis, with
small numbers of both students and teachers.

It would appear, although this is not certain, that the educational programmes as a whole have only been established with
the gradual flow of students through the new department.

Framework of the experiments

All the experiments presented are being carried out within the university framework but at different institutional levels;

- environment is the central theme of the whole university (Green Bay);
- or it concerns only one department (Ulster, Paris VII) or one school (East Anglia) amongst other departments or more traditional schools within the same university;
- or it may even be a division of a department (Waterloo) or a centre within an Education and Research Unit (Tours).

The experiments therefore vary considerably in scale ; consequently their independence and resources are also likely to differ.

Structure and management

In each of the six cases presented, an additional structure has been created to carry out the new functions ; an additional department and not a new department since, as we have already seen, we are dealing here with a university among other universities, or a school, department or section among others of the same.

"Something new" therefore has to be established within the same statutory framework and under the same regulations as governing bodies on the same level.

Why not, then, inside an existing structure ? As "monodisciplinary strongholds", "inward-looking", and "wanting to keep the advantages they have gained", existing departments are accused of being "static", "rigid", and "fossilized".

But how can these pitfalls be avoided? In what ways can these new departments be original?

In the papers from those bodies which have done the most extensive analysis (it should be noted that they are also the ones which aim their different types of education at the widest objectives), four revealing guiding principles emerge;

a) to combat the independence and aloofness of the universities, there is, first of all, an opening to the outside world by means of continual two-way contacts. Non-academics take part in :

- the definition of the problems to be studied and the syllabuses and research programmes deriving therefrom,

147

- the management of the body and the work of the committees which govern it,
- the education as such; similarly teachers and students,
- work outside the university in the field,
- take part in local extramural activities chosen as study
assignments.

(It would be interesting to have information on the ways of
applying this principle of opening the universities, so as to
be able to analyse its consequences more deeply).

This idea is also held by other bodies but their approach to
the outside world is rather more cautious. It may consist
only of :

- calling on teachers from other universities,
- or asking the opinion of non-academics (usually well-
known experts).

b) to end monodisciplinary divisions, in the supplementary
structure work is organized around subjects, thus developing inter-departmental co-operation ;

c) to change and broaden the role of the teacher, he becomes,
vis-à-vis the students, an adviser and a guide and vis-à-
vis the outside, a consultant and a link;

The many facets of this new way of looking at his job
often require the teacher to be only "the first of his students". They also require that he should be permanently
available.

d) as a corollary to the above, the role of the student gains
in importance; he takes part in the definition and development of syllabuses and management; he has a much freer
hand in the orientation, pace, and form of his own work.

It is thus by redistributing roles, by sharing responsibilities, by external help and a pluridisciplinary approach to
the problems that teachers think they will be able to question
almost continuously their own activity and avoid rigidity.

Here again, it would be interesting to have further information in the following :

- by what practical methods can a balance be established
inside educational institutions between the minimum of
collective discipline and stability necessary for any type
of management and the maximum of individual freedom
and critical thought which will enable the desired adjustment to be brought about;

148

- what resources and what degree of independence are available to each institution.

All universities have pointed out that the experiment was difficult, long and costly but only the universities of East Anglia and Tours give precise details of the problems - the former to indicate that its situation is sound and the latter to deplore the very serious difficulties experienced with regard to staff, premises and budgets.

As has been seen, the supplementary structures set up to provide environmental education abandon traditional attitudes and ideas; they wish to innovate. For all of them, except Green Bay, there is the question of ascertaining what these "implants" bring to the universities into which they are grafted and how they are tolerated (and vice versa !).

Is co-existence possible and desirable? The documents analysed all mentioned misgivings, friction and even quite violent clashes among differently oriented departments inside the same university.

Detailed analysis of the proposed course

1. Diplomas : Diplomas are awarded only to students who have completed a full course, i.e. 2, 3 or 4 years' study. The diplomas are similar to those awarded at an equivalent level of study in the country concerned (honours degree - DUEL - Maîtrise...)

As it is the policy of certain universities not to reserve their environmental education for a few specialists but to make it available, if only partially, to all students and also to adults under continuing education schemes it would be interesting to ascertain what steps have been taken to provide a diploma for these two types of students in this discipline.

2. Duration of studies : In the case of subjects which are part of an organised curriculum and for which diplomas are awarded the duration of studies may be 2, 3 or 4 years for students who have completed their secondary school course. A systematic analysis of the appointments obtained by diploma-holders at the various levels will eventually show the comparative value of these qualifications on the labour market.

In the case of students not working for a diploma and adults attending a continuing education course the training period is not less than six months and not more than one year.

3. Potential students : a) working for Environment diplomas :

    - all universities expect students from secondary schools
      to have a reasonably good mathematical background. Only
      three universities have made specific arrangements for
      bringing students up to the required level in mathematics
      if their previous training has been purely literary. No
      statistics are as yet available to show whether this has
      attracted a wider range of potential students.

    - as far as the curriculum is concerned one university
      systematically tries to mix students of different years
      and one other advocates mixing regular students with
      trainees in continuing education. In both cases the aim
      is to enrich the groups concerned and enable first-year
      students to acquire a mature approach more rapidly. Does
      this procedure apply to all subjects ? What results have
      been noted ? Should the idea of having homogeneous groups
      which teachers consider necessary for efficiency be
      reserved for certain types of practical work,or should
      it be dropped ?

      It would be of value to have more systematic information
      on this point.

    b) It is unfortunate that the available documentation does not
       show which sectors of the public would be interested in
       environmental courses as part of a recurrent education
       scheme.

4. Number of students : A sufficient number of students to
operate effectively, but not too many,in order to be able to :

    - develop and adapt syllabuses and teaching methods,
    - find appropriate employment.

This cautious approach seems to have been adopted in five
out of the six experiments analysed : from 50 to 100 students
are admitted each year to the first level of the course. The
objectives, the time allotted for preliminary planning and the
available facilities place the sixth experiment (Green Bay) in a
totally different class.

But although we know the average number of students admitted to Green Bay and the other universities we have no information as to the number of applications received or concerning
admission requirements.

In view of the new teaching methods, is it not essential to make a comparison between :

1. The number of students entering and the number completing the course ?

2. The percentage of students successfully completing an Environment course and the percentage of students doing more traditional courses in the same university ?

5. <u>The teachers</u> . Environment is not a discipline, at least not yet. It covers an extremely wide field of knowledge and overflows the limits of existing disciplines.

The developments of criteria for recruiting teaching staff is therefore a complex matter which does not yet seem to have been closely studied.

The first nucleus of teachers in the recently established departments in existing universities is in most cases composed of volunteers from these universities but nothing particular is known about them.

Teachers who have since been specifically recruited for environment courses seem to have a somewhat similar profile. They are expected to be young, painstaking, open-minded, enterprising, ready to meet any challenge, careful teachers, "resolutely optimistic", full of "dynamic belief in their mission" and "keen but judicious".

The documents in our possession make a point of this aspect.

This attempt to recruit pioneers laying stress on their qualities of leadership rather than the nature of their training and the direction of their research is perhaps justified in the initial stage. But can it be maintained over a long period without prejudice to the objective pursued and without damage to the teachers themselves ? The fact is that if it aims to put the problems of environment into their correct focus and help to solve them an Environment course must be enriched by research (this is perhaps truer for Environment than for any other sector). What are the subjects of research and how is it actually pursued in the new teaching departments ? How is environment linked up with teaching ? Has this problem not been neglected, at least in the preliminary phase, owing to the fact that all universities have given priority to teaching methods ? And yet every teacher in higher education is also a research worker :

- his teaching depends on the research he is doing,

- his contribution depends on the way his research develops,
- his career depends on the ultimate progress of his work.

It is, however, clear that :

- his new role as a permanent and all-purpose adviser to his students makes it necessary for him to be constantly available.
- the integrated teaching which he has to plan as part of a team mobilises a considerable part of his energy.
- his research and the permanent adaptation of his teaching methods to the objectives he has to pursue also call for a considerable effort.

This teaching research (for research has to be done in this field as well) is considered necessary by all concerned but it is still far from receiving recognition in higher education. Until it does receive recognition it can only be carried on pari passu with normal research. Can this really be done without one or other or both of these research tasks suffering while the teacher researcher exhausts himself in trying to meet all these require ments ?   To pursue this analysis fuller information would be required on the teacher/student ratio for each type of activity, recruitment criteria, working methods and timetables etc.

6.   Curriculum. We would rule out any training which unduly restricts the content of the word "environment" (failure to include ecology for example). As regards other training we have so far no more than the subject titles to judge whether an efforts is being made in each case to see the problem as a whole rather than to acquire a smattering of heterogeneous knowledge by dab- bling in everything.

These titles merely show a concern :

- to base the curricula on environmental problems so as to give students an incentive to seek information.
- to acquire methods of study and data analysis.
- to find a guiding concept for the co-ordination of the information acquired.

But what is behind these titles and how are the curricula developing ? Here again the documentation is too brief.

7.   Teaching principles. All experiments in environmental education reveal an urge to reform teaching methods. Teaching reform involves :

- integrated teaching,
- fieldwork,
- receptivity to outside influence,
- practical case studies,

and is reflected in all documentation.

But how are these principles put into practice ? How is the work developed, co-ordinated and evaluated ? What is its cost ? And above all what are the reactions of the students to these innovations ? In practice, they call for more personal work, initiative and freedom and require the students to make a more sustained but more constructive effort.

ENVIRONMENTAL EDUCATION EXPERIMENTS

Section 1

UNIVERSITY OF WATERLOO (CANADA)

DEPARTMENT OF MAN-ENVIRONMENT STUDIES

Address of the university where the educational experiment is taking place :

University of Waterloo - Ontario (Canada)

Documentation used to prepare this report :

OECD - March 1971, 18 pages - Original text in English, French translation - by G. R. Francis, Chairman of the Department of Man-Environment Studies, University of Waterloo.

Motivation of the current experiment :

a) The size and diversity of problems related to the environment : demographic growth ; the awesome potential of modern technologies ; non-renewal of resources of raw materials ; development, deterioration and pollution of urban-industrial regions ; inequality between countries and peoples ; worthwhile way of life for future, etc...

b) Urgent innovations in education to try to begin to solve problems before they become quite unmanageable.

c) Transformation of the role of the university : to look out onto the community.

Aims of course of study :

- to provide complementary training of general interest, within the framework of preparatory education, for all undergraduate students ;
- to widen the pre-vocational training of students in the Schools of Architecture and Urban Planning ;
- to provide specific environmental education.

Year of introduction of course of study :

The University of Waterloo was set up in 1959, while the Division of Environmental Studies providing the course of study described in this report was opened in 1969.

Location of the experiment :

The University of Waterloo is a traditional university comprising five faculties, four professional schools and four Church-affiliated colleges. The mathematics and engineering faculties are the largest of the units. The faculties are divided into discipline-based departments.

Structure and management of the establishment in which the experiment is being carried out :

From the administrative point of view the Division of Environmental Studies is similar to a faculty. It is in continuous communication with the other faculties. At present, the Division is composed of the School of Architecture, the School of Urban and Regional Planning, the Department of Geography and the Department of Man-Environment Studies.

The relationships between the different structures referred to may thus be summarised in the following diagram :

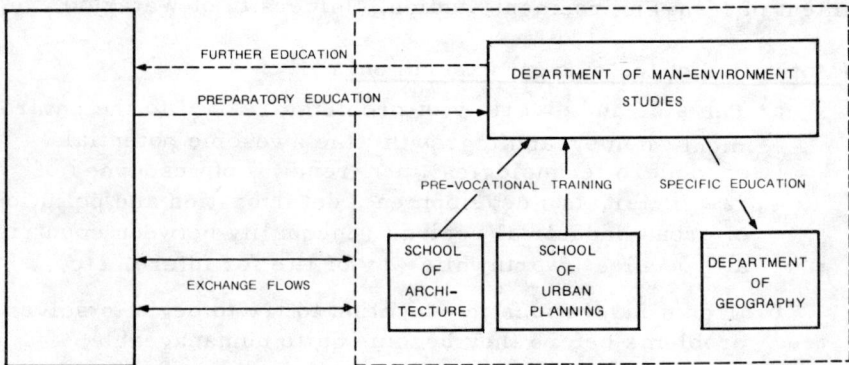

Mr. Francis refers to the administrative difficulties facing this horizontal structure covering more conventional institutions. Pluridisciplinarity is developed much more through the informal network established by the teachers with each other and with the outside world, than by any special regulations.

Detailed analysis of courses offered :

1. Degree course : Bachelor of Environmental Studies
                        (Honours degree)

156

2. Duration of studies : 4 years (undergraduate course)

3. Population : Students

4. Numbers :

    - The University had 1200 students in 1970-71.
    - Courses in the Department of Man-Environment
      Studies began with 3 full-time teachers and 20 students
      in 1969-70, and 10 full-time teachers and an average
      of 60 new students per year since 1970-71.

5. Teachers : about 15 young, full-time teachers in the
   different disciplines, with freshness of mind and flexibility.

6. Programme

Environment is interpreted in the broad sense, but with
no physics or chemistry.

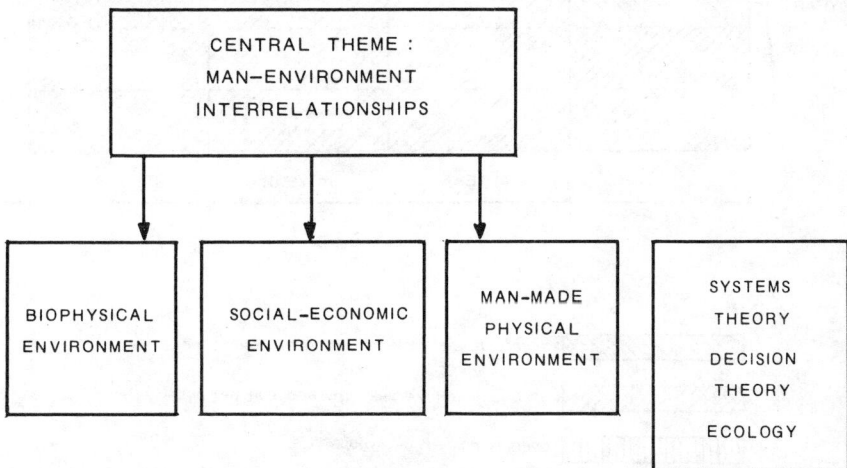

```
          ┌─────────────────────────┐
          │  CENTRAL  THEME :       │
          │  MAN—ENVIRONMENT        │
          │  INTERRELATIONSHIPS     │
          └─────────────────────────┘
              │        │        │
              ▼        ▼        ▼
┌──────────┐ ┌──────────────┐ ┌──────────┐ ┌──────────┐
│BIOPHYSICAL│ │SOCIAL-ECONOMIC│ │ MAN—MADE │ │ SYSTEMS  │
│ENVIRONMENT│ │ ENVIRONMENT  │ │ PHYSICAL │ │ THEORY   │
│          │ │              │ │ENVIRONMENT│ │ DECISION │
│          │ │              │ │          │ │ THEORY   │
│          │ │              │ │          │ │ ECOLOGY  │
└──────────┘ └──────────────┘ └──────────┘ └──────────┘
                                        TRAINING IN REASONING
```

Disciplines included : Biology, Geography, Anthropology,
Communications Science, Economics, Engineering, Fine Arts,
Psychology, Sociology and Social Science ; Statistics, Computer
Science, Documentation.

7. Pedagogic principles :

    - to seek to learn rather than to acquire knowledge
      (research techniques, experimental designs, etc...)

- ability to handle all audio-visual methods as a means of expression,
- to use "real-world" situations to motivate knowledge,
- to move out of the campus to participate in local activities,
- to regard the teacher as a consultant or adviser during a certain period of education, in order to develop student initiative as far as possible round projects which they have to carry out.

8. Pattern of studies :

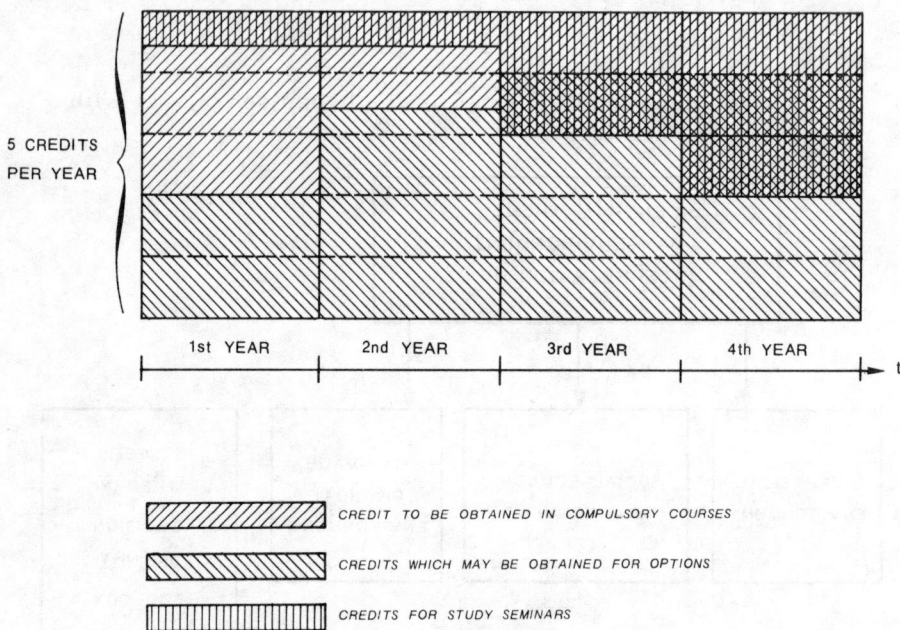

CREDIT TO BE OBTAINED IN COMPULSORY COURSES

CREDITS WHICH MAY BE OBTAINED FOR OPTIONS

CREDITS FOR STUDY SEMINARS

Overlappings between compulsory courses and options indicate that when a student has not obtained the maximum number of credits for his compulsory work he may make up the required number by credits obtained for options.

9. Career openings :

"The potential roles and careers are many, ranging from critic, advocate, initiator, co-ordinator or manager of the

process of social change and adjustment, through to the array
of specialised skills needed to contribute to the solving of individual problems." In fact, since the first students in the Division
will not be graduating till 1974, the career problem has not yet
arisen for them in this university.

Section 2

UNIVERSITY OF WISCONSIN - GREEN BAY

(UNITED STATES)

Address :

   University of Green Bay, Green Bay, Wisconsin, United
States.

Sources used for this data sheet :

1. "The University of Wisconsin - Green Bay" (An example
   of a university oriented towards Environmental problems)
   March 1970 a paper presented by Edward W. Weidner,
   Chancellor of the University of Wisconsin, Green Bay,
   distributed in French and English by CERI, (CERI/HE/
   CP/70.26) , 30 pp., comprising :

   . an introduction by Edward Weidner ;
   . a declaration of principle taken from the 1970-71 Year-
     book of the University of Wisconsin-Green Bay ;
   . an outline of the university's organisation and curri-
     culum ;
   . an address delivered to the American Association for
     Higher Education at Chicago "The University and its
     Environment : the example of the University of Wis-
     consin-Green Bay".

2. Green Bay Students' Handbook 1971-72, 195 pp. ;

3. Green Bay Students' Handbook 1972-73, 144 pp. .

Motivation of the current experiment

   To create within the framework of higher education a
"Communiversity" designed :

161

. to regain and maintain a realistic approach ;
. to meet the needs of the community ;
. to examine the problem of contemporary society and the ecological crisis in particular ;
. to formulate a new set of behavioural patterns so that scientific and technical knowledge can be used to improve the environment

in a word, to "meet the challenge of a new generation of youth who will not be denied less than they have been encouraged to dream".

Educational aim:

To train people in the duties of citizenship. This means combining the world of learning with the real world in such a way that, instead of turning out specialists narrowly confined to their own fields, a sense of social responsibility will be inculcated in every individual and group, by providing basic and advanced education across the broadest spectrum.

Date introduced :

1969 (after three years of preparation).

Background :

The university as a whole which has been set up to deal with environment as the core subject.

Structure :

The University of Green Bay is headed by a Chancellor ; to encourage the intermingling of disciplines it is not divided up into conventional departments or faculties teaching individual disciplines but is organised as a group of colleges, each dealing with one important environmental theme and each administered by a dean.

There are four such colleges :

1. The College of Environmental Sciences (protection of the environment and analysis of ecosystems).

2. The College of Community Sciences (regional and urban problems, processes of modernisation and change).

3. The College of Human Biology (growth and development of man, nutrition, capacity for work and adaptability, population dynamics).

4. The College of Creative Communication (analysis and synthesis, communication and action).

. The School of Professional Studies completes the education provided by the colleges, which here is job-oriented (in company management, public administration, nursery school, primary and secondary teaching, social services and the management of recreational resources). Each college groups teachers and students interested in the particular subject-matter dealt with. Courses, research and community programmes in these areas are the responsibility of the college.

Curricula :

1. Students are prepared for the following degrees :

- Bachelor of Arts or Science, Environmental Science
- Bachelor of Arts or Science, Human Biology
- Bachelor of Arts or Science, Community Sciences
- Bachelor of Arts or Science, Creative Communications
- Bachelor of Arts or Science, Administration.

To qualify for the diploma a student must have a minimum of 124 hours per term to his credit and must have resided for at least one year (years 3 or 4) at the university ; work for an engineering degree can be combined with preparation of one of the degrees listed above.

2. Duration of studies : 4 years

. there is a "semester" system - the first semester lasting from September to December and the second from February to May, coupled with a special period in January ;

. there are between 12 and 18 hours of classes per week depending on the option selected.

3. Enrolment : college students, but it should be noted that

a) a special assistance programme is available for pupils not meeting normal entry standards ;
b) refresher courses are arranged for those returning to study after a long period away.

163

4. Numbers (1971-72) :

   a) Students : approximately 5,000 ;
   b) Teaching staff : approximately 200.

5. Staff recruitment : "In faculty hiring and faculty organisation there is a little concern with the field of a professor's Ph.D, there is much concern with the kinds of
   ecological problems on which he wishes to focus, along
   with students and members of the community."
   Course attendance is reckoned in credits, each credit
   representing two hours of teaching per week during a
   semester.

6. Programme : the general Liberal Education seminars,
   held over four years, include compulsory subjects in
   the first and fourth years only ; apart from these the
   student is relatively free to choose his subjects and
   concentration with the advice of a staff counsellor, according to his interest in some particular environmental
   problem (see table and list in annex).

7. Concentration : the student is required to choose one
   environment-related problem in one of the four colleges
   referred to above, and spend at least half of his time
   of study on the corresponding theme. Teaching throughout the university is based on the study of the environment, the central topic of thought.

8. Educational principles :

   a) learning for the degree is linked with research and
      advisory work ,

   b) as much time as possible is spent off campus ; field
      work takes place in a variety of locations, outside
      teachers are used etc,

   c) the teaching is designed to bring together the various
      disciplines involved in any one theme,

   d) considerable scope is left for students' personal work,
      especially in years 3 and 4,

   e) fuller recourse is had to the spiritual, intellectual and
      material resources of human beings (personal com-
      mitment and devotion, participation, communication,
      sense of reality, the problem-solving approach) ,

f) a flexible credits system ,

g) students are encouraged to take part in "community projects" in which they apply what they have learnt to concrete problems affecting the local community ,

h) student participation in small-scale research programmes applied to problems of the particular region. These programmes are subsidised by the United States government.

TEACHING PROGRAMME AND PATTERN

6 hours per week of general education in the form of Liberal Education Seminars			
Common core for all students: introduction to values, to ecology and to environment-related problems	In each of the colleges: Study of environ-mental problem in the Great Lakes region	Study of the same problems in other regions of the United States	Common core for all students: synthesis

5 to 6 hours per week of courses to be taken in each of the four colleges or special examination attesting to adequate knowledge in these secondary subjects

Acquisition of working tools :	at least 6 credits in each of two subject areas : - data processing and mathematics ; - art and modern languages
	A major environmental problem concentration (1) to be chosen as a main subject for study in one of the four colleges (2)
	One optional subject may be chosen (2) (3) which should be related to the main subject : eg. chemistry and protection of nature, sociology and urban analysis
	Professional applications

Year 1	Year 2	Year 3	Year 4

166

Notes :

1) There are eleven such concentrations, covering all aspects of the environment : analysis and control of the biophysical environment, human adaptability, nutrition, population, growth and development, modernisation, regional and urban development, human identity, environmental values and their communication.

2) In years 3 and 4 the student chooses one of three options to complete his course :

1. 30 credits in one concentration ;
2. 36 credits in a combined concentration/option, of which at least 12 credits must be in the concentration ;
3. At least 30 credits to be chosen by the student with the agreement of the dean of the college of enrolment.

3) List of optional subjects :

Anthropology
Biology (biochemistry, microbiology, physiology, zoology, botany, entomology, ecology)
Business Administration
Chemistry
Communication Sciences
Earth Sciences
Economics
Geography

Geology

History

Literature and Language
(literature and creative use of language in English, French, German and Spanish)
Mathematics
Performing Arts (music, drama, and dance)
Philosophy
Physics
Political Science
Psychology
Public Administration
Sociology
Visual Arts

Section 3

UNIVERSITY OF PARIS VII (FRANCE)

DEPARTMENT OF ENVIRONMENT

Address

Université Paris VII, 2 Place Jussieu, 75005 Paris

Sources used for this data sheet

1. Livret de l'étudiant de l'Université Paris VII - (Students' handbook) 1970 - 71, 300 pp.

2. Students' handbook 1971 - 72, 540 pp.

3. Students' handbook 1972 - 73, 680 pp.

4. "Etude du milieu", a 20-page information booklet (in French, published by the Department of Environmental Studies (Département d'Environnement), describing the objectives of the course as a whole, course programmes, timetables etc. (1971-72).

5. Direct contact with Department authorities.

Motivations of the current experiment

1. To arrest the constant deterioration in living conditions and irreparable degradation of the natural environment.

2. To enable every citizen to understand, choose and fulfil his role as a privileged user of the environment, but also as a long-term manager and protector of an irreplaceable natural asset.

3. To break down, at least in one sector of the University,

the walls between disciplines, which prevent environmental problems from being correctly stated, analysed
and solved.

Educational aim

1. Create among all students, whatever subjects they may
   be studying, an awareness of environmental problems
   and teach them something about the subject. (During the
   first cycle, credits are available to all students on
   various types of pollution, disamenities, communal
   institutions, etc.)

2. To provide a broad, coherent and effective four-year
   course of training to students planning to pursue environmental careers ("environmental studies" stream).

3. To be of service to the community and its various component groups, practical training periods in the field
   are organised on request, teams of staff and advanced
   students can be made available to analyse specific cases
   in the filed, 'think-tank' groups on which academic staff,
   students , officials and community leaders, etc. are
   represented).

4. To develop environment-oriented research during the
   third cycle.

Date introduced

October, 1970.

Background

The reform of higher education in France came into effect
in October 1970 when the new universities, mainly hived off
from previous monolithic faculties (such as Law, Letters, Humanities, Medicine and Science) were ready to operate. The
University of Paris VII was formed by regrouping parts of the
former Paris faculties of Letters and Humanities, Science and
Medicine (on a voluntary basis).

In addition to the usual vertical, monodisciplinary structures imposed by the reform (Teaching and Research Units =
U. E. R. s), Paris VII University has introduced horizontal,
pluridisciplinary structures cutting across all the U. E. R. s
in order to combine all the disciplines :

1. There are <u>Common services</u> grouping all first-cycle
   courses together for management purposes, though the
   U.E.R.s remain responsible for teaching content.

2. <u>Departments</u> whose task is to set up original courses
   and activities to reflect contemporary problems and are
   in line with general university development policy :
   examples are the Department of Environmental Studies
   and the Audio-Visual Department.
   The project described in this data sheet is taking place
   in the Department of Environmental Studies.

1. <u>Structure of the University of Paris VII</u>

(which had 18,000 students in 1970-71 and 22,000 in 1971-72)

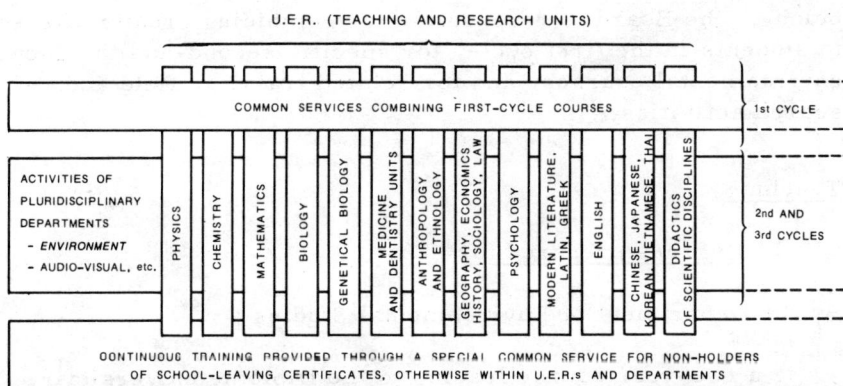

U.E.R. (TEACHING AND RESEARCH UNITS)

COMMON SERVICES COMBINING FIRST-CYCLE COURSES — 1st CYCLE

ACTIVITIES OF PLURIDISCIPLINARY DEPARTMENTS
- ENVIRONMENT
- AUDIO-VISUAL, etc.

PHYSICS | CHEMISTRY | MATHEMATICS | BIOLOGY | GENETICAL BIOLOGY | MEDICINE AND DENTISTRY UNITS | ANTHROPOLOGY AND ETHNOLOGY | GEOGRAPHY, ECONOMICS, HISTORY, SOCIOLOGY, LAW | PSYCHOLOGY | MODERN LITERATURE, LATIN, GREEK | ENGLISH | CHINESE, JAPANESE, KOREAN, VIETNAMESE, THAI | DIDACTICS OF SCIENTIFIC DISCIPLINES — 2nd AND 3rd CYCLES

CONTINUOUS TRAINING PROVIDED THROUGH A SPECIAL COMMON SERVICE FOR NON-HOLDERS OF SCHOOL-LEAVING CERTIFICATES, OTHERWISE WITHIN U.E.R.s AND DEPARTMENTS

- Each U.E.R. has its own teaching and administrative
  staff, its own students, budget, premises and management board ; prepares students for national diplomas in
  its speciality or specialities ; and devises its own con-
  tinuous-training programmes.

- Each U.E.R. also helps, so far as its own subject-matter
  requires, to operate the common services, the pluridisciplinary departments and the special continuing-education

service for non-holders of school-leaving certificates (by defining programmes or "lending" teaching staff etc.)

2. Management of Department of Environmental Studies

The curriculum existed before the structure was established. The Department of Environmental Studies did not acquire official university status until June 1971, whereupon it was able to plan on opening the second cycle of "environmental studies" and to begin preparations for the third cycle.

It was then allocated a budget, premises and administrative staff. It drew up its statutes providing for a Board of Management in which teachers (both university and non-university) active in the Department and students taking the "environmental studies" course are equally represented, and to which university staff representatives and individuals outside the university also belong. The Board is responsible for combining credits offered to students in the first cycle, for specific second-and third-cycle environmental courses, and for related training, field and research activities.

Teaching

1. Degrees prepared for :

By the Department of Environmental Studies :

. a two-year course leading to the Diplôme universitaire d'étude du milieu = D.U.E.M.
   (First degree in environmental studies)
. a four-year course (D.U.E.M. + two years) leads to the Maîtrise des sciences du milieu (Master's degree in environmental science).

It should be noted that during the first cycle it is possible for a student to read simultaneously for a D.U.E.M. and for one of two national diplomas by carefully choosing his optional subjects :

a) First degree in scientific studies (Chemistry, Biology)
   (Diplôme universitaire d'études scientifiques = D.U.E.S.)
b) First degree in Literary Studies (Geography)
   (Diplôme universitaire d'études littéraires = D.U.E.L.)

This means that students who so desire can switch during the second cycle to a more conventional kind of course leading, say,

172

to the teaching profession (secondary school subjects ; natural sciences ; geography, etc.).

2. Course length : 4 years

   - 1st cycle : two years
   - 2nd cycle : two years
   - 3rd cycle, if taken : 2 years.
   - Six-monthly term system (15th September to end of January)
   (15th February to 15th June)

   12 to 13 weeks of classroom teaching per term
   20 hours maximum of classroom teaching per week.

3. Enrolment

   1st Cycle :

   Holders of school-leaving certificates or of equivalent diplomas in all subjects are eligible (refresher courses are provided during the first term for students without a requisite knowledge of subjects) ;

   Candidates unable to satisfy normal requirements can sit the special university entrance examination after one year of continuous training or can apply directly.

   2nd Cycle :

   Operating on an experimental basis, this cycle is only open so far to students holding the D.U.E.M. degree. Later, adequately qualified students are to be accepted from other streams, whether from Paris VII or other universities.

4. Numbers : (forecast for the academic year 1972-73)

   a) Students : 1st Cycle, Year 1 : 90 students
      1st Cycle, Year 2 : 90 students
      2nd Cycle, Year 1 : 40 students

   b) Staff Teaching : some twenty university or non-university staff, working part-time at the Department of Environmental Studies.

5. Staff recruitment

Up to 1972 the Department relied on part-time staff provided by the Paris VII Teaching and Research Units or recruited any additional specialists needed on an overtime basis, expenses being paid by the Paris Rectorate.

In 1972 the Department was allocated one teaching post of its own and is planning to ask for more. Since there is no wish to abolish the double attachment status (to both a U.E.R. and to the Department) of some of its members, the Department will include :

a) mono-disciplinary teachers with U.E.R. posts, enabling subject-matter to be analysed in greater depth and contacts to be maintained with various disciplines and related research ;

b) generalists, which the Department will be able to recruit to fill its own posts ;

c) non-university personnel, which the Department will be able to call upon as necessary.

6. Programme

The 1st Cycle, lasting two years, requires 20 credits to be obtained (fifteen being compulsory and five optional)

- an average of 250 hours of classes per term ;
- one credit varies from 36 to 65 hours in length, depending on whether or not practical or field work is required.

Compulsory Subjects

a) Introduction of the environmental concept (36)[1]
Man as related to the natural environment.

b) The disciplines entering into analysis of the environment : vocabulary, methods, the basic concepts on which they rely, etc. Biology (195) ; Chemistry (130) ; Climatology (36) ; Demography (36) ; Geodynamics (36) ; Physics (115) ; Ecology (50) ; and Sociology (72).

c) Acquisition of working tools : Statistics, one modern language.

---

1) figures in brackets represent the total number of teaching hours over the two years.

d) A field project lasting about eight days in June each year.

Optional Subjects

A student is free to choose the subjects accounting for one fourth of his total credits (as advised by teaching staff upon enrolment). He may either concentrate on the subject areas referred to above or can broaden his training by taking credits in : anthropology, audio-visual techniques, biochemistry, graphics, law, history, data-processing, modern languages, psychology or earth sciences.

The 2nd Cycle lasting two years, requires twenty credits to be obtained.

Year 1 : Field analysis of a specific environment
(in 1972-73 this was the lower valley of the Seine)

a) Practitioners and specialists help in assembling, analysing and processing data ; in visualising and commenting the results (physical and biological environment ; human environment ; utilisation of the environment) ;

b) identification of problems ; choice of specific problems by students ; preparation of analytical plan and documentation file ;

c) instruction in the theory of related disciplines ;

d) field work (4 to 5 weeks spread out over the year) ;

Year 2 : Measures affecting the environment

. Legal and political background of such measures ;
. Planning ;
. Case studies of measures affecting the environment ;
. Pre-career training assignment in an agency concerned with the environment ; the student prepares a project of his own during this period.

7. Major Subjects :

Students do not specialise until the second cycle. Three major subjects are offered :

a) Types of pollution and disamenities
b) Protection of the environment
c) Regional planning

The teaching pattern

1st CYCLE   2nd CYCLE

Outside training

C

1st YEAR   2nd YEAR   3rd YEAR   4th YEAR

COMPULSORY SUBJECTS

OPTIONAL SUBJECTS

FIELD WORK AND TRAINING PERIODS

No major subject will be taken during 1972-73, the course being open on an experimental basis to but a small number of students.

8. Education principles :

1st Cycle : this is based on credits to be taken in the various common services ; while this interferes to some extent with inter-disciplinary teaching it allows the student to reorient himself at any time. Conventional teaching methods (lectures, tutorial and practical work) are used in the various disciplines. Every year a field project is scheduled during approximately one week as to apply and illustrate what the student has learned.

2nd Cycle : teaching is based upon a specific geographical area, which provides the material for environmental study.

     a) Integrated teaching on various topics is provided at the beginning of the term ;
     b) Staff and students arrange seminars and working groups on specific cases ;

c) Four to five-week field projects are held in Year 1
   of the second cycle.

Use of practitioners.
Pre-career training periods in a non-university agency during
the last three months of year 2 of the second cycle.

The student prepares an individual project on some subject
related to his training period.

   9. Career Opportunities :

   "Major environment-related career opportunities will certainly be opening up during the next two years : pollution and
nuisance control, regional planning, management of human
communities and ecology". While these career opportunities
are not yet clear-cut, it is quite conceivable that like present-
day consultancies "the various agencies responsible for planning,
the protection of nature and the management of natural resources"
and industry will increasingly be needing managerial staff with
a solid grounding in a wide set of disciplines.

Section 4

UNIVERSITY OF TOURS (FRANCE)

CENTRE D'ETUDES SUPERIEURES DE L'AMENAGEMENT

Address

Université François RABELAIS, Avenue Monge, Parc Grandmont, 37 - Tours, France.

Sources used for this data sheet

1. "Centre d'Etudes Supérieures de l'Aménagement" (CESA), University of Tours : two 11-page booklets in French, 1969-1970.

2. "U.E.R. Aménagement - Géographie - Informatique", a 13-page booklet in French, undated, available after June 1972.

Motivation of the current experiment

- To prevent uncontrolled interference by man with his environment ;
- Learning to respect the tenuous balance of the ecology
- To compel planners to take account of more than the mere legal or economic consequences of their actions ;
- To satisfy deeply felt needs among the young by undertaking a new teaching approach.

Educational aims

To promote :

1. "a new type of training which will have links forged between the different categories of specialists, so that

they can act in concert ; such specialists to be adequately replaced in dealing with the simple types of case, and the need for calling on a particular c ategory of specialist to be determined" ;

2. a new generation of physical planners and managers which will help to build cities on a more human scale, work together to preserve the landscape and the quality of sites, and help to bring out the best in every type of regional area while not forgetting the people who live in it.

3. courses of study which can better answer actual problems and provide a general form of training enabling the nature of constraints related to both the environment and human activities to be understood.

Date introduced

November 1969.

Background

The projectis being conducted in a section of the Planning, Geography and Data-processing Teaching and Research Unit (U.E.R.) of the University of Tours. This section is called the "Centre d'Etudes Supérieures de l'Aménagement" (CESA). The other Teaching and Research Units which make up the University of Tours are in :

- Human Sciences
- Language, Literature and Civilisation of English-speaking countries
- Classic and Modern Languages, Literature and Civilisation
- Higher Studies of Renaissance Civilisation
- Medicine
- Pharmacology
- Exact and Natural Sciences
- Law and Economics

Lastly, the university also includes a University Institute of Technology (IUT). (1)

---

1) The I. U. T. are short-cycle institutions of two years'duration

Structure and management of the CESA

The "Centre d'Etudes Supérieures de l'Aménagement" is
run by a joint board of teaching staff and students which elects
the Director. An Advisory Council comprising highly qualified specialist and university staff from outside the university
helps to draw up the curricula.

Teaching

1. Degrees prepared for :

   - Diplôme universitaire d'étude du milieu (D.E.U.M.)
     (First degree in environmental studies) of the Univer-
     sity of Tours (1).
   - A four year course (D.E.U.M. plus two years) leading
     to the Maîtrise des-sciences et techniques de l'amé-
     nagement (i.e. Master's Degree in Physical Planning)
     of the University of Tours ;
   - A five year course (the "Maîtrise" plus one year)
     leading to the "Diplôme d'ingénieur ecologiste -
     aménageur" of the University of Tours.

2. Duration of studies : four years

   - Breakdown by year
   - 1st Cycle : two years, each comprising 25 hours of
     teaching over 25 weeks
   - 2nd Cycle : two years, with 15 hours of teaching over
     25 weeks plus field work and individual projects.

3. Enrolment : The CESA is open to holders of school-leaving
   certificates in all subject groups, but the Teachers' Board
   reserves the right to decide whether candidates holding
   the "Baccalauréat" in other than class-"C" subjects
   (science and mathematics) have acquired the requisite
   knowledge by taking refresher courses.
   A remedial course in mathematics, physic and chemistry
   is thus held from 15th September to 1st November (that
   is, before the beginning of the academic year) for prospective students holding the baccalauréat in other than
   class-"C" subjects.

---

1) It should be noted that students can, having taken the D.U.E.M.,
   opt for the University Institutes of Technology (IUT) and obtain the
   "Diplôme de Technicien Supérieur" after an additional year.

4. Numbers : Students (whole university)   : 11 000
            Teaching staff (whole university) :   400
            Students CESA   :   300
            Teaching staff CESA   :   25

5. <u>Staff Recruitment</u> : Breaking with the traditional isolation of faculty teachers, the CESA not only draws heavily on staff from the various established faculties (Exact
   Sciences, Human Sciences, Law and Economics) but also
   upon practising specialists.

6. <u>Programme</u> : Curricula are worked out by committees of
   specialists and approved by the Boards of the CESA, Faculty and University

   1st Cycle : Three major subjects (all these courses are
   compulsory) covering two years.

   a) <u>Data relating to the environment and to the nature of
      man</u> (120 hours of lectures, 23 hours of tutorial work,
      87 hours of practical work) :

      - Physical aspects of the environment (air, soil, sub-
        soil, water)
      - The functioning of living beings (producers, consu-
        mers, reducers, man).

   b) <u>Data relating to human activities</u> (111 hours of lectures,
      111 hours of tutorial work) :

      - Demography (distribution and movements of the
        population)
      - Problems of economic geography (energy, raw
        materials, communications)
      - Economics (micro-economics and macro-economics,
        behaviour of economic agents)
      - Sociology (sociological structures, mobility, culture,
        and working population).

   c) <u>Functioning of the biosphere of ecosystems and of
      man-adapted at their various levels of integration</u>
      (163 hours of courses, 93 hours of tutorial work,
      6 hours of practical work) :

      - Functioning of the biosphere,
      - Functioning of ecosystems,
      - Major types of man-adapted areas,
      - Studies of an area at continental scale.

182

The first cycle also includes :

d) Acquisition of working tools : Data processing and
   foreign languages (96 hours of lectures, 224 hours
   of guided work) :

   - Map analysis (48 hours of tutorial work),
   - Graphics and mapping (32 hours of tutorial work),
   - Statistics and data processing (50 hours of lectures
     and 100 hours of tutorial work),
   - English (90 hours of tutorial work).

2nd Cycle

Year 1 : Two certificates (C1 + C2) are prepared for :

a) C1 Environmental planning and protection (230 hours) :

   - Regional planning (90 hours),
   - Civil engineering (25 hours),
   - Synthetic cartography (25 hours),
   - Elements of law (25 hours),
   - Pollution and waste (15 hours),
   - Protection of the environment, landscapes and
     archaeological sites (50 hours).

   Teaching is in the form of lectures, visits, training
   periods and field work.

b) C2 Human ecology (125 hours of lectures, 15 hours of
   tutorial work, 30 hours of practical work)

   - Elements of psychology (75 hours),
   - Psychosomatics, population trends,
   - Aesthetic needs, background and life-style,
   - Stress and hostility due to disamenities,
   - Social medicine and hygiene.

   Students wishing to take as their second year option
   the certificate "Town and Country Planning Law"
   substitute Introduction to Planning Law (175 hours
   in total) for Human Ecology in C2. All courses are
   compulsory.

Year 2 :

The student prepares for certificate C3 and works up a
"project" enabling his aptitudes and what he has learnt
over the preceding years to be assessed.

C3 at the choice of the student (with a "project" in the same field) :

- Regional planning
or- Development planning of reserves, parks and sites
or- Town and country planning law

Five other options can be taken outside the University of Tours by agreement with other French universities (Development planning of coastal, mountain, Mediterranean and tropical areas).

7. Special Subject : The CESA is geared to problems of development planning.

8. Educational principles :

- Conventional courses which however partially overlap with neighbouring disciplines, or group disciplines together under some co-ordinating topic ;
- Tutorial work and practical work in the field ;
- Off- campus training periods ;
- Extensive individual work by the student in Year 2 of the second cycle ;
- Compulsory courses each year ;
- The purpose is to introduce the students promptly to concrete problems and teach them to deal with subjects requiring a synthetic approach.

9. Course layout

1st CYCLE   2nd CYCLE

YEAR 1   YEAR 2   YEAR 3   YEAR 4

COMPULSORY

OPTIONAL

FIELD WORK AND TRAINING PERIODS

10. Career opportunities : It is not the purpose of a university, generally speaking, to provide professional
training as such. In any case, a country's management
needs are difficult to ascertain, and are apt to change
from year to year. So these remarks can only be a
tentative guide. A CESA form of training should fit the
student for public administration or for the various
public, semi-public and private agencies which are now
engaged in land-use planning and in implementing such
projects, such as the G. E. P. (1), the O. R. E. A. M. (2),
various regional commissions, regional and departmental services of the Ministry of Equipment and the
Ministry of Agriculture, municipal services, town and
city planning agencies, new town commissions, consultancies, town-planning firms, the "Committees for
expansion", chambers of trade and of agriculture,
nationalised undertakings (Electricité de France, Gaz
de France, national parks), banks, etc...

---

1) Groupe d'Etudes et de Programmation
2) Organisation d'Etudes d'Aménagement de l'aire metropolitaine.

Section 5

UNIVERSITY OF EAST ANGLIA (United Kingdom)

SCHOOL OF ENVIRONMENTAL SCIENCES

Address of the university where the educational experiment
is taking place :

- University of East Anglia, Earlham Hall, Norwich
  NOR 88 C (United Kingdom)

Documentation used to prepare this report :

1. OECD   1969   "Innovation in Higher Education :
                       New Universities in the United Kingdom".

2. "University of East Anglia" - 1972-73 : Science
   prospectus (June 1971).

3. OECD 6 March 1971   "Environmental Sciences at the
                        University of East Anglia" : 8
                        pages, original version in English,
                        French translation, prepared by
                        K.M. Clayton, Dean of the School
                        of Environmental Sciences at the
                        University of East Anglia ...

Motivation of the current experiment :

1. To create, within the University, structures making possible a closer relationship between disciplines and their
   subsequent integration.

2. To develop educational innovations.

3. To broaden the range of instruction for students.

Aims of the course of study

1. To provide a good scientific training for students concerned with the physical environment ;

2. To give students specialising in environmental sciences a spread of knowledge and an ability to relate the approaches of different disciplines to problems which arise. This knowledge should extend to the study of man and his activities.

Year of introduction of course of study :

The School of Environmental Sciences at the University of East Anglia was opened in 1968.

Location of the experiment :

Like the University of Ulster, the University of East Anglia is one of the new universities created after the last war to cope with the influx of students due to demographic growth and the raising of the school-leaving age. It opened in 1963. The School of Environmental Sciences was created five years later, as soon as the first group of Schools was sufficiently developed to be viable. The aim was to exploit fully, over a wide range of subjects, the possibilities of integration offered by the Schools system.

The University of East Anglia is at present composed of seven Schools, each of which covers at least two traditional disciplines, and the School of Environmental Sciences which is more broadly pluridisciplinary :

- School of Biological Sciences,
- School of Chemical Sciences,
- School of English and American Studies,
- School of Environmental Sciences,
- School of European Studies,
- School of Music and Fine Arts,
- School of Mathematics and Physics,
- School of Social Studies.

This model differs in the following way from the two traditional models of the older English universities :

Model of a collegiate university: in this model (Oxford, Cambridge), the College is an autonomous structure ; all teacher and student activities are housed in the college.

MODEL OF A UNIVERSITY WITH A SCHOOLS STRUCTURE

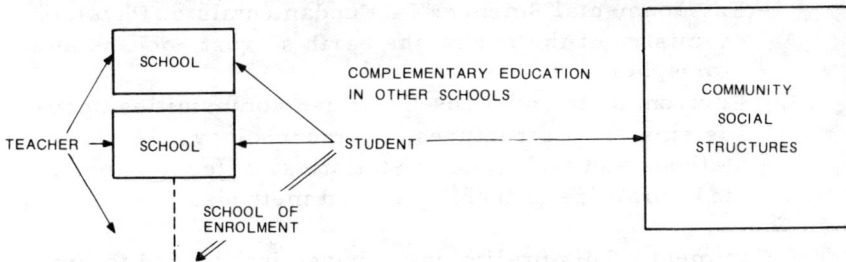

Model of a civic university : in this model (all the city universities) students and teachers work in a single faculty or department. No social structures are provided.

Detailed analysis of courses offered at the school of environment science :

1. Degree course : Bachelor of Science with Honours.

2. Duration of studies :

   - undergraduate course : 3 years
   - possibility to continue to post-graduate studies.

3. Population : students who have completed their secondary education (the preliminary courses in the first and second terms enable sixth form Arts students to transfer to science).

4. Student numbers : undergraduate 150
                                        graduates about 20

5. Teaching staff : 18 lecturers.

6. Programme : centred mainly on earth sciences and geography, or "some (and by no means all) of the Environmental Sciences" ; there is, in particular, no ecology, this science is regarded as another approach to the problems of the Environment, but as it has been unable to come to terms with the human problems it would at present represent an unhelpful approach for a School of Environmental Sciences which has included man in its curriculum.

a) <u>Programme of the broad survey course during the first two terms</u> :

- Environmental Sciences I : Fundamentals of Physics, chemistry of the earth, the earth's crust, oceans and atmosphere.
- Environmental Sciences II : Human communities, eco-systems, soil structures, geomorphology.
- Methods and techniques : Statistics, calculus, mechanics, practice in techniques and methods.

<u>Comment</u> : This preliminary course is intended to give students the necessary foundation for a scientific study of the environment and to introduce them to the practical problems of measurement and experimentation.

b) <u>Programme of options in second and third years</u> :

Options I : Earth sciences (applied), biology and paleo-biology, economic geography and locational analysis ; geophysics and earth structure ; hydrology and fluvial geomorphology ; meteo-rology and climatology ; oceanography ; Qua-ternary studies ; rock chemistry ; soil science surface processes ; tropical resources and development ; urban and regional planning and development.

Options II: Planning and pollution ; mathematics and computer science.

<u>Comment</u> : Teachers are endeavouring to reduce the number of options to impose the integration of disciplines around a single theme (e.g. : geomorphology + sedimentology = surface processes).

7. <u>Dominant</u> : Geology, geography.

8. <u>Pedagogic principles</u> :

a) no hierarchy of courses in the Options, to promote the mix of second or third year students and help the former to mature more quickly ;

b) considerable freedom for students in their choice of options in order to ensure the strong motivation which leads to high-quality work ;

c) retention of the lecture formula supplemented by work in seminars with a limited number (15) of students ;

d) development of laboratory and field work ;

e) preparation of a project (a dissertation of about 10,000 words, the marks for which count for about 10 per cent in the final assessment).

9. Timetable :

Preliminary course 20 hrs. per week	18 hrs. per week	Presentation of project
	6 options to be chosen from list I (one of these 6 options may be chosen from list II or another School). Project proposed during the summer holidays	
1 st year	2 nd year	3 rd year

10. Career Openings : forecast.

Section 6

NEW UNIVERSITY OF ULSTER (UNITED KINGDOM)

SCHOOL OF BIOLOGICAL AND ENVIRONMENTAL STUDIES

Address of the university :

New University of Ulster, Coleraine, County Londonderry, Northern Ireland - United Kingdom.

Documents used to prepare this report :

1. The New University of Ulster - Prospectus 1973-74. Student Handbook - 124 pages - in English.

2. Geography, Biology and Environmental Science at the New University of Ulster - 12 pages booklet in English,

3. Human Ecology at the New University of Ulster - 8-page booklet, in English.

Motivation of the current experiment :

To reappraise man-environment relationships. This reappraisal must begin with an educational change in which these relationships become the central theme of education.

Aims of course of study :

"Training of environmental scientists who will have responsibility for research and management activities directly related to the environment." The course aim is to produce graduates who have a knowledge in depth of the physical environment and who also understand how the environment may be safely manipulated.

193

Year of introduction of course of study :

October 1968, opening date of the University.

Location of the experiment :

The School of Biological and Environmental Studies of the University of Ulster.

The New University of Ulster is one of the new universities created after the last World War, particularly in the 1960s, in the United Kingdom. In contrast to the old "classical" universities organised in "colleges" (e.g. Oxford) or in faculties or departments (civic universities), where disciplines are kept separate, these new universities are divided into "schools" (1). As teachers and students can spread their activities over several schools, these universities encourage pluridisciplinarity.

The New University of Ulster is composed of four pluridisciplinary schools, divided into Departments, and an Education Centre :

- School of Physical Sciences comprising the departments
  of Chemistry, Mathematics, and Physics ;
- School of Biological and Environmental Studies : Biology,
  Geography and Psychology ;
- School of Social Sciences : Economics, Social Organisation,
  Social Anthropology and Sociology ;
- School of Humanities : History, English, Greek and Latin,
  Modern Languages, Linguistics, and Philosophy ;
- Education Centre, responsible mainly for teacher train-
  ing , adult education and teachers' refresher courses.

"Biological and Environmental Studies lie at the heart of developments at the New University" as shown in the following diagram.

This diagram also shows, for studies centering on biology, geography and environmental science, the wide range of possible transitions from one course to another and programme adjustments at undergraduate   level (see page 3 and note above)

---

1) Reference : OECD : Innovation in higher education : New
   Universities in the United Kingdom - 1969.

UNIVERSITY STRUCTURE AND MAJOR LINKAGES
BETWEEN DISCIPLINES IN THE SCHOOL OF BIOLOGICAL
AND ENVIRONMENTAL STUDIES

(from the booklet "Geography, Biology and Environmental Science")

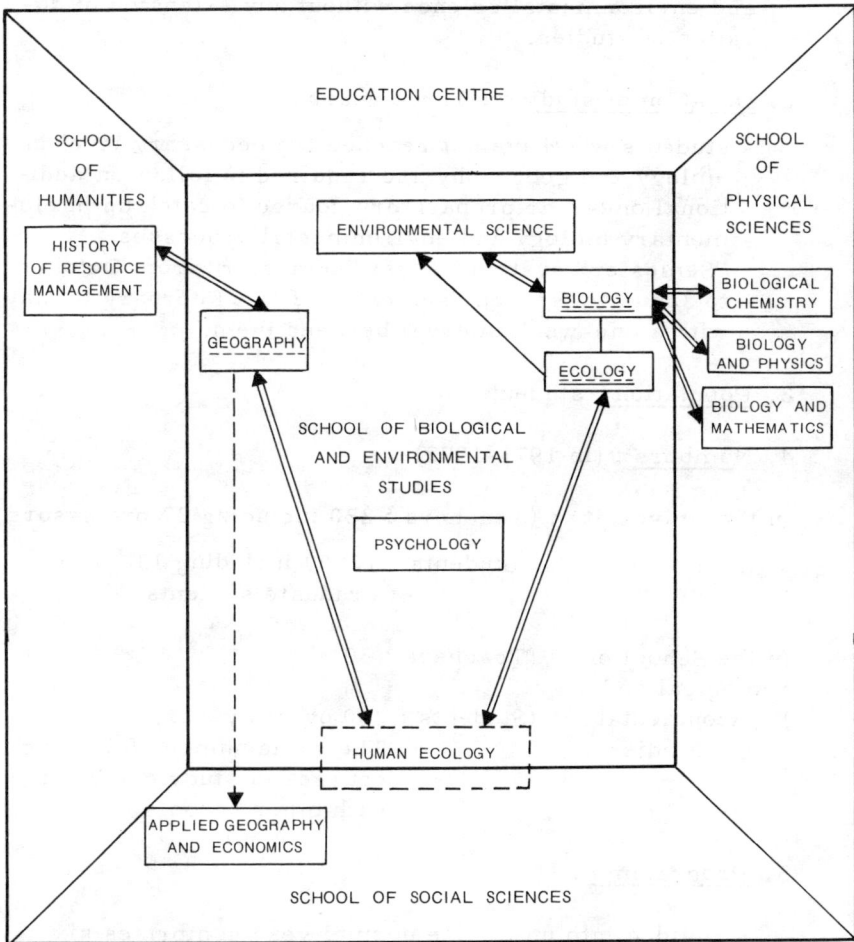

EDUCATION CENTRE

SCHOOL OF HUMANITIES

SCHOOL OF PHYSICAL SCIENCES

ENVIRONMENTAL SCIENCE

HISTORY OF RESOURCE MANAGEMENT

BIOLOGY

BIOLOGICAL CHEMISTRY

GEOGRAPHY

BIOLOGY AND PHYSICS

ECOLOGY

BIOLOGY AND MATHEMATICS

SCHOOL OF BIOLOGICAL AND ENVIRONMENTAL STUDIES

PSYCHOLOGY

HUMAN ECOLOGY

APPLIED GEOGRAPHY AND ECONOMICS

SCHOOL OF SOCIAL SCIENCES

COURSE NOW AVAILABLE

COURSE AVAILABLE IN 1973-74

COMBINED PROGRAMME (OVER 3 OR 4 YEARS)

TRANSITION POSSIBLE AT THE END OF THE 1st YEAR

TRANSITION POSSIBLE AT THE END OF THE 3rd YEAR

UNDERLINED : Course making it possible to combine a degree in the discipline with a diploma in education (necessitating one year's further study)

UNDERLINED: "Sandwich" courses possible (further six months in a governmental or private laboratory)

NOTE : The normal duration of under-graduate studies is three years.

195

Course of study

1. Degree course : Bachelor of Science in Environmental Studies. Possibility of a combined degree in biology and environmental science without any extension of duration of studies.

2. Duration of studies : Three years
   - students who have not reached the necessary level in biology and geography are required to follow an additional one-year preparatory course to catch up in elementary biology and environmental processes.
   - "Semester" system : First "semester" from October to January, second "semester" from February to May, with a one-week interval between them.

3. Population : students

4. Numbers : (in 1971-1972)

In the University ; (Teachers : 220 including 27 professors
                    (Students : 1,600 including 130 postgraduate students

In the School of   (Teachers : 30
Biological and
Environmental   (Students : 200 over 3 years.
   Studies   The same number following courses of study combined with other schools

5. Programme :

   - Divided into units (one normal year comprises six units).
   - Combines courses already organised under Geography and Biology programmes and special courses in Environmental Science.

1st Year : 4 compulsory units : Physics and Chemistry for Environmental Studies, Introduction to Geology, Elementary meteorology and climatology, Introduction to ecology.

          2 option units

2nd Year 2 compulsory units : Geomorphology, Biogeography,

196

and either	2 compulsory units in planning : Applied Geography related to environmental planning, Quantitative techniques in geography,
and/or	2 compulsory units in biology/ecology : Comparative anatomy and Physiology of plants and animals.

- 2 option units if necessary to complete the year.

3rd Year	2 compulsory units : Conservation, Dissertation (project for which the field work is done during the long vacation between the second and third years).

- 4 option units from among the following :
  Fluvial processes, micrometeorology
  and applied meteorology, advanced soil studies,
  Pleistocene ecology, water ressources, Pleistocene stratigraphy and sedimentation, systems
  analysis in environmental studies, organisms
  and environment, ecosystems, population
  dynamics, town planning.

6. Teacher Recruitment : Teachers come from the Geography and Biology Departments.

7. Dominant subjects : Biology and Physical Geography.

8. Pedagogic principles : In addition to the traditional lectures the emphasis is placed on :

- practical instruction,
- instruction in small groups,
- student participation in instruction in seminars,
- field work and instruction for groups or individuals.

The wide range of field stations, experimental areas, habitats and sites in the vicinity of the University develops aptitudes for experiment, observation and data collection.

9. Pattern of studies :

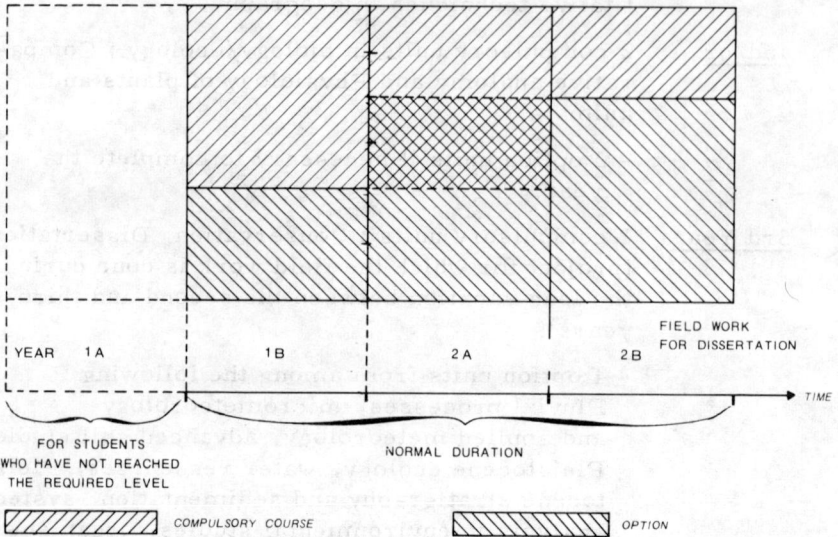

YEAR 1A   1B   2A   2B

FIELD WORK FOR DISSERTATION

TIME

FOR STUDENTS WHO HAVE NOT REACHED THE REQUIRED LEVEL

NORMAL DURATION

COMPULSORY COURSE   OPTION

Part Two

SURVEYS ON ENVIRONMENTAL EDUCATION
IN OECD MEMBER COUNTRIES

Chapter I

STUDY ON ENVIRONMENTAL EDUCATION
IN OECD MEMBER COUNTRIES (1)

By Jean-Marie ABILLON
Director of the Department of Environment,
University of Paris VII, France

1) except the United States

SUMMARY

STUDY ON ENVIRONMENTAL EDUCATION IN OECD MEMBER COUNTRIES

(except the United States and Australia)

I. OBJECT AND SCOPE OF THE STUDY

At the Workshop on Environmental Education at University Level held in Tours, France, from 4th to 8th April 1971 under the aegis of the OECD, participants agreed that it might be well to augment the published record of proceedings with up-to-date information on environmental education in Member countries.

A questionnaire (1) was accordingly sent to all recognised (2) higher education institutions in these countries, except Australia (not yet a member at the date of mailing) and the United States, for which a special survey was undertaken (3).

The purpose of the questionnaire was to compile specific information on :

1. the organisational structure on universities or other institutions of higher education teaching environmental subjects ;

2. the percentage of enrolments in environmental courses ;

---

1) The questionnaire, reproduced in Annex 1, covers the months of June and July 1971.

2) The questionnaire was sent to an establishment appearing in the "World List - Universities and other Institutions of Higher Education, University Organisation" (1969) published by the International Association of Universities.

3) See Chapters II and III

3. the classification of courses in terms of one or several disciplines (unidisciplinary or interdisciplinary courses) ;

4. the various educational levels at which courses are offered ;

5. the settings in which the courses are presented ;

6. the links between institutions teaching environmental science and outside bodies or communities ;

7. access to courses by non-students ;

8. participation by university teachers in environmental programmes at secondary level.

The information thus gathered on the present state of environmental teaching in higher education among OECD Member countries was used as a basis for a working document to enable further investigation and, possibly, for a later workshop on higher environmental education. In this context it is important to take additional note of :

1. Difficulties reported by respondents ;

2. Ambiguities in the answering of certain questions ;

3. The fact that some of the replies could not be fully analysed because insufficient information was provided. Most often the perhaps too general nature of the question was the reason, but in such questionnaires this is often hard to avoid.

Item (1) is considered in the following overall analysis of replies ; the remainder are discussed case by case in the detailed analyses.

II. OVERALL ANALYSIS OF REPLIES TO THE QUESTIONNAIRE

Initial analysis of the 249 replies to the questionnaire revealed a number of difficulties encountered by various respondents in framing their answers. Nevertheless, it has been possible to classify the replies within a few well-defined categories and, following the elimination of some, to compile a set of statistics by individual countries.

1. Difficulties encountered by some respondents

Certain of the institutions of higher education stated that it was either difficult or impossible to answer the questionnaire without a precise definition of "environmental education or studies" (1). Some even said that a great many courses might come under the title "environment" since a very wide area was covered by the term in its broader sense (2).

Such comments illustrate the tendency of many respondents to include under "environmental education" the teaching of traditional subjects that impinge on this area.

2. Classification of replies

As already implied, the very broad interpretation given to "environmental education" made the questionnaires somewhat difficult to process. The replies were finally arranged in three categories.

1. Positive replies (129) : The only replies regarded as appropriate to this category were those mentioning :

a) some subject or set of subjects dealing with environmental matters, for example, pollution, land-use planning, effect of pollution on public health, conservation of resources on environmental aesthetics ;

b) one or more specific courses directly dealing with some environmental problem such as air pollution, ecology as applied to the human environment, urban management or economic analysis of the environment.

Such positive replies here sub-classified in a number of types that are analysed in paragraph II.3. below.

2. Unspecific replies (50) : These have one or another of the following characteristics :

---

1) Examples are Aberdeen University, College of Agriculture (U.K.); Sheffield Polytechnic (U.K.) Liverpool Polytechnic, College of Building and Engineering ; National University of Ireland (Dublin)

2) Two characteristic replies were those from the University of Sussex (U.K.) and the Institut Industriel du Nord (France).

a) they state that environmental education is provided, without commenting any further ;

b) they use some vague descriptive term for this field of education (e.g. environmental studies, environmental science or the human environment) ;

c) they mention a set of traditional courses that might be considered environmental education but there is no evidence of these being correlated. Student enrolments may vary considerably from one such course to another.

Some of these replies, especially those coming under (b) above, have nevertheless been counted and analysed as positive replies for that part of the questionnaire that does not deal with education itself.

3. Negative replies (103) : These fall into two groups :

a) those stating that no environmental courses are offered in the institution. These are by far the most common in this category :

b) replies mentioning or describing some long-established traditional course. Examples are courses in pharmacy, forestry, regional geography, and so on.

3. Various types of positive reply

The positive replies are of two distinct types :

1. In the first type, full-time education is mentioned, extending over one or more years and co-ordinating several disciplines in a fairly broad environmental theme, usually at some clearly specified educational level. Replies of this kind were accompanied by a brochure or booklet containing detailed information. Institutions offering or planning such instruction, as well as the main features of each course, are listed in Annex 2.

2. In the second type, a partial or fragmentary form of environmental instruction covering a broad range of subjects is described. This may be a set of courses (or a single course) in one or more of the traditional departments and covering one or more of the traditional fields. It may be open to all students and even to non-students. In fact all possible combinations were encountered in this type of answer, which cannot be further classified unless qualified by more detailed information indicating :

- the field of study in which the course is taught
- the diploma or degree conferred
- the amount of time spent on the course
- whether or not the course is of an informational nature.
  If it is, towards what kind of public is it directed.
- the disciplines involved.

Owing to the great diversity of replies and the impossibility of assessing the weight of courses offered, the analysis attempted in the following pages is necessarily largely qualitative in approach.

4. <u>Breakdown of replies according to country and type of institution</u>

Table I shows a breakdown of positive replies by countries and type of institution. For purposes of comparison, the latest known student enrolment figures and the number of universities and institutions of higher education in each country are given.

In the column "Number of positive replies" four countries are especially prominent - Canada, France, Japan and the United Kingdom. The large number of positive replies from "other institutions of higher education" in France may however be attributed to its many engineering schools, most of which have a low student enrolment (averaging less than 200).

Of far more significance is the weight of positive replies calculated in relative terms. Table II whenever possible shows the number of positive replies received per thousand students. Non-university institutions of higher learning and universities and colleges have been considered together, since in spite of the wide disparity in total enrolments per institution when both categories are compared, in each the numbers taking environmental courses are much the same.

Table II indicates that <u>for most countries the ratio of positive replies per group of thousand students averages 5 per cent and that no great dispersion occurs around this average.</u>

III. DETAILED ANALYSIS OF QUESTIONNAIRES

Table III is provided for guidance. It covers most of the questions asked by the survey as analysed by countries. Questions omitted in the Table are dealt with separately.

1. Percentage of students enrolled in environmental courses
(questions 4 and 5)

Calculation of the ratio by taking the answers to questions
4 and 5 shows that on average environmental subjects are studied
by 6 per cent of the students in the institutions that replied positively. This figure must be used, however, with reservations,
since numbers enrolled in a complete environmental course
extending over at least one year can be accepted as such, while
those given for students exposed to the subject on a partial basis
cannot. The number of student hours spent on environmental
subjects as plotted against total student hours would no doubt
come closer to expressing the true position. The only conclusion
that can be drawn from this part of the survey is that some 6 per
cent of the students attending respondent institutions have been
brought into contact with some aspects of the environment.

Of greater value and significance are enrolments in environmental courses in ratio to the total student population in each
country. This figure can be obtained by simply comparing the
total under question 5 with the sum of the figures in column 3
of Table I (number of students). The figure is extremely low :

In most OECD Member countries the student force enrolled
in a full or partial environmental course during 1971 was not
more than 2 per cent of the total student population of that country as recorded around 1970

2. Breakdown of courses according to degree of integration
and educational level (questions 6 and 7)

Table IV shows how the courses break down in terms of
their type, whether disciplinary, interdisciplinary or a combination of both according to country and educational level. The
Table brings out certain significant features :

- in each category, the percentage of cases mentioning a
  course at graduate level is shown to be constant ;
- the percentage of cases as between undergraduate and
  postgraduate level is largely reversed when "interdisciplinary" rather than "disciplinary" courses are considered.
  (See definition of 'interdisciplinary courses' in the questionnaire, Annex 1).

The features which are illustrated in Figure I can be accounted for fairly easily. Interdisciplinary education consists in integrating a number of disciplines into a single course taught by

208

a generalist or by a team of teachers from different disciplines. At postgraduate level, where specialisation is highly developed, integration involves a relatively small number of disciplines. Not only is integration easier on this account ; it also requires that knowledge acquired has to be combined and this is something that can better be achieved after the undergraduate stage when the student is still learning the fundamentals.

Yet if both interdisciplinary courses and the combined type are set against the total replies in terms of educational level, the following result is obtained.

At undergraduate level 25 per cent of positive replies mention interdisciplinary courses. The percentage with regard to the remainder considered in the questionnaire is 22 per cent.

Subject to a quantitative check (relative extent of the various types of course), the following qualitative assessment would seem to apply :

Course integration increases with the level of education. Considerable efforts are however being made (in 25 per cent of cases) to introduce interdisciplinary courses at undergraduate level.

The different characteristics quoted above are illustrated in Figure 1.

3.   The settings in which environmental courses are taught (Question 9)

Question 9, dealing with the organisational structure of environmental education, was variously interpreted.

Does this mean, as implied in 9 (a), an institute or centre purposely set up for undertaking environmental educational and research activities ? Or does it mean a broader framework in which partial instruction is provided (such as an engineering college adding a section on pollution to its usual curriculum) ?

Difficulty was moreover experienced in distinguishing between an interdisciplinary institute and a centre for environmental teaching and research. Some respondents checked both questions.

It was therefore thought best to combine (b) and (c) under a common heading. Thus, Table III shows that establishments with fairly loosely co-ordinated disciplines compare about evenly with interdisciplinary institutes and teaching centres.

Such a state of balance between the two types of structure is hardly surprising at a time when environmental education is still in the development stage.

Links with organisations or communities outside institutions of higher education (question 10)

Question 10 could be interpreted in two ways :

Where do the funds for environmental teaching and research programmes come from ?

Are such programmes linked (in the broad sense) with the community, government, industry, etc. ? For example, is there co-operation (not necessarily enumerated) between teachers and/or students and the organisations or communities outside the institution?

Based on the broader interpretation, it is interesting to note that relations of institutions of higher education with the outside world are divided to a surprisingly even extent among regional and local communities, industry, government and non-university institutions.

Access to courses by non-students and participation by teachers in secondary education (questions 8 and 11)

In 31 per cent of cases institutions stated that their courses were open to non-students. It may be pointed out that universities and colleges alone account for 21 per cent of these. It would be interesting to know what sort of people are attracted to such courses (whether professionals concerned with environmental problems, civil servants, the general public or whom).

The support given by university teachers to environmental education in secondary schools is far from negligible, 23 per cent of the institutions sending in positive replies state that they participate in developing programmes for environmental teaching in such schools.

Breakdown of the disciplines concerned in environmental education

In view of the general nature of the questionnaire it was not always possible to determine the number and nature of the disciplines involved in the environmental education referred to in the positive replies. Nevertheless, in general terms one can see that if certain disciplines are dominant simply from the number of courses in which they are included ; interesting characteristics can also be noted in the particular disciplines grouped for a given course.

Table V shows the frequency with which disciplines are quoted in the positive replies. It may be felt that the term "discipline" is not entirely appropriate for such subjects as ecology or public health which already embrace a number of traditions of learning and research to which this word has for long been applied. Nevertheless, the term has been adopted in its widest sense for the sake of simplification.

It will be seen from this table that certain disciplines (biology, ecology and public health) constantly recur and that the "experimental" sciences (biology, chemistry, physics, public health, and so on) appear 125 times, whereas the humanities and social sciences (law, economics, human geography, etc...) appear only 28 times.

In the environmental courses available in OECD countries emphasis is placed in more than half the cases (54 per cent) on the main disciplines concerned in the study of nature (biology, ecology) and the protection of human beings (public health). However, the "experimental" sciences very definitely outweigh the humanities and social sciences (4.5 : 1)

Figure II is a histogram of the number of disciplines included in the various environmental courses. It has two striking features :

- When the number n of disciplines is low (less than 7) the number of cases quoted in which the course concerned comprises n disciplines is inversely proportional to n. In this case the course is generally fragmentary.

- In excess of n = 7 the histogram shows a definite peak. The cases comprising this peak are homogeneous co-ordinated courses covering at least one university year.

It may therefore be concluded that :

When an environmental course is fragmentary (for example, a partial course that is part of a traditional syllabus) the number of disciplines concerned is small. Complete co-ordinated courses represent a minimum of seven disciplines.

Breakdown of subjects comprising a course

Table VI gives the list of subjects reported in the positive replies, their frequency and their component disciplines. The

211

main subjects are regional or urban planning (20 cases) pollution (16 cases), and the protection of nature and resources (18 cases). Human problems (human ecology, public health) are more difficult to present in the form of subjects because they are more complex and comprise disciplines that have only recently been explored in depth (e.g. sociology, social psychology, epidemiology).

Finally, it was noted on analysing the questionnaire that no country seems to have laid special emphasis on a subject specifically involving environmental studies. Japan was found to be the only country that stresses public health and aesthetics.

IV. CONCLUSIONS

The very general nature of a questionnaire which was primarily designed for prospective purposes and the vagueness of a relatively large number of the replies make it impossible to draw anything other than qualitative conclusions. However, these provide a sufficiently detailed picture of the state of environmental education in OECD countries. In particular, they show that the general emerging trend is to some extent consistent with the requirements defined by the participants in Tours Workshop who were themselves mostly engaged in experiments with the teaching of environmental sciences (1). These requirements are contained in the recommendations agreed on the conclusion of the workshop (2) but reproduced here for purposes of annotation :

- Recommendations 1 and 2 : That there should be organisation of environmental education at all university levels and for all categories of students and emphasis on environmental problems in the teaching of each discipline. The OECD study revealed that few universities or institutes of higher education offered even a fragmentary course in environmental studies at the time the workshop was held. When such courses did exist they affected only a negligible fraction of the student population.

---

1) It should, however, be noted that a large number of institutions of higher education have started environmental courses since the date of the survey.

2) See pages 31 - 35

- Recommendation 3 : The development of general environmental courses open to all students in a number of universities in each country.

The survey showed that such courses were practically non-existent and that a considerable effort has still to be made in this respect.

- Recommendation 4 : One or more universities in each country should focus on man and his environment, if possible with the help of organisational structures based on new conceptions of learning. Here, too, cases of students receiving special training as "environmentalists" are relatively limited. If the OECD countries only are considered and Australia and the United States (1) excluded, examples are only to be found in Canada, Denmark, France and the United Kingdom.

- Recommendation 5 : General content of environmental education. This aspect was not covered by the questionnaire.

- Recommendation 6 : Importance of interdisciplinarity in environmental education and research. No small effort is already being made by universities or institutes of higher education to promote interdisciplinarity in environmental education and research.

- Recommendation 7 : Pedagogical techniques. This matter was not raised in the questionnaire.

- Recommendation 8 and 9 : Relationships between institutes of higher education and the outside world and participation in secondary education. Much has also been done by institutes of higher education to keep in touch with outside bodies and communities, to make courses available to the non-student public, and to co-operate in extending environmental education in the secondary school system. Although few in number - which is surprising in view of the seriousness and urgency of environmental problems - the experiments recorded in the survey were to some extent consistent with the recommendations of the Tours Workshop regarding new types of education and outwardly-oriented institutions.

Finally, the survey shows that environmental education is provided in two forms :

---

1) See in this connection Annex 2 at the end of this study and also the six experiments at undergraduate level analysed in Chapter II, Part One.

- a fragmentary course comprising information or specialisation in the application of a discipline or technique,

- a homogeneous course over at least one year generally
involving the detailed study of one or more of the following
subjects :

. Land use,
. Pollution and nuisances,
. Protection of nature and use of natural resources,
. Human ecology.

In the latter type of course no less than seven disciplines
appear to be involved. This figure, which emphasizes the complexity of environmental problems, seems high and it may indeed
be a useful first step to determine the effective contribution of
each of the disciplines at present concerned.

QUESTIONNAIRE ADDRESSED TO UNIVERSITIES
AND HIGHER EDUCATION INSTITUTIONS

Survey on Present Status of Interdisciplinary
and Specialised Environmental Teaching in Higher Education

1) Country...

2) University or
   Institution...

3) Name of
   Respondent ....

4) Total Number
   of Students ....

5) Number enrolled
   in Environmental Courses ....

6) Special or Disciplinary
   Courses in Environmental Education (1)
   List subjects and number of students
   enrolled in each)..

   a) undergraduate

   Subject/Number   Subject/Number

   ..../.....   ..../.....
   ..../.....   ..../.....
   ..../.....   ..../.....

_____

1) Disregard traditional courses. Include only those which
   emphasize application to present environmental problems.

215

. . . ./. . . . ./. . . . .
. . . ./. . . . ./. . . . .
. . . ./. . . . ./. . . . .
. . . ./. . . . ./. . . . .
. . . ./. . . . ./. . . . .

b) graduate

Subject/Number   Subject/Number

. . . ./. . . . ./. . . . .
. . . ./. . . . ./. . . . .
. . . ./. . . . ./. . . . .
. . . ./. . . . ./. . . . .
. . . ./. . . . ./. . . . .
. . . ./. . . . ./. . . . .

c) postgraduate

Subject/Number   Subject/Number

. . . ./. . . . ./. . . . .
. . . ./. . . . ./. . . . .
. . . ./. . . . ./. . . . .
. . . ./. . . . ./. . . . .

7) Interdisciplinary Environmental Courses (1)

a) undergraduate

Subject/Number   Subject/Number

. . . ./. . . . ./. . . . .
. . . ./. . . . ./. . . . .
. . . ./. . . . ./. . . . .
. . . ./. . . . ./. . . . .
. . . ./. . . . ./. . . . .
. . . ./. . . . ./. . . . .
. . . ./. . . . ./. . . . .
. . . ./. . . . ./. . . . .

---

1) 'Interdisciplinary' means

   a) representatives of different disciplines teaching jointly
      an environmental course, or
   b) one teacher giving a course on a unifying environmental
      theme (e.g. ecology, systems theory ....) to students
      of different disciplines

Subject/Number   Subject/Number

. . . ./. . . . ./. . . . .
. . . ./. . . . ./. . . . .
. . . ./. . . . ./. . . . .
. . . ./. . . . ./. . . . .
. . . ./. . . .   ./. . . . .
. . . ./. . . . .

b) postgraduate

Subject/Number   Subject/Number

. . . ./. . . . ./. . . . .
. . . ./. . . . ./. . . . .
. . . ./. . . . ./. . . . .
. . . ./. . . . ./. . . . .

8) Are environmental courses open to non-students ?

Yes ☐   No ☐

9) Organisational Structure

    a) Loosely co-ordinated working group ☐
    b) Interdisciplinary institute ☐
    c) Centre for environmental teaching and research ☐

10) Are environmental teaching and research linked with :

    a) local community ☐
    b) region ☐
    c) industry ☐
    d) government ☐
    e) non-university institutes ☐

11) Do members of the university participate in development
    programmes for environmental teaching in secondary schools?

Yes ☐   No ☐

Annex 2

LIST OF INSTITUTIONS THAT REPLIED TO THE QUESTIONNAIRE AND OFFERED A COHERENT COURSE OF STUDY ON (SOME) ENVIRONMENTAL PROBLEMS

The experiments at undergraduate level referred to at the Tours Workshop are not included in this list.

DENMARK :   Royal Veterinary and Agricultural University (106 students)

Interdisciplinary course at graduate level (ecology, biology, pollution, social and economic aspects of environmental control).

UNITED KINGDOM : University of Southampton (was scheduled to begin in 1972)

Pluridisciplinary course at undergraduate level (ecology, ethology, biography, geology, biology, economics, resource management, rural and regional development).

SWITZERLAND :   Ecole Polytechnique Fédérale, Lausanne (Most courses were scheduled to begin in 1972)

Pluridisciplinary and interdisciplinary course in land-use planning (1st and 2nd cycles), ecology (course open to all 1st cycle), hydrology and atmospheric pollution (3rd cycle).

FRANCE :   Ecole Nationale Supérieure Agronomique Rennes (was scheduled to begin in October 1971)

A one-year course at third-cycle level : ecological factors, population, biocenoses, ecosystems, biological equilibria, principal world biocenoses, cartography, sociological and economic problems concerned in the conservation and planning of the natural environment, land-use planning and its biological aspects.

FRANCE :   **Université Claude Bernard - Lyon I**
(Project for 1971-1972)

Preparatory cycle at 1st-cycle level : mathematics, meteorology and climatology, chemistry, ecology, physiology and hygiene, human and economic geography, dynamics of human societies, cartography, foreign language. Pluridisciplinary course at 2nd-cycle level based on land-use planning, environmental techniques (nuisances and pollution, ecology, geodynamics, technology), planning of landscapes and built-up areas, economic and legal aspects, social psychology of the environment, case studies.

FRANCE :   **University of Orleans**

Interdisciplinary third-cycle course on applied ecology (30 students). Common core : ecology, pollution, planning legislation, aerial photography, management of natural resources, cost of pollution, hunting, re-afforestation, town planning Options : wildlife ecology and water pollution, plant ecology, soil science and landscaping, atmospheric pollution and climatology, legal aspects of pollution, land-use planning, computer science.

CANADA :   **The University of Western Ontario. Faculty of Engineering Science** (27 students in 1970-71)

Pluridisciplinary course at graduate level : air pollution, water pollution, industrial processes, environmental biology, pollution legislation, political sciences, resource utilisation, medical effects, micrometeorology, seminars, pratical work and projects on the environment.

219

CANADA :   University of Ottawa (16 students in
                       1970-71)

                       Pluridisciplinary course at graduate level:
                       regional development, town planning,
                       ecology, law planning, PPBS, resource
                       management, transport and communica-
                       tions, leisure, applied computer science.

UNITED KINGDOM :   University College, London - School of
                       Environmental Studies

                       i) One year pluridisciplinary course for
                       specialists professionally concerned with
                       problems arising from the rapid growth
                       of towns in developing countries : basic
                       studies : development economics, socio-
                       logy of modernisation, political and ad-
                       ministrative sciences, physical environ-
                       ment, ergonomics, systems analysis and
                       design methodology, statistics. Optional
                       subjects : planning and strategy of urba-
                       nisation, housing policies, planning and
                       construction of educational premises.

                       ii) A pluridisciplinary and interdiscipli-
                       nary course at post-graduate level leading
                       to a degree of Master of Science (Conser-
                       vation), has existed since 1960. About
                       10 students a year. This theoretical and
                       practical course focuses on conservation
                       problems. In addition to courses on eco-
                       logy, geomorphology, climatology, biology
                       and land use, students are particularly
                       brought into contact with real conservation
                       problems.

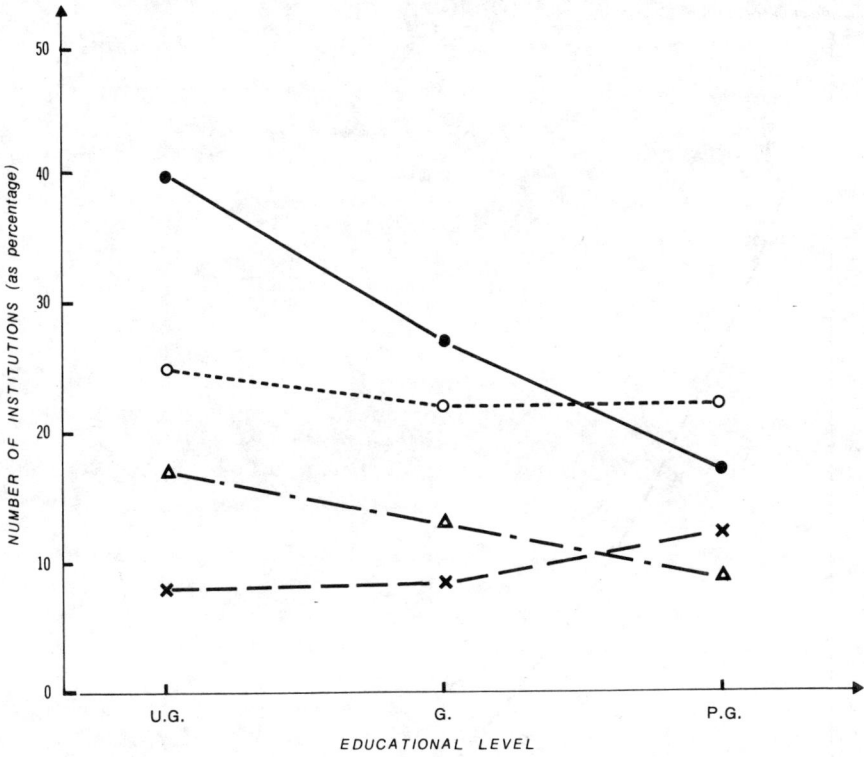

Figure I

EXTENT OF INTERDISCIPLINARITY
IN ENVIRONMENTAL EDUCATION

● INSTITUTIONS ONLY TEACHING DISCIPLINARY COURSES

✖ INSTITUTIONS ONLY TEACHING INTERDISCIPLINARY COURSES

▲ INSTITUTIONS TEACHING COMBINED–TYPE COURSES

○ INSTITUTIONS TEACHING COMBINED–TYPE OR INTERDISCIPLINARY COURSES

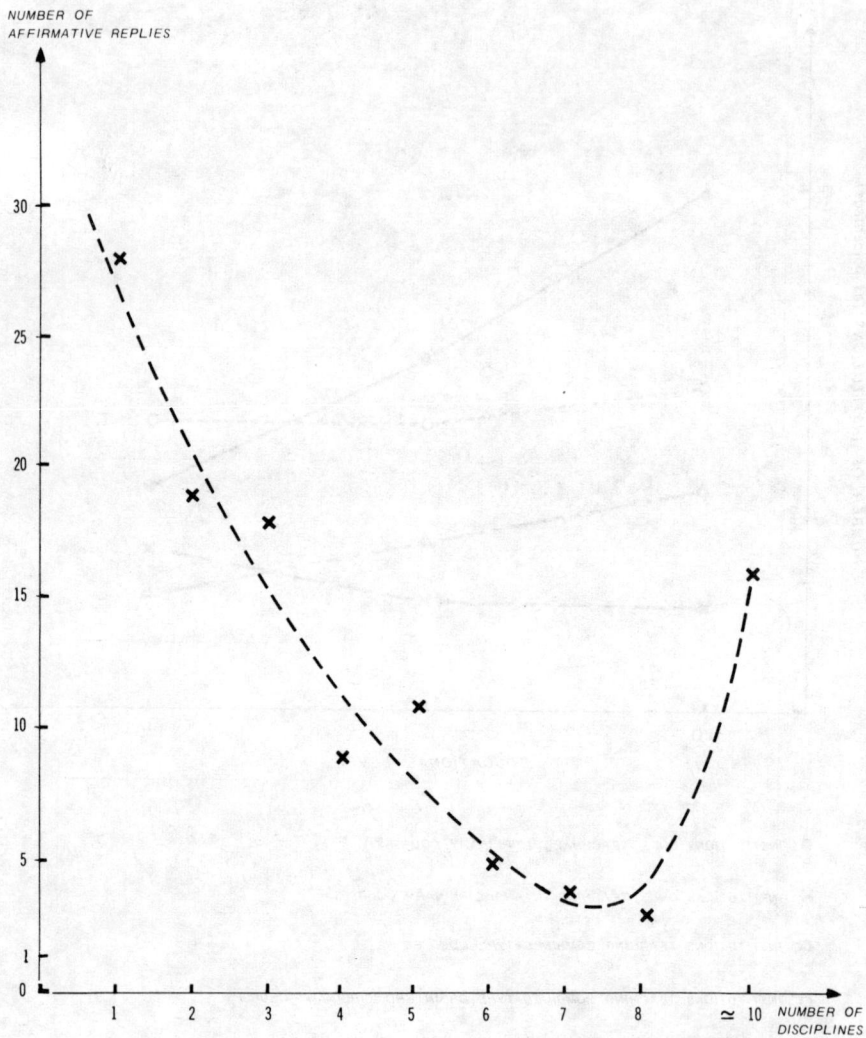

Figure 2

DISTRIBUTION OF AFFIRMATIVE REPLIES
AS A FUNCTION OF THE NUMBER OF DISCIPLINES CONCERNED

Table I. BREAKDOWN OF POSITIVE REPLIES BY COUNTRIES
AND TYPES OF INSTITUTIONS

Country	Number of Institutions (a)		Number of Students (b) (thousands)	Number of replies received	Number of positive replies	
	Universities or Colleges	Other Institutions of Higher Education			Universities or Colleges	Other Institutions of Higher Education
Austria	6	5	52.0 (1969/70)	2	1	1
Belgium	5	9	84.0 (1965/66)	11	2	-
Canada	52	-	427.9 (1967/68)	19	14	-
Denmark	5	14	60.3 (1968/69)	12	2	4
Finland	11	8	66.1 (1969/70)	12	4	2
France	63	269	749.0 (1969/70)	51	16	20
Germany	37	-	445.0 (1968/69)	11	2	2
Greece	4	6	-	2	-	-
Iceland	1	-	-	1	1	-
Ireland	6	3	20.0 (1967/68)	3	1	-
Italy	34	5	-	2	1	-
Japan	57	323	1525.4 (1968/69)	29	9	4
Luxembourg	4	-	-	-	-	-
Netherlands	13	6	124.0 (1965/66)	6	-	4
Norway	4	4	38.6 (estimation)	3	1	1
Spain	19	25	236.4 (1968/69)	9	2	1
Sweden	8	17	123.0 (1968/69)	14	3	2
Switzerland	9	-	-	1	1	-
Turkey	8	44	-	4	1	-
United Kingdom	48. univ. 48. coll.	53	529.0 (1967/68)	56	18	8
Yugoslavia	7	-	261.2 (1967/68)	19	14	-
TOTAL	401	791	For guidance 4742.7	249	82	49

a) The number of institutions was compiled from the World List - Universities and other Institutions of Higher Education ... published by the International Association of Universities 1969
b) Source : OECD 1971

223

Table II NUMBER OF POSITIVE REPLIES PER
THOUSAND STUDENTS, BY COUNTRIES

Country	Number of positive replies per thousand students
Austria	40 %
Belgium	24 %
Canada	33 %
Denmark	100 %
Finland	90 %
France	48 %
Germany	9 %
Ireland	50 %
Japan	8, 5 %
Netherlands	32 %
Norway	52 %
Spain	12, 5 %
Sweden	38 %
United kingdom	49 %
Yugoslavia	3, 8 %

Table III ANALYSIS BY COUNTRIES OF QUESTIONS
8, 9, 10, 11 AND CERTAIN ASPECTS OF QUESTION 7
IN QUESTIONNAIRE

Country	Positive replies		Courses open to non-students		Structure(1)		Links (2)					Partici-pation in secondary education	Planned (3)	Inter-disciplinary Courses (4)	
	Univer-sities	Other	Univer-sities	Other	a	b + c	a	b	c	d	e			Univer-sities	Other
Austria	1	1	-	1	2	-	1	-	-	1	1	-	-	1	-
Belgium	2	-	2	-	-	1	-	-	-	1	-	-	-	1	-
Canada	14	-	5	-	4	6	7	10	5	6	3	7	2	8	1
Denmark	2	4	1	2	4	2	-	5	6	3	3	2	-	2	2
Finland	4	2	3	-	4	2	3	4	3	2	5	2	-	4	1
France	16	20	6	6	9	22	7	12	14	9	7	8	2	5	6
Germany	2	2	1	-	1	1	1	1	1	2	2	-	-	2	-
Iceland	1	-	-	-	1	1	-	-	1	1	1	-	-	-	-
Ireland	1	-	-	-	-	1	-	1	1	1	-	-	-	1	-
Italy	1	-	-	-	-	1	-	-	-	-	-	2	-	-	1
Japan	9	4	2	1	5	2	4	6	6	4	4	-	-	2	-
Netherlands	-	4	1	2	1	3	2	2	3	4	4	2	-	1	1
Norway	1	1	-	-	1	-	1	1	1	1	1	-	-	-	-
Sweden	3	2	2	-	-	3	1	1	2	2	2	4	1	2	1
Switzerland	1	-	1	-	1	1	1	1	1	1	1	-	-	1	-
Turkey	1	-	-	-	-	1	1	1	1	1	1	-	-	-	-
United Kingdom	18	8	3	-	8	8	9	8	7	7	9	4	2	8	-
Yugoslavia	1	-	-	-	1	1	-	1	-	1	1	-	1	-	-
Total partial	80	49	27	13	41	57	43	50	44	47	45	30	8	38	10
Total general.	129		40											48	

1) Replies to question 9, parts (a) and (b) + (c).
2) Replies to question 10, parts (a), (b), (c), (d) and (e).
3) Some replies indicate that the course is in the planning stage.
4) Some replies mention interdisciplinary instruction at various educational levels. They are only counted once in this Table but at all levels in Table IV.

Table IV BREAKDOWN INTO DISCIPLINARY,
INTERDISCIPLINARY OR COMBINED COURSES
BY COUNTRIES AND EDUCATIONAL LEVELS

Country	Disciplinary courses			Interdisciplinary courses			Combined courses		
	UG	G	PG	UG	G	PG	UG	G	PG (a)
Canada	5	6	2	1	1	1	6	3	0
France	6	10	8	1	5	7	3	8	3
Japan	10	3	2	-	-	-	3	1	1
United Kingdom	14	2	4	4	-	2	5	1	6
Other	17	14	6	4	5	6	5	4	2
TOTAL	52	35	22	10	11	16	22	17	12
Percentage in terms of level	48 %	32 %	20 %	27 %	30 %	43 %	43,5 %	33 %	23,5 %
	100%			100%			100%		

a) UG = undergraduate level
   G = graduate level
   PG = postgraduate level

226

Table V   FREQUENCY OF THE DISCIPLINES MENTIONED
IN THE POSITIVE REPLIES

Discipline	Frequency
Anthropology	2
Bioclimatology	3
Biology	29
Chemistry	11
Law	2
Ecology	28
Economics	4
Physical geography (a)	9
Human geography (b)	13
Geology	7
Soil Science	2
Physics (c)	8
Public Health (d)	26
Sociology	7
Statistics	2

(a), (b), (d) ; the following individual disciplines which would
have unduly lengthened the list if they had all been quoted
have been grouped under a general heading :

a) Geophysics, hydrology, climatology ;
b) Demography, town planning, economic geography ;
c) Of the 8 cases listed under physics, 5 were more particularly related to radioactivity ;
d) Parasitology, toxicology, industrial health and hygiene.

Table VI FREQUENCY OF THE SUBJECTS CONCERNED IN ENVIRONMENTAL EDUCATION

Subject	Frequency
Agriculture	4
Regional Development	11
Architecture - Town Planning	9
Chemistry of water resources and the environment - Pollution (a)	16
General ecology and ecosystems	18
Resource Conservation Human ecology (a)	6
Physical environment - physical geography	10
Hygiene - Public Health	4
Oceanography	1

a) The subjects underlined may be considered new, i.e. specially created for environmental studies. The other subjects mentioned were already taught before emphasis was laid on environmental problems. It was often difficult to determine whether these subjects were taught in such a way as to highlight the complexity of environmental problems. Example : does the teaching of architecture and/ or town planning include social psychology and or ecology, etc... ?

Chapter II

A SURVEY OF ENVIRONMENTAL SCIENCE EDUCATION
IN THE UNITED STATES

By Karl E. SCHAEFER

Department of Environmental Physiology,
University of Rhode Island, Connecticut, United States

A SURVEY OF ENVIRONMENTAL SCIENCE EDUCATION
IN THE UNITED STATES

The Subcommittee on Science, Research and Development of the Committee on Science and Astronautics of the 91st Congress published, in December 1969, a survey on "Environmental Sciences Centers at Institutions of Higher Education."(1) The subcommittee had prepared a questionnaire on environmental sciences centers and sent it to 1,300 accredited colleges and universities in the United States. Of the 500 responses received, 106 were utilized since they concerned pertinent environmental programs.

Structure and Composition of the environmental centers showed many different patterns. "The establishment of a center may be originated by faculty, students, Government agencies, or private organizations and industrial enterprises". These findings correspond with the multiplicity of relations of environmental programs to institutions inside and outside the university in the other OECD countries mentioned in Chapter I.

Moreover, it was observed that in the United States "many programs of environmental centers are action-oriented rather than theoretical in nature. In fact, an environmental center often appears to reflect a university's degree of involvement in the social, economic and political issues of the community, state and nation". It was concluded that "for these reasons, as the survey indicates, environmental science centers often are initiated in response to proposals coming from faculty groups, civic or government agencies or industry on a specific local or regional environmental problem".

Anyone who is at all familiar with the university situation in the United States can confirm these findings and their indication that the initiative for instituting environmental education programs in the universities came largely from without the universities. The environmental problems grew and forced themselves on the universities. As it will be shown later, the universities were and still are ill-prepared to provide an appropriate environmental education wich really deals with environmental problems in a decisive way.

The existing academic departments provide the majority of research and instructional programs in environmental education. Initiatives for environmental quality instruction started in those departments which are directly involved with environmental problems such as :

1 . departments of engineering, urban planning, land use and transportation,
2 . public health departments of medical schools and,
3 . departments of biological and chemical sciences with ecology as a focal point.

In some universities forestry and agricultural and marine sciences have taken a lead in environmental research and education programs. When the complexities of the man-environmental relationship are probed more deeply, other disciplines such as mathematics, social sciences, psychology and law are drawn more and more into environmental science center curricula.

There are the greatest varieties of Interdepartmental Environmental Science Centers, from simple "paper institutes", where the faculty is still completely linked with the individual departments, to fully budgeted centers with their own faculties. It is a common experience that the existing university structure with its departments exert great constraints on the development of environmental centers. The survey indicates that centers which "insist originally on interdisciplinary activities seem to be more successful from the start than institutes which evolve gradually from their parent departments".

It is also noted that "Environmental Science Centers", in addition to regular faculty members, have drawn liberally on "professionals in government and industry or private organizations for everything from course teaching to development of symposia and organizing of field expeditions".

Environmental Programs are largely action-oriented, probably because of the stimulus from the outside to do something about the environmental problems. But many centers recognize that "basic research and intensive investigation of the multitude of factors which contribute to an environmental problem are necessary before action programs can be carried out". The latter represent, frequently, an activity which is helpful in motivating the students but does not produce any lasting results.

The future scope of environmental programs as envisioned

in many environmental centers in 1969, at the time of the survey, would include a broadening of studies and instructions to include social and behavioral sciences and also include undergraduate environmental education, which in 1969 was practically non-existent. There was also a recognition for the need to go beyond the training of environmental specialists and to develop programs for the training of an environmental generalist who could effectively coordinate the activities of specialists.

The report on "Environmental Studies at the CIC Universities" (2) gives a fairly clear picture of how the Big Ten universities in the Middle West (Universities of Illinois, Indiana, Iowa, Michigan, Minnesota and Wisconsin, and Chicago, Michigan State, Northwestern and Purdue Universities) approach environmental education. The general direction is the development of a policy of utilizing existing departments to educate and train environmental specialists. Programs of environmental education are predominantly created at the graduate level. The report noted that "seven out of eleven CIC universities have established or are in the process of establishing university-wide Environmental Studies Centers or Institutes". These centers play more or less the role of clearing houses, in which a multitude of environmental research and instruction programs of individual departments are coordinated. They are specifically neither set up nor planned as competitive units in relation to existing departments. As a matter of fact, the Institute for Environmental Quality of the University of Michigan is an example of a new institution set up to strengthen the research capabilities of special departments.

The Institute started with a grant of $ 750,000 from the Rockefeller Foundation in December, 1969. The Foundation had decided to concentrate its efforts in environmental education in universities which had already proved themselves capable of research and graduate education of a high calibre. The grant was given to support integrative efforts.

The program of the Institute consists of twenty graduate fellowships in environmentally oriented research work carried out in existing departments. In addition, "seed money" is provided during the academic year 1971-72 for over twenty faculty-student research projects. This institute supports graduate students only in career-professional work on one or more environmental problems and is not formally involved in undergraduate education. The Institute for Environmental Quality at the University of Michigan has the distinct advantage of being able to support environmental research projects along nontraditional lines which, as far as funding is concerned, represent "high risk" projects and would probably not find support.

A similar example is the Institute of Environmental Health of Purdue University, founded in 1965, to provide a coordinated management for an interdisciplinary research and educational program in environmental sciences. The staff of ninety members hold titles in the schools and departments with which they are affiliated and not with the interdisciplinary Institute of Environmental Health. In other words, the members of the institute are bound up with the reward structure of the individual departments. The institute does not have facilities of its own, and programs in research and instruction are carried out in the facilities of the individual departments.

The Institute for Environmental Studies at the University of Wisconsin was organized along similar lines. Its director reports to the Chancellor of the university. It serves as the administrative organization for groups and other centers active in environmental research and education, such as the Marine Studies Center, the Center for Climatic Research, Remote Sensing Study Group, etc. The institute is responsible for developing environmental research at the undergraduate, graduate, and postgraduate levels.

Several innovative approaches in curriculum development in environmental sciences were reported, among them a Bachelor's degree program at the University of Michigan in which the student will graduate with a joint degree (B. A.) in a discipline like Geography, and Environmental Studies. The student has to satisfy the usual requirements for a B. A. degree and in addition he elects a special program in environmental sciences consisting of introductory courses at the freshman level, a seminar series on problems of environmental quality during the sophomore-junior years, and a "senior" practicum in environmental science.

At Michigan State University a "System Science Program" has evolved with the active participation of many departments. Interdepartmental Ph. D. programs have been developed in ecology (University of Michigan) and in environmental biology (University of Illinois).

The report concluded, "With so many research institutions involved in environmental sciences it is believed that short term research will be effectively accomplished without major organizational changes. However, the long term research related to the "future of man"and the" quality of life" requires the stability and stimulation that should be provided by new instrumentalities at our universities".

Some general comments were given which are reminiscent of the remarks on generalist and specialist environmental education made at the Tours workshop. It is pertinent that an attempt was made to give a perspective in environmental education which is quoted in the following :

"The dilemma, which must be reconciled, is that the theoretical solution of environmental problems may lead to nearly every discipline at a university, while without a generalist viewpoint the proper questions may never be raised".

The report lists also some very interesting student quotations which throw some light on the environmental education programs. It had already been stated in the congressional subcommittee report (1) that students were rarely involved in the development of environmental programs. This is also borne out in other quoted remarks :

a) On student participation :
"If positive pressure were exercised to bring students in and seek their opinions, rather than just their benedictions, student input might begin. But just opening the doors is not enough; students are too cynical and many of the good ones, whose opinions could really help, will not come".

b) On curriculum development in environmental sciences :
"There is no consideration of an end goal in the design of the environmental courses we see popping up. A course is put together and when it is over and doesn't lead anywhere then we decide, oh well, that was for awareness".

"Where can a person go for a generalist background? Courses and curriculums both suffer from the common ill of being no more than a "laundry list" of topics with little to tie them together".

"Team teaching would be fine if there were a team rather than a collection of faculty".

"Project-oriented courses suffer from three major ills : ill defined projects, lack of leadership, and too little time".

"The job of developing curriculum has fallen to the students and young faculty because the established people can't work across disciplinary lines".

c) <u>On research in environmental sciences</u> :
   "After seven years of research into the problem of animal waste disposal, we've finally come to the conclusion
   that it's better to spread it around than to pile it up".

<u>Faculty quotations on disciplinary and problem-oriented
interdisciplinary research and education</u> :

"Anything to break down compartmentalization is needed".
(Professor of Engineering).

"The peer system contributes to specialization--we need
mission-oriented subcultures". (Professor of Engineering)

"There is a general difficulty in relating a discipline to a
problem--that is, the faculty--either they were not trained
in problems or they forgot". (Center Director).

"I would emphasize the importance of "Historical Accident"
in setting up academic disciplines". (Dean of Arts).

The Steinhart report on "The Universities and Environmental Quality--Commitment to Problem Focused Education" (3)
was prepared for the President's Environmental Quality Council in 1969 and has had an influence on the development of plans
for Interdisciplinary Institutes for Environmental Quality as
indicated in the report on the CIC Universities (2) cited earlier.
This report was based on an analysis of the material collected
in the survey of the congressional subcommittee (1) and on
detailed site visits to six larger institutions with ongoing environmental programs.

   It was recommended that the Federal Government support
formation of schools of the Human Environment at colleges and
universities for the purpose of establishing <u>problem-focused
education</u> and research programs. Since a considerable resis-
tance on the part of the established disciplines and departments
against problem-oriented education was observed at most universities, it was recommended that the programs considered
worthy of funding should meet at least two important criteria :

   1) Substantial or complete control of the faculty reward
      structure.
   2) Freedom to be innovative in introducing course material,
      educational programs, work-study programs, and curri-
      culum requirements for degree.

   These requirements are obviously difficult to meet in universities dominated by departments. Of the environmental programs

of the CIC universities, only one center at the University of Wisconsin offered its own courses but none of the environmental institutes awards degrees. (2).

It has been pointed out by Hare (4) that "when we propose to introduce a broad-spectrum, synthesizing effort like environmental studies we run full tilt into all these vested interests of the traditional departments and the largely analytical disciplines they profess. We also bang ourselves against the clan spirit of the traditional faculty groupings".

Hare, a professor of geography at the University of Toronto and former president of the University of British Columbia, comments further on the difficulties encountered with environmental problem-focused programs :

"The political interest in the environment demands proposals for action--on all time scales, from the immediate assault on pollution problems to the long-term reconstruction of society in a better relation to environment. At present we are not action-oriented, and on every campus there is a dead weight of opinion that regards action-oriented programs as hostile to the academic life.

"I must also stress the incompetence of the established disciplines to tackle society's real problem. What we mean by discipline is an agreed tested body of method--usually analytical--that we bring to bear on problems of our own choosing. The essence of our thinking is that we cannot tackle problems that don't fit the competence of our own discipline".

Steinhart pointed out that problem-focused activities have existed at the universities in the schools of agriculture and public health for fifty to one hundred years, which "succeeded in spite of their reputation of being second-rate intellectual efforts". In looking at environmental programs connected with schools of public health and medical schools he observed that "no professional medical people seem to be directly involved with the environmental programs on a continuing basis". In his studies Steinhart found that "more than half of the students participating in such problem-focused environmental programs have held jobs for several years and have returned to the university" They were attracted by these multi-disciplinary programs and hoped to be able to obtain some broader knowledge to deal with the problems society faces today. In an Appendix to the Steinhart report (3), D. E. Cunningham reviews the funding of university interdisciplinary research.

The results of these efforts have been mixed. In particular, attempts to support interdisciplinary research involving social sciences with science-oriented disciplines have been considered to be a failure. The question is raised whether truly interdisciplinary research is at the present time "alien to the discipline-oriented structure of the university". One of the important problems is that the "reward system for the individual faculty member at a university is almost totally ungeared to interdisciplinary activities".

Cunningham brings some very interesting suggestions for future action. At the present time there are resources in depth but not in breadth. A mechanism is needed to bring these in-depth resources to bear on the complex environmental problems; maybe new types of "functional academic departments" are needed for this purpose.

Commenting on the historical development of the national laboratories in which a mission dictated personnel requirements and the use of unique equipment, the question is raised whether "the analysis of the environmental problems we face in the next decade will require this type of unique, expensive equipment or, for that matter, the deep specialization that characterizes fundamental research in the national laboratories. The personnel connected with such institutions has skills not readily transferable to interdisciplinary environmental investigations needed".

There is apparently a feeling that requirements for a more synthetic knowledge demanded by the environmental problems cannot be fulfilled by the heavily specialized researcher. In order to produce the right match in administration of funding and execution of programs for interdisciplinary research at the university, Cunningham suggests consideration of coordination of different federal funding agencies.

Reference is made to the study of Eric Jantsch entitled, "The Emerging Role of the University, "(5) in which he proposes a new purpose of the university in a three-fold role in enhancing society's capability for continuons self-renewal through unification of the educational, research and service function of the university. He states that,

"The disruptive forces threatening the university--and indeed society itself--may be expected to act as cohesive forces once a number of structural changes have been introduced, both within the university and in its relationships with society at large and with various elements of the surrounding community.

"It is necessary to deal with causes, not with symptoms. The general concern over the university, and above all the student's concern, cannot be resolved with patchwork and compromising shock absorbing strategies. There are no clear-cut problems to be solved--the classical single track and sequential problem-solving approach itself become meaningless today. This may come as a cultural shock to our pragmatic and efficient society, valuing nothing higher than 'know-how' ".

Let us turn to the new ventures in environmental education at the new colleges, where environmental studies have been put on an equal footing with the sciences and humanities.

It is characteristic that the development of a broadly based curriculum, oriented toward environmental problems, required a change in the conventional college structure. In the following, three examples are discussed : The University of Wisconsin at Green Bay, Huxley College and Evergreen State College, Washington :

The new approach to environmental education in Green Bay has been described in the position paper of Chancellor Weidner during the proceedings of the OECD workshop, as well as in the report of Peterson (See Chapter III). Only a few essential points are mentioned here for the purpose of comparison with the other new colleges.

The University of Wisconsin-Green Bay originated as a Community College with a special focus on Man-Environment. There are two outstanding features :

1) The selection of a problem-focused education--Man-Environment--made it necessary to depart from the traditional disciplines and led to the creation of four "Theme" colleges, each college having an aspect of the environment as its special focus, e. g., College of Environmental Sciences Colleges of Community Services, Creative Communication, Human Biology and a School of Professional Studies. Within each college, the faculty was grouped into concentrations which represent more specific environmental problem areas. Thus, the University of Wisconsin in Green Bay has been organized from the start along interdisciplinary lines as a logical consequence of a problem-focused educational plan.

2) Concentrating education on specific problems requires a necessary complementation to do something about the problems-action programs !

238

This is embodied in the community-university relationship. Students are involved in community work, pollution probes, anti-poverty work, etc., and citizens of the community who have pertinent experience in environmental programs teach at the University, even if they don't have the usually required academic credentials.

Following the authorization of the new institution by the Wisconsin State Legislature in 1965, it took four years to get the school into operation in 1969. According to all reports the school has been quite successful.

The Evergreen State College in Washington, located in a thousand-acre forest on the shores of Puget Sound, started its first year of school in 1971. The State Legislature of Washington created this college in 1967 with the request that it should not be a carbon copy of existing institutions. The resulting new experiment in education, with emphasis on environmental problems, is based on a design to which the well-known industrial consultant, Arthur D. Little, greatly contributed.

The experiment consists in a radical departure from a conventional college structure. There are no departments, no schools, no examinations. The program consists of two types of studies :

1) Coordinated studies related to basic questions : What is Man? --a full year program called Causality, Chance and Freedom, which seems to reflect the theme treated in Monod's book on "Chance and Necessity" (6). Another coordinated two-year studies program is entitled, Human Development. These coordinated studies are based on interdisciplinary seminars. Lectures do not play a role but there are computer-assisted instructional programs where students and faculty interact via computer. In this way background material, previously covered by traditional lectures and suggested readings, is handled.

2) The contracted studies program involves mostly environmentally-oriented projects such as inventory of plant and animal species, soils and geology, status of environmental pollution with contribution to an environmental inventory computer data bank.

Special laboratory facilities are under construction, housed in a five million dollar science center containing teaching-research modules. Moreover, mobile minicampus units consisting of commissary, laboratory and dormitory trailers will enable groups of students and teachers to travel. Collaborative team efforts are emphasized rather than "competitive individualism".

Huxley College of Environmental Studies, in Washington, has attempted a compromise between the traditional college structure and a new environmental college, such as Green Bay, Wisconsin, by attaching a "cluster college" for environmental studies to the existing Western Washington State College, which is organized along traditional lines. The "cluster college" concept has been advanced by Gaff, et al., 1970 (7) The student would obtain, during his first two years, an education in the traditional disciplines at Western Washington State College. Those students interested in getting a degree in environmental studies would enter Huxley College at the Junior level. A major would be selected in a concentration such as environmental control and tailored to his background, e.g., chemistry (environmental control-chemistry), resulting in a double major.

Huxley College is an adisciplinary college where faculty members with diverse backgrounds work together. Most of them have full time appointments in the college. Some joint appointments strengthen the ties with Western Washington State College.

The previously mentioned problems related to the control of the faculty reward structure 'Steinhart (3)) have been avoided with this system of the "cluster college" for environmental education. Research is considered an important aspect of Huxley College. Programs are being developed both for undergraduate and graduate levels. Community involvement is an essential component of the educational program and consists of an Environmental Reference Bureau which provides free information on environmental problems, on request, to anyone in the Community. A recycling center has been started.

How can a small liberal arts college of high standing develop a quality program in environmental education at the undergraduate level and to this within the existing structure of the college? This was the basic question asked at a conference on "Undergraduate Education in Environmental Studies" held at Dartmouth College in April 1970 (8). This is a most pertinent question in view of the rush of hastily organized environmental courses with which many colleges and universities across the United States responded to the public concern about the environmental crisis. Such courses have been characterized aptly by students as "a laundry list of topics with little to tie them together".

Based on the proceedings of this conference, Dartmouth

College adopted an "Environmental Studies Program" which includes a "modified major" representing a series of interdisciplinary environmentally-focused courses, coupled with a conventional major in one of the established disciplines. This program was similar in scope to that developed by the "Center for Environmental Studies" in neighboring Williams College which had been in existence since 1967 (9). The Williams proposal for an undergraduate program in environmental studies was presented at the conference by Reidel and Scheffey (10) and attests to the authors' experience with, and perception of, the real problems in environmental education.

The proposed Williams curriculum consists of an introductory course, a concentration sequence and a core sequence. The four introductory courses in environmental studies are offered in the departments of Economics (Title : Resource Allocation), Art (Title : Environmental Planning and Design), Biology (Title : Environmental Biology-Ecosystems) and Political Science (Title : Politics, Bureaucracy and the Public Environment).

The first core course in environmental studies offered in the Junior year requires all four introductory courses as prerequisites and is given by the members of the Center for Env mental Studies. This course, entitled "Environmental Perception and Planning", focuses on a synthesis--"an inquiry into the essential correlations and interrelationships between various modes of environmental perception and awareness". Then follows a concentration sequence, composed of courses offered by the departments, which varies depending on the options selected.

The Senior core course in environmental studies (Environmental Planning and Policy) deals with topics like natural resources appraisal and administration, the economic forces, ecological consideration and cultural attitudes affecting the planning process, as well as analysis of regional and national environmental policies in an expanding urban environment. For those seniors who major in environmental studies, there is a final core course offered in Environmental Problems in which experience in actual environmental planning is gained through independent and group studies of local environmental problems.

The Environmental studies Programs developed at Williams College has been described in more detail because it seems to fulfill the requirements for a quality program in environmental education in a small college. Utilizing the strength in the existing departments, the students receive a grounding in specific knowledge before an effort is made to achieve a synthesis. This corresponds well with the experience of R. Dubos (11) who told the author that it is extremely difficult to teach first-year students a general approach to environmental problems. They must first have some grounding in a discipline or some field to be able to ask the right questions.

The concentration sequence in the courses offered by the departments, following the general environmental course focus-ing on a synthesis, can contribute to the further deepening of the understanding of environmental problems. The final core sequence on environmental planning and field studies of environ-mental problems seems to round out an excellent program in which courses of a more specialized nature are astutely balanc-ed with general environmental courses.

According to the student and faculty response given in Peter-son's report, the Williams College program in environmental studies seems to be one of the best in the country. The only difficulty with such a program lies in the structure; it requires an ideal cooperation between departments and an Environmental Center which so far, according to all reports (e.g., 2,3), has not been accomplished anywhere.

A. Scheffey, the former Director of the Center for Environ-mental Studies at Williams College, gave a very pertinent paper on "Policies and Pitfalls in Organizing a Curriculum" (12) at the Dartmouth conference. He points to the hectic activities on many campuses dealing with man-environment problems and warns that the academic landscape is cluttered up with paste-on institutes to give a superficial environmental education pro-gram. He himself has had long years of experience and com-bines the knowledge of specialists in a number of areas with that of a genuine generalist.

He points out the long lead-times necessary between the beginning of an exchange of ideas among members of different departments and the time when an agreement is reached and a formal program in environmental education can be instituted. There are enormous difficulties in achieving an organic rela-tionship between individual departments in regard to environ-mental education programs. Scheffey states that the elements needed to succeed in the existing framework of a college involve-administrative initiative, faculty involvement, capacity for curriculum change and student participation. He goes on to say that "there is a final and indispensable requirement, the presence of a small but critical grouping of individuals whose primary concern is with environment as an area of synthesis".

All these elements are needed to develop a "quality program" in environmental education, but it appears that permanency of a quality environmental education program cannot be assured without a change in the university structure, giving environmental education programs control over the faculty reward structure and making them independent of the departments, as stated in the Steinhart report (3).

The very fact that Dr. Scheffey and Dr. Reidel, Director and Assistant Director of the Center for Environmental Studies at Williams College, who developed a most successful program in environmental studies, have left Williams College underscores again the importance of the Steinhart demand requiring environmental programs to have control of the faculty reward structure. Scheffey also mentions a desirable pedagogical innovation for environmental studies--that blocks of time could be devoted exclusively to environmental topics taught from different disciplinary viewpoints.

A curriculum in Human Biology has been proposed at Stanford University, Palo Alto, California, in response to the challenging environmental problems (Kretschmer (13)). For many years physiology has been taught as a "frog physiology", then moved on to a "dog physiology", and now we are supposedly entering the area of "human physiology". Kretschmer points out that during the last 30 years increasing emphasis has been placed on research that deals with man himself. This new body of knowledge is considered to provide enough resources to each biology with a primary emphasis on the human example.

The new proposed curriculum in Human Biology is designed with two far-reaching objectives in mind. (1) to "humanize" biological studies, e. g., teaching physiology based on studies of human subjects, and (2) to provide a biological perspective of behavioral sciences to attempt a unification among disciplines like psychology, sociology, anthropology and politics (Kretschmer (13)).

It is interesting to note that such goals, requiring fundamental changes in approach, are thought to be reachable through a reorganization of the curriculum with an emphasis on description of human experiments. Taylor's book, "The Biological Time Bomb" (14), expresses a public concern that biological research as practised in certain laboratories today could lead to "dehumanizing" conditions in the future. In the face of this concern, underlying attitudes and modes of thinking in biological research would have to be evaluted in an effort to "humanize" biological studies. Such attempts have been made in the Allpach Symposium of 1968 which was published under the title, "Beyond Reductionism" (15) in 1970, in Rene Dubos' "So Human an Animal" (16) and in Bertallanffy's "Robots, Men and Minds" (17), 1967.

Some of the details of the proposed curriculum in Human Biology are mentioned. The core subjects in biology consist of Molecular and Cellular Biology, Organismal Human Biology, Man and Nature and Population, Food and Environment, while the core subjects of Man and Society are taught as interdisciplinary, biologically-oriented courses in the behavioral sciences. After completing the core subjects, the students can choose advanced courses in either of two tracks--Biology of Man or Human Populations, The Environment and Policy--but are required to take courses in both sequences with emphasis in one.

This is an example of a type of curriculum revision which is made as an adjustment of the university to the problems brought from the outside. Whether such adjustments are sufficient to meet the demands for environmental education will depend on the extent to which they are successful in changing attitudes and values in regard to the man-environment relation. All too often, adjustments of universities in the field of environmental education represent, in the words of Arnstein (18), "old wine in new bottles" which does not get to the heart of the problem.

Lynton K. Caldwell has expressed very succinctly the real issue in a short article entitled, "A Crisis of Will and Rationality" (19) from which some passages are quoted :

"Our country faces a crisis of the mind and spirit, more profound and more threatening than the crisis of the environment..."
"The environmental crisis in America can have only two explanations. Either Americans are incompetent to manage their natural heritage, or they are indifferent to its future".
"To surmount this crisis of will and rationality, a major effort will be necessary to orient and motivate the coming generation of decision-makers...."
"If undergraduate education is to help resolve the inner crisis of purpose which underlies the external crisis of environment a more valid set of goals and objectives will be required".

Considering all the aspects of environmental education which were brought out in the different reports and surveys discussed so far, two major conclusions seem to emerge. An environmental education which really deals with the underlying causes of the environmental crisis requires (1) a university structure which enables environmental education programs to develop free of the constraints of the conventional departments and disciplines, and (2) interdisciplinary teaching of a great variety, with the unifying theme of a man-centered science providing new aspects in the relationship of man-environment.

244

REFERENCES

1. Environmental Policy Division, Legislative Reference Service, Library of Congress. Environmental Science Centers at Institutions of Higher Education. A survey prepared for the Subcommittee on Science, Research and Development of the Committee on Science and Astronautics, U.S. House of Representatives, 91st Congress, Washington, December 15, 1969.

2. Ragland, Kenneth W. and Thomas W. Smith. "Environmental Studies at the CIC Universities". January, 1971.

3. Steinhart, J.S. and Cherniack, S., "The Universities and Environmental Quality". A report to the President's Environmental Quality Council from the Office of Science and Technology, Sept. 1969.

4. Hare, J.K. "How Should We Treat Environment". Science, 167, 352-355, 1970.

5. Jantsch, Erich. "Integrative Planning for the "Joint Systems" of Society and Technology--The Emerging Role of the University". CERI/HE/CP/70.08.1970. OECD.

6. Monod, P. "Chance and Necessity", A. Knopf, New York, 1971.

7. Gaff, J.G. and Ass. "The Cluster College". Jossey-Bass Inc., San Francisco, California, 1970.

8. Reiners, A. and F. Smallwood, Eds. "Undergraduate Education in Environmental Studies", a Conference Report. The Public Affairs Center, Dartmouth College, Hanover, New Hampshire, 1970.

9. W. Carney. "Man, Land." Williams College Center for Environmental Studies, the first two years. Williams College Williamstown, Mass., 1969.

10. Reidel, C. and A. J. W. Scheffey. "Williams Proposal for an Undergraduate Program in Environmental Studies".

    "Undergraduate Education in Environmental Studies" Conference Report. Reiners, A. and F. Smallwood, Eds, Dartmouth College, 1970.

11. René Dubos, October 1971, personal communication.

12. Scheffey, A. J. W. "Environmental Centers in a Crowded Landscape", "Policies and Pitfalls in Organizing a Curriculum" in "Undergraduate Program in Environmental Studies", Conference Report. Reiners, A. and F. Smallwood, Eds., pp. 38-51, Dartmouth College, 1970.

13. Kretschmer, N. "Human Biology". In : Environmental Education, pp. 14-15, 1970. Scientists' Institute for Public Information, New York, N. Y. ".

14. Taylor, G. R. "The Biological Time Bomb". The World Publishing Co., New York, 1968.

15. Koestler, A. and J. R. Smythies, Ed. "Beyond Reductionism". Macmillan, New York, 1970.

16. René Dubos. "So Human an Animal". Scribner's Son, New York, 1968.

17. Bertallanffy, L. von, "Robots, Men and Minds". George Braziller, New York, 1967.

18. Arnstein, G. "Seminar on Environmental Issues". Southern Conn. State College, New Haven, Conn., Dec. 9, 1971.

19. Caldwell, L. K. "A Crisis of Will and Rationality", pp. 18-19, in "Environmental Education 1970". Scientists' Institute for Public Information, New York, N. Y.

Chapter III

SURVEY AND EVALUATION OF ENVIRONMENTAL EDUCATION PROGRAMMES OF SELECTED UNIVERSITIES OF THE UNITED STATES

By Lee PETERSON,
University of Rhode Island, United States

INTRODUCTION

In late October, 1971, we were commissioned by the Center for Educational Research and Innovation of OECD to initiate a survey of selected university level environmental education programs in the United States. Throughout the months of November and December we collected and compiled information from a limited, but what we felt was a fairly good cross-section of environmental programs offered by U.S. universities.

We obtained our information by means of personal interviews, questionnaires, replies to Conservation Foundation questionnaires, and university brochures and monographs. We strongly emphasized personal interviews and attached particular importance to student response.

Our choice of programs to cover was influenced by a list of those institutions contacted by the Conservation Foundation in its recent survey of environmental studies program, and the proximity of these institutions to our Connecticut base of operations. These researches included programs from the following universities :

Dartmouth College, Hanover, New Hampshire
Hampshire College, Amherst, Mass.
Williams College, Williamstown, Mass.
College of the Atlantic, Mount Desert, Maine
Cornell University, Ithaca, New York
University of Wisconsin, Madison, Wisconsin
University of Wisconsin, Green Bay, Wisconsin
University of Indiana, Bloomington, Indiana
University of California, Santa Cruz, California
Evergreen State College, Olympia, Washington

During the course of our studies we found that virtually every program included student participation in community action projects. A few universities had programs which offered no off-campus activities and confined themselves to in-class problem solving. Others went to the other extreme and offered a large

248

number of community action oriented courses but a minimum of in-class work.

We felt that the programs which were the most effective in giving their students a solid background in environmental studies and pointing out the directions the students should take in order to arrive at solutions to environmental problems were those that had achieved a good balance between these two poles of theory and practical application.

We have tried to refrain from making value judgments on any of the offered programs in the universities investigated; but when we have, we have used this as a "measuring stick" for the program's success.

	University of Wisconsin-Green Bay	Hampshire College
1. Scope of program	Involves the entire University	Environmental Quality Program.
2. Objectives	To reorganize academic principles to a problem-oriented, socially-concerned, and integrated educational plan which would preserve and rejuvenate the environment.	Combining environmental education with public service.
3. Theme	Man and his environment	Ecography, a synthesis of various disciplines including ecology and geography; man's relationship to the natural world, other men, and himself.
4. Structure	Interdisciplinary	Interdisciplinary
5. (a) form of teaching	Problem oriented	Problem solving and practical application
(b) subject matter	Concentrations that deal with man and his total environment	Student-faculty formed courses concerning local problems and projects - waste disposal, urban ecology, public health problems, etc.
6. Community-University Interaction	Great emphasis is placed on the University's ability to contribute to the community and the reciprocal value of the community contribution to the university.	Strongly emphasized

College of the Atlantic	Evergreen State College	Kresge College, University of California-Santa Cruz
Involves the whole college	Involves the whole school	Whole college involved
The study of man and his environment, both natural and man-made ; to arrive at a good definition of human ecology	To provide an educational alternative that takes into account the dilemmas of contemporary life. Emphasis on individualized program of study	To evolve new teaching methods
Human ecology	Man and his responsibility to his total environment	Man and his relationship to his social and natural community
Interdisciplinary	Interdisciplinary	Interdisciplinary
Heavy emphasis on problem solving	Book learning and evaluations	Workshops
Ecology, human behavior, law, history and philosophy of science	Man and his total environment	Group dynamics methods of education
Emphasized student involvement in local and regional issues, internship program	Very little as yet	The university is concentrating first on its own community

	University of Indiana	University of Wisconsin-Madison
1. Scope of Program	Environmental Studies Program	Institute for Environmental Studies
2. Objectives	To convey a comprehensive view of the operation and interaction of socio-economic and natural systems	To educate undergraduate and graduate students who will participate in professions which relate to the man-environment system : emphasis on research
3. Theme	Influence of science and technology in society	Man-environment systems
4. Structure	Interdepartmental	Interdepartmental
5. (a) form of teaching	theory with emphasis on sciences	Subject matter, in-class issue oriented
(b) subject matter	pollution oriented	man and his relationship to his natural environment
6. Community-University Interaction	Little community interaction	Advisory function

Dartmouth College	Williams College	Cornell University
Environmental Studies Program	Center for Environmental Problems	Departments of Environmental Education
Sensitizing program, concentrates on giving future lawyers, politicians, businessmen, etc., a background in the understanding of the environment	To acquaint students training to be professionals in various disciplines with environmental problems and an interdisciplinary approach to problem solving	Train natural history and conservation teachers.
Man's interaction with the natural environment; emphasis on implementation of better policy vis-à-vis the environment	Interdisciplinary environmental problem solving	Ecology
Interdepartmental	Interdepartmental	Interdepartmental
Predominantly subject matter in-class issue oriented	Both subject matter and problem solving oriented, strongest emphasis on problem solving	Subject-matter oriented with emphasis on natural sciences
Core courses in environmental studies. Optional courses in resource management, environmental law, general sciences, population dynamics, politics.	Natural sciences, chemistry, political science, history, art, economics, field projects	General science, communications, and education (theory and practical courses)
A limited number of student research teams are involved with local problems. A few teach in lower schools in the surrounding area.	Very pronounced: strong emphasis on student participation in community projects	Emphasized student teaching

The Environmental Education program at Cornell is designed to train environmental educators rather than to introduce
students to general environmental studies/problems. The goals
of this program are quite specific and the people involved are
highly qualified. As a result, it is accomplishing what it sets
out to do. For over fifty years it has been training exceptional
teachers of natural history and conservation.

The Division of Environmental Education awards degrees
on both the undergraduate and graduate level. The program
aims to train students in the natural sciences and communication skills that will prepare them for professional careers. To
this end, work experience that supplements the academic program is strongly encouraged. This is not just an offical policy
that has little effect. Graduate students are employed in active
teaching situations. The interests of students enrolled in this
program are such that regardless of official encouragement,
they are actively involved in a variety of educational programs
in nature centers, museums, conservation organizations and natural history publications outside of Cornell/Ithaca.

The Division of Environmental Education comes under the
auspices of the Department of Education. In order to major in
the program a student must complete specific requirements in
chemistry, biology, geology, natural resources, entomology,
education and communication arts. In addition, the student may
elect to take any number of courses from other departments
that are relevant to his particular career interests.

There are a number of faculty members that infuse the program with its exceptional spirit and vigor. They have been res-
ponsibile for preserving the emphasis on applying academic
training in a professional manner. As one student put it, "once
you graduate, who cares what you know. What counts is how you
can apply it". As a whole, the student response to the program
has been very enthusiastic.

UNIVERSITY OF WISCONSIN - MADISON

In January, 1970, the Institute for Environmental Studies (IES), which had been a graduate research unit, was restructured to coordinate and initiate graduate and undergraduate environmental studies. The function of the institute is threefold : first, it is to develop interdisciplinary curricula that deals with man and his relationship to the natural and man-made environment. Secondly, it functions to improve communications between departments within the university as well as between the university and the community. Thirdly, it is to continue to support the extensive research projects and facilities with which it is related. These facilities include the Center for Climatic Research; the Water Resources Center, and the Biotron--a unique structure incorporating laboratories in which any environment on earth can be completely recreated.

The Institute was not designed to become a separate entity with its own faculty but to develop new combinations of expertise from the disciplines already existing at the university. Consequently, a student must receive his degree from a traditional department as well as from IES. Courses offered by IES are taught either by its own faculty or in conjunction with faculty from other departments. A prerequisite for many of the courses is that students are required to do projects. However, since the projects can be either research or applied, they do not require that the student work with his knowledge outside the academic community. As a result, the problem-solving orientation remains in class.

The curriculum consists of a core course and a selection of courses from the traditional disciplines that are related to man and his dealings with his environment. The core course selects a principle such as "energy and its use" and explores the technical, social, and philosophic implications of it. A few examples of supplementary courses are : paleoclimatology, environmental resource management, physical system of the environment, river basin planning seminar, etc. At present most of the courses offered emphasize man's relation to his natural environment. Only a few deal with the cultural and man-made environment.

The Institute is strengthening its ties with the community. The faculty have been extending themselves as consultants for governmental committees; faculty and students staff Environment Wisconsin, a central community action organization that serves as an information center and clearing house for many of the environmental groups throughout the state.

IES is beset by the usual problems of the budjet pinch, limitations it places on research, and faculty and program expansion. Moreover, one of the most important assets of IES is its emphasis on prodding and stretching the existing disciplines to new programs of integrated application of their knowledge. However, counter to this is a dangerous pressure to solidify, institutionalize and gain departmental status in order to attain recognition for professionalism equal to that of the traditional departments.

COLLEGE OF THE ATLANTIC

College of the Atlantic is a small, coeducational institution awarding the Bachelor of Arts Degree in Human Ecology. It will accept students at the beginning of the 1972-1973 academic year. Although the college will strive to provide the student with a broadly-based education, the educational format departs considerably from those of traditional liberal arts colleges. Rather than offering a random assortment of disciplines from which a student may sample, the college is offering a curriculum organized around a central theme--human ecology.

The primary function of the College of the Atlantic as an academic community will be to study the various relationships which exist between man and his environment, including the natural and man-made environments. Rather than beginning with a fixed definition of human ecology, the goal of the college will be to develop one.

As the curriculum of College of the Atlantic will be strongly problem-oriented, an integral part of the program will be the workshops. "The first-year workshops, problem-oriented group projects, will deal with both real and simulated issues. Besides providing an overview of the complexity of real problems, the workshops will encourage a realization of the interdependency of all fields of knowledge". A number of basic courses in vital areas of information relevant to environmental problem-solving will also be offered.

Along with the workshops and basic courses there will be seminars, skill courses, tutorials and independent study programs. Furthermore, the college has planned an internship program which will enable more advanced students to leave school and receive on-the-job training in their special field of interest while continuing to receive college credit. A typical first-year program at the college will consist of : the introduction to human ecology (the only required course); one workshop, and one seminar or special skill course.

Courses which will be offered during the 1972-1973 academic year include : classical ecology, composition (an English writing course); creative arts, economic determinants, production and use of energy, history and philosophy, human behavior, legislature, literature, mathematical skills, music, photography, political power, the limits of science, scientific laws and methods.

All, or almost all, of these courses will be presented in a way that will tie them in with the school's central theme-- human ecology.

EVERGREEN STATE COLLEGE - OLYMPIA, WASHINGTON

Evergreen State College accepted its first students for course work in the fall of 1971. Early planning of the college was initiated by the trustees of the college with the help of A.D. Little Associates as consultants, together with the president, provost, deans and directors of the college. It is a four-year college offering a Bachelor of Arts degree at the completion of the course.

The college has eliminated the conventional academic structure, dispensing with courses, departments, grades or major requirements and has focused on coordinated learning communities involving some 100 students and five faculty members. Faculty members have been drawn from different backgrounds and will bring their special experience to cut across the usual boundaries between academic disciplines. Students join with faculty to define problems, to develop skills, and to search for answers. Credit at Evergreen will be earned by work well done in two kinds of total-immersion, full-time activities : Coordinated Studies and Contracted Studies.

The coordinated studies are divided into two courses ; the first deals with the basic problems of society "What is Man?"; and the second "How Does Man Develop?". These two programs are supplemented with a Contracted Studies program which allows students to work more individually and to further their knowledge in a more specific area of interest.

The over-all program to date seems to be highly natural-history oriented.

Inasmuch as the educational program for Evergreen College has just been inaugurated it is too early to make any kind of an analysis of the program or how effective it has been.

UNIVERSITY OF CALIFORNIA AT SANTA CRUZ

The University of California has now been divided into a number of separate colleges--the most recent being Kresge College set up to include the broad concept of ecology--man and his relationship to his community (natural and social).

The college is still in its experimental stages--having no fixed campus--and is, at present. housed in temporary quarters. The faculty-student ratio is 1 to 20 (one teacher to 20 students) who work together as an educational and administrative unit.

The study courses are organized into workshops such as :

1. Studying organization, group dynamics, human relations, self values, and the application of these to understanding our developing community.

2. Studying the physical environment and the relationship of life styles to that natural environment.

3. Studying and experimenting with methods of education.

Kresge College is so juvenile and so new in its concepts that no evaluation of the college or its program, and its effectiveness, can be made at the time of this report.

HAMPSHIRE COLLEGE

Hampshire College is an experimental college inaugurated in 1969. It is a member of the five college system which includes the University of Massachusetts, Amherst, Holyoke, and Smith. Its overall guiding philosophy is innovation and interdisciplinarity in education.

Hampshire's Environmental Quality Program (EQP) is essentially an outgrowth of one of the college's three schools-- the School of Natural Science and Mathematics. The program is strongly problem oriented. Furthermore, a great deal of emphasis is placed upon the student's participation in off-campus projects. In fact, one of Hampshire's primary goals is to combine education with public service.

In the first year of the program's operation, 1970-1971, the students responded to the obvious need for study and action to local environmental problems by focusing on the Concord River, one of New England's historic and much-abused waterways. Along with their work on the Concord River the students participated in a number of seminars :

Chemistry and the Analysis of Pollutants : principles of chemistry were learned by analyzing pollutants.

No Deposit--No Return : A study of political, social and operational aspects of the Amherst sewage system with a view to finding improved methods of waste disposal.

Campus Design : Investigation of architectural proposals for the Hampshire campus, testing plausibility and ecological soundness.

Man-made Environment : A study of form and design in man-made environments and their effect on man.

Environmental Law : A study of governmental decision-making which affects the environment.

Based upon the experiences of this first year, students in the Environmental Quality Program proposed that the program be expanded into the study of urban problems. Having decided

259

upon the city of Holyoke as the focal point of their attentions, two students spent the summer of 1971 compiling information on the city's economics, politics, sociology, population, business, public health, sewage system, and general ambiance. Using this information, Hampshire students and faculty developed the following areas of concentration for the 1971-1972 curriculum :

1. A chemical laboratory for the City of Holyoke.

2. Public Health Problems of an urban community : the establishment of a small diagnostic screening laboratory which can be used to identify and study the incidence of various kinds of pollution-related public health problems in the City of Holyoke.

3. Theatre, Art, and Music as Environment : Designing and developing events (plays, paintings, sculpture, models, musical performances) using environmental motifs and techniques. Students will also work with Holyoke school children in initiating this program.

4. Urban Ecology.

5. Waste Disposal in Holyoke : Examination through field trips, literature and in the laboratory of disposal problems of sewage and solid wastes.

The strength of the program lies within the degree of student participation in the community projects.

The weakness is certainly the let-it-happen-naturally school of thought-and then formulate a course program.

WILLIAMS COLLEGE

The Center for Environmental Studies at Williams College was founded in 1967 "to provide a focus for undergraduate teaching and faculty research in environmental topics and to relate the resources of the college to the needs of the surrounding region". During the first three years of its existence the center concentrated most of its efforts on research and assisting the surrounding region to deal with its environmental problems. An undergraduate environmental studies program was instituted in the fall of 1970.

There are basically two ways in which such a program can be set up within the college with a traditional academic structure. The first is to have interdisciplinary courses taught primarily by the members of one department or center. The other is to bring together a program in which the courses are actually taught within the different departments. Williams has adopted the latter approach.

The program has not been established as a major. The student must coordinate this environmental program with a major in one of the traditional disciplines.

Each student in the program is required to take an introductory course in each of the following subjects : ecology, economics, planning and design. Students majoring in one of the physical sciences are required to take an additional course in the social sciences or humanities; students majoring in the social sciences or humanities are required to take an additional course in the physical sciences. During the junior year each student is required to take a core sequence course in Environmental Studies, entitled "Perspectives on Environmental Analysis", which encourages each student to arrive at a synthesis of the knowledge gained from courses in the traditional disciplines in order that he or she may make an interdisciplinary approach to environmental problems. Each student must also take one advanced course dealing with environmental topics in his/her major field, and during the senior year to take a second core sequence course on "Environmental Planning and Policy". This last course "seeks to involve the students in three to five person interdisciplinary groups undertaking planning or analysis projects for such organizations as planning boards and watershed associations".

A number of courses offered within different departments are complementary to, but not actually a part of, the environmental studies program. These include courses in the departments of economics, geology, history of science, history, and art. There are also two advanced ecology courses. There is a trend towards increasing the environmentally related courses offered within the college; and this trend is expected to continue.

The Williams program appears to be a particularly successful one. In part, this success appears to be due to the fine balance that has been achieved between classroom work and community action. An even greater reason for the program's success may be found in the limitations which have been placed on its goals. Rather than teach environmental studies outright the program is designed to teach an interdisciplinary approach to environmental problems. This subtle shift in emphasis has allowed the program's planners to formulate a far more tightly knit and sequential curriculum. Students graduating from the program do not leave with the final answers to environmental problems, nor do they leave with even the knowledge to answer these problems in the future. Rather, the students leave with the ability to utilize knowledge they have gained, and in the future have an interdisciplinary approach to environmental problem solving.

INDIANA UNIVERSITY -- BLOOMINGTON

The Environmental Studies Program at the University of Indiana was initiated with the general purpose of providing students with intellectual and technical proficiency, to supply them with an overall view of the way the socio-economic and natural systems operate and interact.

The program was initiated by the faculty in response to the growing concern that scientific knowledge should be applicable for governmental policy decisions about environmental issues; and secondly, to the growing student demand for relevance in higher education. The program was set up in the fall of 1971 for undergraduates and organized within the existing structure of the university.

In other words, students who receive a degree in environmental studies must also major in an established discipline. Required courses are selected from individual departments and are taught by the professors in those departments.

The Environmental Studies Program presently has only two professors on its own staff who teach the core courses. These are taught with a systems approach to pollution problems. The established departments have shown great interest in and cooperation with the formation of this new program. However, any increases in course offerings in the future will probably come under the auspices of the regular departments.

The program is subdivided into two options : one for the students of the biological and physical sciences; and the other for students of the social sciences, behavioral sciences or the humanities. In order to complete a major in Environment Studies, majors in the sciences must take additional courses of which the following are examples; environmental or urban geology; conservation of natural resources, microbial ecology,

262

general ecology. The other option, for the humanities majors, requires courses such as public finance, politics of environmental management, economic geography, public policy analysis.

Even though the Environmental Studies Program at Indiana is one of the most recently instituted efforts, it has not avoided the problems that generally plague environmental education programs. There are problems with communicating between the traditional disciplines, coordinating their efforts toward joint projects; and dealing with a reward structure that encourages departmentalized research and teaching. The perennial problem of finance hinders the program in terms of additional faculty, courses, and facilities.

In addition there are problems peculiar to the Bloomington campus. First, library resources are limited; second, there are no agriculture, architecture or engineering departments to augment the program. Third, there is little community interaction.

A shool of public and environmental affairs has been proposed for the future which would offer graduate studies and function to coordinate centers and institutes already existing throughout the state in an effort towards community service.

Those students who have taken the introductory course (first offered this year) in environmental pollution are all planning to use the environmental orientation they have received from this program in the future. However, they agreed that there was no vigor in the social sciencies/humanities aspect of the program.

Students have been involved in the formation of the program to the extent that there are two students on the forming committee. However, at present there does not seem too much active student involvement as they are waiting to see what the program is all about. The Environmental Studies Program is starting on a small scale, working within the existing university structure, attempting to apply traditional disciplines to environmental problems. Nevertheless, everyone expects it to evolve-but slowly.

UNIVERSITY OF WISCONSIN -- GREEN BAY

University of Wisconsin at Green Bay is a university established solely for environmental studies. The goal of the university is to establish interdisciplinary education that applies skills and knowledge to solving problems of man's total environment. The university, originated by the citizens of Green Bay and surrounding communities, persuaded the state government to give them funds to establish their own university which would be relevant to their region, time and problems. In 1968 the academic plan was approved.

The organization was to be transdisciplinary, focused on the theme of man and his environment. Moreover, knowledge was to go hand in hand with experimental application and should be student initiated. This was to be a "communiversity"--a university contributing to the community and a community that contributed actively to the university. There is a citizen-faculty advisory committee for each concentration in the university. Citizens who don't have academic credentials but who do have pertinent experience are asked to teach. Students are also engaged in antipoverty work--working full time for 12 months for academic credit rather than salary. They also participate in legal counselling, economic development, pollution studies, or similar community projects.

The university is organized along general concentrations rather than traditional disciplines. The student is encouraged to develop his own specific program. Students get credit for learning outside the classroom and faculty are expected to extend their teaching and time available to students beyond the classroom.

The concentrations are grouped under four colleges : The College of Community Services includes modernization process, regional and urban analysis; The College of Creative Communication incorporates analysis, synthesis and communication action; The College of Human Biology groups growth and development, human adaptability, nutritional sciences and population dynamics; and finally, the School of Professional Studies which includes managerial systems, social services and leisure sciences. These concentrations are supplemented with options of the more traditional disciplines and preprofessional programs.

Every student, whatever his program, must take the four year basic seminar. The second focuses the environmental issues into a required off-campus experience in the region. The third year requires selected studies in another culture and also requires off-campus experience, if possible. And then in the senior year the student integrates his knowledge into a project that deals with a subjects of continuing concern to society.

University of wisconsin-Green Bay graduates have had great success finding jobs or being accepted into graduate schools. They have been able to successfully compete in basic competence with students trained in the more traditional fields. So actually, this educational focus of man to his environment has been an advantage.

However University of Wisconsin-Green Bay has had its share of problems as well. First, the University gets funded on a per student credit which does not encourage experimenting with new educational programs, nor does it lighten the faculty load in order to leave faculty time to improve the quality of their teaching and contact with the students. As in all of the new environmental programs there is a problem of professional recognition for faculty as well as students. University of Wisconsin-Green Bay has tried to emphasize teaching abilities and community involvement as much as publishing criteria by which it selects and keeps its faculty. At the same time, tenure is granted only to faculty with Ph.D.s. Because Green Bay is such a departure from traditional academic structures, it is finding it particularly difficult to get incoming students to take responsibility for their own educational programs.

DARTMOUTH COLLEGE

First opened to students during the 1970-1971 academic year, the Environmental Studies Program at Dartmouth College may be described as a sensitizing program designed to "open the minds of potential leaders in a wide variety of professions to the complexities and dangers of environmental problems". To achieve this aim and "to make the most effective use of its resources". Dartmouth has begun its program at the undergraduate rather than the graduate-research level.

The program has not been designed as a departmental major, autonomous from all other existing departments, but rather as a series of interdisciplinary courses which can be coupled with a conventional departmental major. Undergraduates major in one of the regular departmental majors and modify that major with a program in environmental studies. Although a very limited number of new faculty members have been appointed to the program on a full-time basis with no formal affiliation with a traditional academic department, the majority of the faculty appointed to the program serve only part time and are selected by their respective departments.

The program's core curriculum consists of the following four courses :

Environmental Studies 1 : Man's dependence and effect on his natural environment (i. e., the interaction between population dynamics, technology and basic resources - taught by faculty from biography, engineering sciences and chemistry).

Environmental Studies 2 : Earth as an Ecosystem (i. e., geological, physical, chemical and biological cycles in relationship to one planet as a finite environment--taught by faculty from biological sciences, chemistry and earth sciences).

Environmental Studies 3 : Social and political aspects of the environment (ie : Man's attitudes and perception of his environment and an evaluation of economic, political and legal approaches--taught by faculty from art, anthropology, economics and political sciences.

Environmental Studies 4 : Environmental policy formulation--students work together in 8-10 man groups to formulate and justify policy measures which they feel would be appropriate to deal with a problem they have detected and analyzed.

In addition to the four core courses a number of optional advanced seminars are offered by interested faculty on such topics as "Environmental Perception", "Environmental Law", "Land Resources Policy", and "Control of Man-made Diseases".

The major weakness in the program, according to faculty members, lies in its administrative structure rather than its academic orientation. Due to its lack of organizational status the program has little or no control over the faculty reward structure. "Leadership has been on a part-time basis and other faculty are also primarily committed else-where".

As yet Dartmouth has had little difficulty in funding its environmental program. However, if in the future money becomes less readily available, it is felt that difficulties will arise between the various departments, with the environmental program being the loser. The current director of the program indicates that steps are being taken to solve this problem "within the framework of the college".

The weakness in the curriculum seems to center around the

emphasis on man's relationship to the natural environment rather than the total environment, and the lack of emphasis placed upon off-campus activities (community projects, local research, etc.). Although there is some indication that a humanities course may be included in the core curriculum, it doesn't seem likely that it will markedly alter the program. On the other hand, it does appear likely that there will be greater emphasis on community involvement in the future (Environmental Studies 4 has just recently been incorporated into the core curriculum).

On the whole, student reaction to the program has been favorable although they all felt that the courses, as they were presented last year, were somewhat less than adequate. However, they feel that the necessary adjustments have now been made and all is well.

SUMMARY

Without exception every program that we examined was structured on the principle that an interdisciplinary approach must be used when teaching environmental studies. However, the methods which each university employed to achieve this interdisciplinary approach varied. The two basic structural variations we encountered among environmental studies programs were directly related to the overall structuring of the institution in which they were located. If the institute had an interdisciplinary structure, so did the environmental studies program. If the institution used the traditional departmental structure, then the environmental studies program usually had an "interdepartmental" structure where teachers and courses were shared between the departments and the program.

Within an institution with a traditional departmental structure there are basically two ways of setting up an environmental education program. The first is to have the courses taught primarily by members of an environmental studies department or center who try to pull all the multi-disciplinary aspects of their subject matter together themselves. The other is to construct a program within which the courses are actually taught in the different departments. Neither of these alternatives has seemed to be particularly attractive to those universities which have departmental structures. All of them have chosen to take a compromise course.

Thus, most institutions have established a center for environmental studies which offers a number of interdisciplinary courses (most often taught by someone who has been appointed to both the center and one of the traditional departments); and then a variety of related courses are taught in other departments. It is interesting to note, however, the degree to which each program stresses the courses taught within the center.

While Dartmouth College does not have an official environmental studies center, it does have a program with a core sequence of four interdisciplinary courses. These four courses

269

must be taken by each of the program's students while those offered by the separate departments are optional.

The program at the University of Indiana, Bloomington, is
much the same as Dartmouth's. The only difference lies in the
fact that the core courses at Dartmouth are taught by faculty
members who hold appointments in other departments where
they share teaching time, while the core courses at Indiana are
taught by men who have been appointed to a center for environmental studies and do not share teaching time.

On the other hand, the majority of the core sequence courses
at Williams College are taught in departments outside of its
Center for Environmental Studies. Only two courses are taught
within the Center at Williams. Like the core courses at Dartmouth, these courses are taught by faculty members who hold
joint appointments. However, they differ from those at Dartmouth in that they are not designed to teach environmental studies outright but rather to encourage the students to arrive at a
synthesis of the material and approaches they have learned in
their other courses.

The program offered at the University of Wisconsin, Madison, is similar to that at Williams in that it offers only a few
interdisciplinary courses taught within the center itself. Like
the courses at Indiana they are for the most part taught by men
appointed to Madison's Institute for Environmental Studies. These
courses are general in nature. They serve to give the student
an introductory glimpse into a wide range of environmental problems before he or she goes on into the more specialized courses which are associated with the center--but offered by the
departments. In this respect the program at Madison is more
closely allied with those at Dartmouth and Indiana than at Williams.

The final example of an environmental education program
set up within a university with a traditional departmental structure is to be found at Cornell University, Ithaca, N.Y. This
program differs from all the others in that virtually all its core
courses are taught by men specifically appointed to the Department of Environmental Education. However, this is a bit mis-
leading as the Cornell program is designed to produce environmental teachers while the others are designed only to give students a general background in environmental studies. As a result, Cornell's Department of Environmental Education was
formed to serve a very specific function, with limited goals,
and shouldn't be compared with the others.

Programs offered by institutions with interdisciplinary

structures tend to vary more than those in institutions with departmental structures. Invariably, they are themselves inter-disciplinary in their structure. Either they are a school for en-vironmental studies which forms only a part of a college, as in the case of the Environmental Quality Program at Hampshire College, or they are an entire college whose theme is environ-mental studies, such as College of the Atlantic, Evergreen, or the University of Wisconsin-Green Bay. In each case the tradi-tional departments have been abolished in favor of new multi-disciplinary forms which better develop the subject matter. The variations arise from the differing themes upon which each col-lege is founded and the different methods which each employs to achieve its goals.

Another aspect of each program that we examined and which remained fairly constant was the use of off-campus, community-action projects as an important teaching aid. There are only a few programs--such as those offered at Dartmouth, Indiana, and to a lesser extent the University of Wisconsin at Madison--which do not include student participation in off-campus projects as an integral part of the teaching program. However, in each of these institutions there are definite plans to move in that direction.

While the majority of the environmental education programs strongly encourage student participation in community action projects, there is a good deal of variation in the degree to which it is emphasized. The Environmental Quality Program at Hamp-shire College is constructed almost entirely around the idea of getting the student off the college campus and working on speci-fic projects in the surrounding communities (i. e. , Holyode, Mass.). One of its stated goals is to combine education with public service. Unfortunately, Hampshire's program seemed to us to have gone too far and sacrificed a solid background in theory for practical application. As a result, its students seem destined to graduate with the ability to apply solutions to local problems, but without the ability to theorize solutions to larger problems. In a sense, they are no better off than graduates of the Dartmouth program who can only think while the Hampshire students can only act.

The Williams program seems to have taken a more sensi-ble course. There the students are first given a strong base in theory, then taught in class how to make an interdisciplinary approach to problem solving, and finally sent into the surroun-ding community to learn the pragmatics of achieving a solution using the tools they have already learned.

271

Our overall impression of the environmental studies programs we examined is that they are still very much in the experimental stages. The greatest shortcomings in these programs seem to lie in their curriculum and not in their structuring. There has been a great deal of public and student pressure to start programs at once--now. As a result, most programs were hurriedly put together with far more attention placed upon structuring and financing than upon the actual curriculum. At the same time too few questions have been asked as to what each student is expected to be able to do with his environmental education. No one has found out what careers are available to students coming out of environmental studies programs, much less plan a curriculum to prepare students for those careers.

At present virtually every environmental studies program is only designed to make students more environmentally conscious and they are not prepared, as a result, to take action on more than a limited scale. It is good to be aware, but an environmentally aware public is only half of what is needed to solve our problems; at the same time we need mean and women who can lead that public in the right direction. That should also be the function of the university environmental program.

RECOMMENDATIONS

Most of the environmental programs offered in the United States are in their first two years of operation. The few that have been in existence longer, such as Green Bay, Wisconsin, have only produced one or two graduating classes. As yet it is far too early to judge their true effectiveness. Questions such as what are the career opportunities; how are local communities being affected; and which is the most effective program have yet to be answered.

We strongly recommend that a far more complete study than this be undertaken in a year or two. If such a study is begun we suggest that personal interviews with both faculty and students be emphasized. Only in this way can the investigator discover the discrepancies between the stated objectives and what is actually happening.

Furthermore, the investigative study should not limit itself to responses from the academic community but should broaden its scope to include responses from government agencies, conservation groups, businesses, local societies and possibly concerned individuals.

272

Conclusions

PROBLEMS POSED BY CERTAIN ASPECTS OF ENVIRONMENTAL EDUCATION

By Jean Marie ABILLON
Director of the Department of Environment,
University of Paris VII, France

Before concluding this first study on environmental education at post secondary level, or rather, before presenting some thoughts and unresolved questions relating to the subject in the light of personal experience, it may be well to attempt to clarify the term "environment" or at least to outline its principal aspects.

In simple terms, according to the dictionary, the word environment refers to all or part of an object's or a living being's surroundings. Without going beyond the most urgent problems created by man's presence on earth, namely, demographic growth and the intensive use of natural resources (soil, mineral wealth, air, water, etc.), it is obvious, then, that environment becomes everything that surrounds man, hence, everything that is used by man, including man himself !

It is impossible to disregard the over-riding importance of man in the environment and argue that it can be discussed without taking the human dimension into account : as now approached, the protection of nature is a will -o' -the wisp chased by well-meaning citizens and a myth manipulated by governments. Environmental problems give rise to economic and political problems. As long as these are not resolved in terms of man's better use of the environment, technological solutions can only be makeshifts barely able to delay ultimate disaster, as forecast, for example, by MIT's System-Dynamics Team (1).

The environment can be somewhat more closely defined as a system of interacting elements, including man as an element occupying a very special place in the system. Thus while his remarkable adaptability enables him to avoid the effects produced by other elements in the system, he can also exert undue influence on them.

Any study of a problem arising from man's use of the environment, therefore, technically boils down to a system's dynamic analysis, which must be carried out in three steps :

1) by determining the different elements in a system and the laws that govern interactions between them, to the greatest possible quantitative extent and at least in

---

1) The limits to Growth - D.H.Meadow, D.L.Meadows, J. Randers W.W.Behrens III. Universe Books - New York, 1972.

qualitative terms;

2) by then determining the evolution of the system and, more precisely, by predicting how changes made to the system will affect its evolution;

3) once a goal has been set - taking political and economic choices into account - by finally settling upon the action for best achieving this goal, i.e. those least damaging to the environment.

Any form of environmental education must comprise a human as well as a physical and a biological part; its aim should be to show the complexity of environmental problems, especially by pointing to the relations between environmental factors and enabling these factors and their respective importance to be determined. These aims correspond to step 1) above. Given the present state of our knowledge, steps 2) and 3) may very often be out of reach.

Granted that this is the goal to be achieved, analysis of the answers to the OECD questionnaire (1) has shown that the term environmental education too often refers to a conventional or very fragmentary type of education in no way suited to the objectives just specified. Here I intend only to consider those problems that relate to environmental courses that really attempt to achieve these objectives. Most of these are experimental and very recent, so little information is yet available about them. Many questions, therefore, are still to be answered, the principal of them being :

- the level of such education
- curriculum content
- teaching methods
- job outlets
- the effects of environmental education on university structures
- teachers
- research, especially educational research
- the problems of continuing training and of information.

These are all questions that might well be proposed for discussion during some future workshop on environmental education.

---

1) See Chapter I, Part Two.

Educational Level

Opinions on this point are very divided. Some are in favour of teaching environmental subjects in the first university cycle, while the majority are in favour of a specialised training in the second or third cycle. Both solutions have their advantages and disadvantages :

i) Education in the first university cycle :

Advantages : As the purpose of environmental education is not only to provide sound qualifications but to teach a completely new way of thinking and of grasping problems, this training should start as early as possible. The proposition should be considered of so broadening the first cycle as to make it accessible to all students of the university. So far, this has been tested for a limited number of students only (except at Green Bay, Wisconsin). A compulsory course could provide a common core where students would be made aware of environmental problems before later branching off into the more traditional specialised fields of which they could be offered a choice. In short, there shall be a broad form of training at the beginning with an opportunity for specialisation later on.

Disadvantages : What is proposed is, largely, a venture into uncharted territory. The risks could be avoided, however, by giving the student the opportunity to branch off at any time into a more traditional course. There is, too, a danger in an unduly pluridisciplinary education.

ii) Education after the first university cycle :

Advantages : The least costly way of producing environmental specialists is by training students who are already strongly oriented towards some relevant subject (chemistry, biology, geography) and have a good basic knowledge of it.

Disadvantages : It is difficult to reconcile pluridisciplinary education with recruitment from very heterogeneous student backgrounds. Ultimately this might not even prove possible.

Hitherto there have not been the data seriously to compare these two kinds of training - first cycle or post-first cycle. Now that a certain number of experiments have been completed, however, such comparison becomes possible and would be most useful. I suggest, in the following respects :

- training (aptitudes and knowledge at the end of the student's studies),
- teaching difficulties encountered (due for instance to the heterogeneous recruitment of students),
- job outlets (e. g. how these open out in relation to the kind of training received).

Curriculum Content

Even if teaching methods seem more important than content in training environmentalists or environment specialists, a minimum amount of the subject matter to be learned must, nevertheless, be defined. Furthermore, the recent proliferation of environmental courses makes it timely now to think of harmonizing them so that students can promptly be exchanged between countries and specialists, and wherever they come from, can use a common language when discussing environmental problems outside their own national frames of reference.

One way of solving this problem might be the method suggested by Marcel Boisot at the OECD Workshop in Nice in September 1970 (1), namely that, by comparing the different curricula, the minimum common content for a given type of training could be determined, the rest being left free for adjustment to the specific problems any particular course had to resolve.

Teaching Methods

These have a twofold effect : On the general approach to how knowledge should be presented where the notions of pluri-, inter - and transdisciplinarity (2) come into play, and on the actual form of presentation adopted by the teacher in the lecture room, laboratory or the field.

Pluridisciplinarity, interdisciplinarity and transdisciplinarity :
While environmental education must, by definition, be pluri-disciplinary, and while the resolution of environmental problems can only be transdisciplinary, the question still remains as to when these different concepts should be applied. In the case of courses that begin in the first university cycle, as no synthe-

---

1) Interdisciplinarity : Problems of Teaching and Research in Universities, OECD Paris, 1972, pp. 89 et seq.
2) See also the definitions of these terms restated by P. Duguet, ibid. pp. 38, 39 .

sis is possible until all the factors of a problem are known, the wisest method in the present state of integrated education is to proceed in three stages :

First Cycle : acquisition of basic knowledge :
p luridisciplinarity
Second Cycle : integration of this basic knowledge through an understanding of environmental problems : interdisciplinarity
Third Cycle : study of environmental problems as systems : transdisciplinarity.

The first cycle in this method is disliked by students because they fail to see how the groundwork in each discipline can later be integrated in the study of environmental problems. The real cause of this, though, is the difficulty so many teachers find in introducing environmental concepts into their monodisciplinary teaching. Once some of these first cycle courses are revised in this respect, the students' objections may well disappear. However, whatever the level at which interdisciplinarity begins, the question of how integrated teaching should best be conducted still remains.

While it may as yet seem illusory to undertake any integrated form of teaching except for case studies where separate disciplines are used to solve specific problems, it has been suggested that unifying themes such as the study of ecosystems, exchanges of energy and so on could be used to facilitate this kind of teaching. This, though, is not a method; it is more an educational plan or a guideline.

Unfortunately information and reports on experiments in integrated education are totally lacking. The first thing that should be defined by those responsible for these experiments is the "language" that must be used, since without a common "language" the integration of disciplines remains no more than a figment. But "languages" such as these, however, imperfect they may be, do already exist. One, for example, is "DYNAMO" (1). The language of graphs may be another (2)

---

1) See on this subject : J. W. Forrester : Principles of Systems, Wright-Allen Press and A. L. Pugh III : Dynamo II User's Manual M. I. T. Press
2) See the document presented by Marcel Boisot at the Workshop on Environmental Education held at Tours : A tentative organisational approach to the problems of environment. See also: The theory of graphs in terms of systems as described by P. Delattre in : Système, Structure, Fonction, Evolution; Masson, Paris.

At a time such as this when so many teachers are urging the advantages of integrated education a serious confrontation on the subjects is urgently called for, especially to resolve such questions as :

- How can the necessity of acquiring a minimum of know-ledge in each discipline be reconciled with integrated education ?
- In what circumstances is integrated education possible ?
- How does integrated education work ?
- What are the languages to be used ?

Teaching in Practice. Apart from conventional teaching methods which may still be used to some extent, theoretical instruction and the reality of environmental problems can only be linked by case studies and field activities playing a larger part. The latter can take various forms, for example :

pluridisciplinary field work under the guidance of a teacher ; surveys or studies of a local or regional kind carried out by students on their own ; or the teaching of theoretical subjects in the field, e.g. biology courses in biological research stations.

Such outside activities are very popular with students be-cause they enable them to test their knowledge, to understand the value of the training they receive, to criticise the course in the light of their own experience and to acquire an easier grasp of a subject that might otherwise seem somewhat dry. But for the teacher they require a considerable effort of organi-sation ; the costs of field trips are usually high and these are rarely budgeted for in his department.

It is also advisable to allow the student great scope for initiative by affording him an opportunity to do personal work on the environmental problems of communities or organisations outside his university - possibly by means of contracts negotia-ted between the body concerned and the university. Lastly, a policy of extramural courses in laboratories, development agencies and the like would further the student's pre-professional training. It should be possible to include all these activities within a programme of environmental education.

Teaching methods can thus vary considerably, but they should all be guided by a concern to promote contact between the university and the outside world. Much can still be learned by comparing experiments that various universities have been making in this field.

Job Outlets

This topic is only brought into the present discussion for the record because the earliest experimental curricula will not have run their course until July 1973 at the earliest. Job outlets therefore, can only be tentatively forecast at the moment. They will only become clear as students trained in environmental subjects come onto the labour market. However it is a matter that students engaged in environmental training are already seriously concerned about, possible outlets being as yet so ill-defined. Within a year it may indeed be possible to review the situation and usefully to discuss the following topics, among others, in relation to the actual position in each country :

- types of employment for the various kinds of training received (i.e. for generalists, environmentalists, specialists, environmental technologists, etc.)
- the emergence of new kinds of job ;
- the ease or difficulty with which environmental graduates compete for similar jobs with students who have received a more conventional education ;
- bringing training in line with the requirements of the job market.

UNIVERSITY STRUCTURES

As environmental education is pluridisciplinary and deals with real problems arising outside the university, it cannot make do with traditional monodisciplinary university struc - tures. When it is well established, it is, in fact, found in one of two kinds of organisation :

- in a pluridisciplinary organisation, co-existing with monodisciplinary university units of a more or less conventional type (it is relevant to observe that the structures of most new universities encourage the creation of such pluridisciplinary structures) ;
- in new universities entirely dedicated to education that is directly geared to problems posed by the environment.

The first type of organisation has definite advantages, provided the university in question is sufficiently pluridisciplinary. Traditional disciplines benefit from the synthesis achieved by teachers and researchers concerned with environmental subjects

as well as from the different mental approach they introduce.
The way is smoothed because such teaching and research staff
also belong to mon odisciplinary departments where they still
do some of their work. Conversely, environmental education
and research should not alienate itself from the more advanced
research being carried out in traditional disciplines. The major
disadvantage is obvious : pluridisciplinary types of organisation
often run into difficulties because, in co-existing with monodisciplinary types, some overlapping necessarily occurs that tends
to interfere with the traditional disciplines. This may cause
serious delay in their proper development.

The second kind of organisation (that specifically devoted
to environmental education) guarantees innovators a free rein
and freedom to plan university structures to suit their own
particular goals. But, unless care is exercised, there is danger
of their becoming isolated from the traditional disciplines at a
time when environmental science, which is still in its infancy,
cannot hope itself to offer the full range of opportunity that is
due of teaching and research staff in universities of this newer
type.

Lack of information makes it hard to say at present whether
the unit of environmental education should be an organised body
within a university or the entire university itself, nor can we
be certain about its method of operation beyond the fact that it
should be governed by a concern for pluridisciplinarity and for
contacts with the outside world. What is now imperative is that
these questions should be answered. Put succinctly, they are :

- How are relations between the environmental education
  organisation and the traditionally structured departments
  organised (budgetary and non-budgetary resources, position of the organisation within the university, etc.) ?
- What is the mode of operation of the organisation and how
  can it promote contacts with the outside world (e.g. do
  people from outside share in management, in planning
  curricula) ? How can it also promote interdisciplinarity ?

TEACHING STAFF

In the absence hitherto of any special training courses, all
those now teaching in the field under consideration have specialised initially in a single discipline ; and those who, through
their own determination and drive, were first to take part in the

more outstanding experimental projects were formerly active
in mono-disciplinary types of organisation. Most of them had
been engaged in research in their own traditional discipline -
often for career purposes, as in France where teachers are
promoted within a traditional disciplinary framework. Nevertheless, these men have also devoted a great amount of their
time to environmental education, it now being well known that
integrated education and the new teaching methods are deeply
absorbing matters.

But in spite of much goodwill on all sides, communication
between disciplines is still difficult. This is due to differences
in training, hence of language, and to the fact that communication techniques such as group dynamics are not used. The resulting loss of time is apt to be frustrating, especially as the
time is borrowed from research activities.

It is obvious that, in order to retain their autonomy, while
also developing their teaching and especially research activities,
environmental institutions must specially recruit all or part of
their staff. The criteria for such special recruitment appear
to be :

- motivation, attitude, state of mind ;
- specialisation in environmental subjects, the chemistry
  of pollution for a chemist, physical planning for a geographer, etc.) ;
- aptitude and experience in field work,
- and, no doubt, others.

The next question is who should be responsible for selection :
a pluridisciplinary committee made up of representatives of
the disciplines concerned and subordinate to the recruiting
organisation ? Or a monodisciplinary committee made up of
representatives from the particular discipline concerned ?

The answers to all these questions may differ from country
to country and it will be necessary to compare them if erroneous
general conclusions are to be avoided.

Other problems remain :

- To what organisation should the majority of staff teaching
  environmental subjects be attached : to monodisciplinary,
  to environmental, or to both types of organisation at the
  same time ?
- Will the training of students as environmentalists enable
  future teachers of environment to be recruited from among

them ? Should all future teachers be recruited from this source or should a mix be maintained with specialists in the disciplines concerned ?

RESEARCH

Although environmental research is expanding, it is still in its infancy. It is primarily carried out in laboratories and organisations heavily endowed for the purpose where research is mainly of a technological kind converted from traditional laboratory practice.

In traditional disciplines research and education seem to be largely separate, although teaching activities may be helped by research. This is, however, no longer true for environmental courses. It is hardly conceivable that real-life cases or urgent, factual environmental problems should be tackled without trying to provide an answer ; hence the links between research and teaching must be close. While such research is at present limited to small-scale projects that can be incorporated in a wider context, it cannot yet be predicted how much their scope may become enlarged with time.

Similarly, it is still difficult to tell what kind of research students of environmental subjects will embark upon after their training. Although, quite clearly, it can be undertaken only as part of a pluridisciplinary team, it is so far hard to see what the position and activities of future environmentalists working in such teams will be.

CONTINUOUS TRAINING AND EDUCATING THE PUBLIC

While it is important to expand the training of environmental specialists, thought should also be given to retraining professionals whose work can affect the environment and, additionally, to keeping the public informed.

As to the retraining of professionals, the way Sweden (1)

1) See Appendix 2, p.299: A short Report of Environmental Education at Swedish Universities and Institutes of Higher Learning. Office of the Chancellor of Swedish Universities, April 1971.

has met its most urgent requirements until qualified environ-
mental-research staff have been trained is an example worth
following. Other experiments are under way, and it would be
advisable to take an inventory of them.

Although extending somewhat beyond the scope of university
education as such, the job of keeping the public informed can
become an important aspect of the university's or university
environmental institute's activity. The public can be informed
in several ways. Those that come first to mind are :

- providing instruction designed to initiate the public or
  make it aware of environmental problems,
- organising lectures or seminars on practical themes or
  problems,
- making documentation and technical reports accessible to
  the public,
- showing how various kinds of human activity can affect
  the environment through simulation programmes that would
  be readily accessible and relatively simple to arrange.

Once again, a review and exchange of information on these
aspects of environmental education would be of great value.

CONCLUSIONS

Since it breaks new ground on every count, environmental
education means that knowledge must be reorganised in terms
of present problems and the needs of the community. This calls
for the revision of curricula, teaching methods and university
structures, regarding all of which much remains to be discussed
and much has yet to be done.

If the methods used for such reorganisation prove adequate
as well as effective, they should be given opportunity to prosper.
Any sterile conflict with the traditional disciplines must be
prevented. Will the solution then consist of setting up new universities or in reorganising existing universities along pluridisciplinary lines ?

Appendix 1

REPORTS OF THE THREE WORKING GROUPS
OF THE WORKSHOP OF TOURS

REPORT OF THE WORKING GROUP N° 1

Chairman : H. MISLIN (Germany), Rapporteur : V. LABEYRIE, (France)

RECOMMENDATIONS

I

To ensure that no one with a university education is unaware of the importance of environmental problems : our awareness of these questions should be promoted, for example, by seminars in all institutions of higher education.

To enable the various professions called upon to deal with the environment to understand environmental problems, compulsory courses designed to foster an understanding of the environmental effects created by the selected field of activity should during an initial stage at least be introduced into universities and institutes of higher education which emphasize some scientific, technical or social theme.

An optional course relating to the environmental effects of this type of activity should be organised in at least one institution of each of these types in each country.

II

Noting that the problems of developing and managing the human environment cannot but increase in the coming decades, it is urgent to train "co-ordinators" who can take action among the groups responsible for such problems as indispensable counterparts of the specialists previously referred to. Their role should be to coordinate the work of the various specialists and co-opt other specialists to deal with specific problems.

The co-ordinators should undergo a newly designed university course which would include the basics of environmental,
social and economic subjects. Training must not consist in
juxtaposing disciplines or parts of disciplines but in integrating
all the factors needed for an understanding of the problems, i.e.
the impact of man on the environment and of the environment
on man. It must include not only a considerable proportion of
practical field work carried out by teams of students, teachers
and people from outside, but also ensure proficiency in communication techniques and data analysis.

These types of training should be organised experimentally
in a number of special institutes and begin as soon as students
enter the university in order to cover at least four university
years.

III

In order to expedite these recommendations, such practical
action should be taken as the preparation of retraining programmes open to all, refresher courses for teachers, the organisation of documentation and symposium centres, etc.

IV

As environmental education, like any other, is inseparable
from research, it is recommended that it be promoted and sup-
ported by the creation of specialised documentation centres.

V

To limit the process of trial and error often associated
with the creation of new types of education, the exchange of
information on environmental education should be encouraged
and organised.

VI

To enable the world as a whole to benefit from the errors
made by industrialised countries, it is hoped that these teaching
and research centres can contribute to the study of environment
problems as they affect developing countries.

REPORT OF WORKING GROUP N° 2

Chairman : G. R. FRANCIS (Canada), Rapporteur : P. J. NEW-
BOULD (United Kingdom)

1.   The University context

University-sponsored environmental education falls into
certain slots in the scheme shown in diagram 1. The position
of the vertical lines (undergraduate, M. Sc., etc) differs from
one country to another but does not affect the general plan. Cross-
hatched areas show the location of general environmental courses. All the types of environmental education shown are actually
happening somewhere, and are therefore presumably all feasible. Different institutions will, and should accord priority to
different slots. Environmental education for all undergraduates
for general teachers and for the general public is a propaganda
exercise, and those receiving it do so on a voluntary basis.

2.   The definition of environment

There is a clear divergence between those mainly concerned with the physical/biological aspects and those mainly concerned with socio-economic aspects. There are differences of
concept and vocabulary and communication is imperfect. Ultimate convergence is desirable but at present the divergence
must be recognized and accommodated. It is appropriate for
different institutions to adopt different emphases.

3.   Institutional structure and constraints

Any major attempt to introduce environmental teaching requires some organisational basis, money, manpower and a position in the structure of the university. This may grow from
small beginnings or be introduced directly as a major component.

289

Institutional constraints, varying from one institution to another, include organisation, finance, staff expertise, the definition of environment which is employed (see 2 above), student demands, initiatives and capabilities, possibilities for employment of those receiving environmental training, and the narrowmindedness of the other members of the institution.

4.   A general environmental course.

Four main components are identified in diagram 2. This course may be flexible as to time or structure (1 year is a typical duration, but the same framework could contract to 10 or even 4 weeks, or expand to 3 years). It involves some element of progression, possibilities being shown in 2a. The degree of student choice would vary but a typical pattern is shown in 2b. Part 1 of such a course would normally be taught by staff from existing departments and might take the form of programmed learning or prescribed textbooks. One useful way of planning such a course is to start from Part 4, the projects, and work back, finding what problem areas, main subjects and basic subjects are most appropriate (see 6c below).

5.   Subjects and disciplines as related to general environmental courses. Several possible patterns are shown in diagram 3 ; again no time scale is specified.

6.   Some alternative models were put forward. Without elaborating them in full, the following points can be made.

   a) emphasis not only on community-oriented projects but on feedback of the results to the community, leading to the development of new projects.

   b) an important and continuing role for experts (professions or single discipline training) and for co-ordinators, and in general for the development of teamwork.

   c) Definition   necessary   necessary   Institutional structure
      of problem   knowledge   disciplines and teaching programme
      objectives

   d) skills of communication are vitally important, also decision theory, operational research and statistics.

7.   A shopping list of problem or theme areas not mutually exclusive but representing different emphases. Not meant to be exhaustive.

a) Man and environment, especially human variability, adaptability and perception.
b) Energy systems, natural and man-manipulated
c) Systems theory
d) Natural resources, conservation
e) The physical environment
f) The biological environment, ecology
g) Urban environments
h) Environmental pollution
i) The equilibrium society, including equilibrium population (ZPG) and equilibrium economy
j) Relevant problems, e.g. world population
k) Course totally project oriented.

8. Three project areas and the disciplines needed to support them. **Traffic in a community,** including social and economic pressures generating it, road planning, parking, regional planning, accidents, medical problems, economic problems, pollution, noise.

engineering
chemistry
ecology
sociology
systems theory
landscape architecture
economics
psychology
planning
statistics

A coastal recreation area including social and economic pressures, ecology and nature conservation carrying capacity, safety, pollution including litter and sanitation, regional planning, management.

ecology
economics
sociology
planning
landscape architecture
engineering

River pollution, including water supply, effluent disposal, fishing, general recreation, navigation, population, industry.

chemistry
biology
engineering
ecoromics
human physiology

Diagram 1

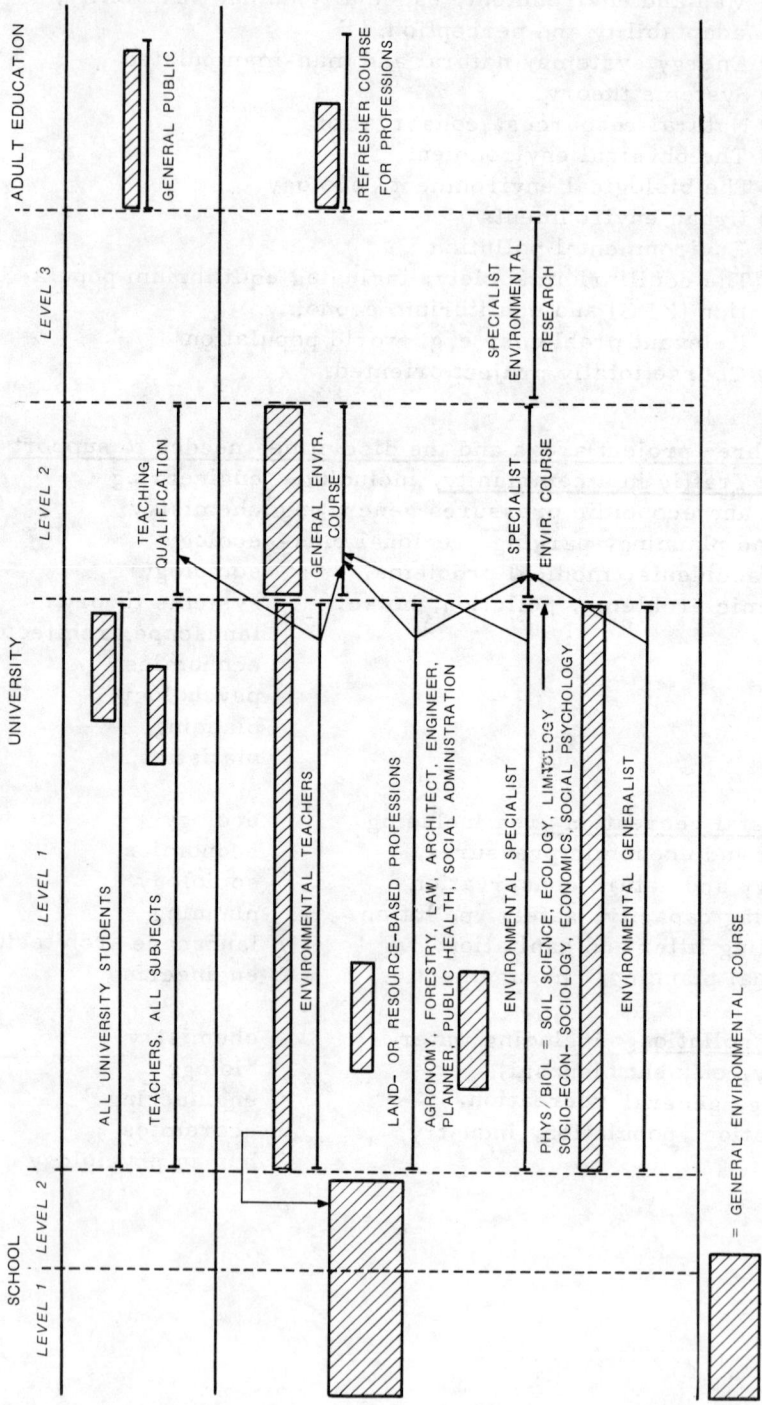

The thickness and length of this represents only a very tentative suggestion of the amount and duration of such a course.

SCHOOL — LEVEL 1 — LEVEL 2

UNIVERSITY — LEVEL 1 — LEVEL 2 — LEVEL 3

ADULT EDUCATION

ALL UNIVERSITY STUDENTS

TEACHERS, ALL SUBJECTS

ENVIRONMENTAL TEACHERS

LAND- OR RESOURCE-BASED PROFESSIONS

AGRONOMY, FORESTRY, LAW, ARCHITECT, ENGINEER, PLANNER, PUBLIC HEALTH, SOCIAL ADMINISTRATION

ENVIRONMENTAL SPECIALIST

PHYS/BIOL = SOIL SCIENCE, ECOLOGY, LIMNOLOGY
SOCIO-ECON = SOCIOLOGY, ECONOMICS, SOCIAL PSYCHOLOGY

ENVIRONMENTAL GENERALIST

TEACHING QUALIFICATION

GENERAL ENVIR. COURSE

SPECIALIST ENVIR. COURSE

SPECIALIST ENVIRONMENTAL RESEARCH

GENERAL PUBLIC

REFRESHER COURSE FOR PROFESSIONS

= GENERAL ENVIRONMENTAL COURSE

292

Diagram 2. A GENERAL ENVIRONMENTAL COURSE

1. Basic subjects

Biology	Geography	Chemistry
Sociology	Human biology	Biochemistry
Interscience	Systems theory	Statistics
Psychology, etc.		

Students would select certain of these
to supplement their own needs

2. Main subject　　　　　　　An alternative structure specified :

Ecology　　　　　　　　　　　Nature conservation
Environmental science　　　　　Land management
Socio-economic organisation　　Human welfare

3. Problems Integrating themes

Human tolerances
Energy resources
Growth of population

4. Project

Diagram 2a

POSSIBLE STRUCTURES

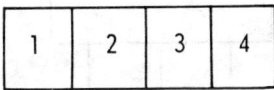

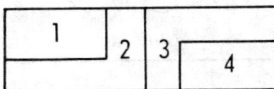

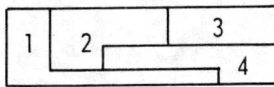

but not

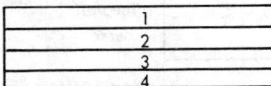

TIME

Diagram 2b

POSSIBLE SYSTEM OF OPTIONS

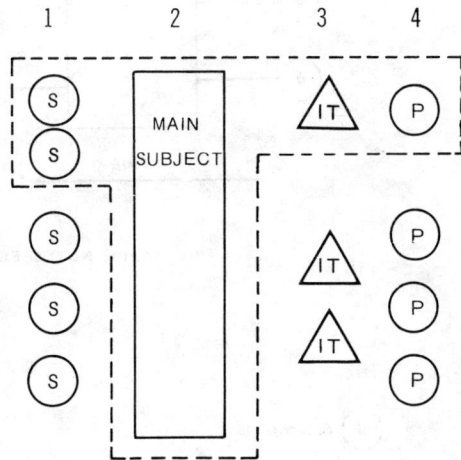

$\frac{1}{2}$ ONE STUDENT'S COURSE

Diagram 3

POSSIBLE RELATIONSHIPS OF SUBJECTS
AND GENERAL OR INTEGRATING COURSES

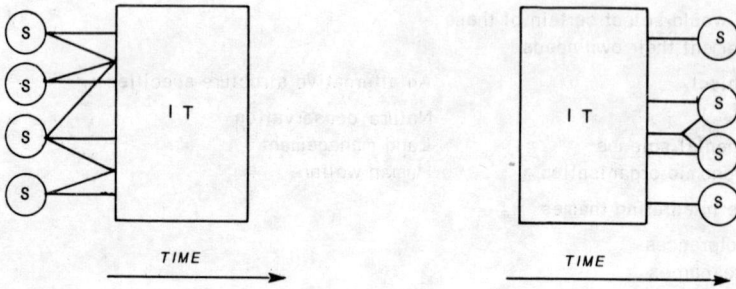

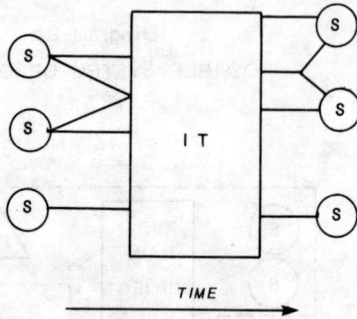

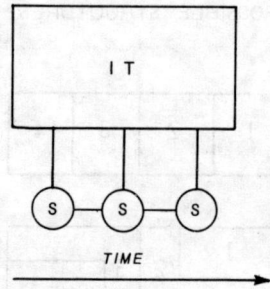

TIME

TIME SCALE NOT SPECIFIED

(S) Subject

| I T | Integrating course

294

REPORT OF WORKING GROUP N° 3

Chairman : O.I. RØNNING (Norway), Rapporteur : K.M. CLAYTON
(United Kingdom)

Working Group 3 abided by the best ecological principles
by recycling the same topics and the same arguments throughout
the day in a most economical way. In the end, a series of recommendations was reached, and it will focus this report if these
are set out first.

1.   The Swedish One-Year programme for graduates, set out
in Appendix 2, the Fornstedt report (1), represented a useful
example of the sort of course that could be offered at this level.
(Some detailed comments are set out below).

2.   A course teaching Environmental Studies could not be based
wholly on lectures, but would require other forms of tuition,
in particular work in laboratories. It would also require seminars or discussion groups, work by small groups in the field,
and possibly also questionnaires, simulation games, and participation in projects involving local problems.

3.   The teaching of such a broad course must necessarily be
carried out by a group of teachers working as a team, and that
the mutual instruction of such a team was quite as important
as the instruction offered to students taking the course.

4. International exchange of teachers and also of students would
assist both in the training of teachers in environmental subjects,
and also in the propagation of this approach to interdisciplinary
training. It was also thought that these international exchanges
would aid the adoption of a truly international view of environmental problems, for it is often impossible for countries to act
alone in these matters.

These, then, are the main conclusions reached at the end
of our discussions. They represent the unanimous opinion of

---

1) See Appendix 2.

this Group, although naturally there were minor reservations, particularly about the details of the Swedish programme. The Group was swift to adopt an agreed position on two main points, and these were taken for granted in the rest of the discussion. First, that it was convenient to accept three levels of instruction in Higher Education in which environmental studies were required :

i) the undergraduate degree level where many students might be introduced to environmental problems, while in other cases special comprehensive courses should be provided

ii) the immediate post-graduate level where a year might be available to give an environmental orientation to students trained in other subjects - the Swedish One-Year programme falls at this level

iii) the need to provide some instruction in environmental problems to such critical groups as leaders of public opinion, industrialists and politicians, not to mention the ordinary citizen. Some of the instruction provided at this level could reasonably be regarded as education, but some of it would have more the quality of propaganda.

The second point on which early agreement was reached was that there was no point in pursuing a discussion of the differentiation in educational requirements of specialists and generalists. This question was put aside at the beginning of the discussion, and the resolve and determination of the Group was so great that it was never seen again.

In the morning's discussion a distinction was drawn between courses that top up the training already received by (say) biologists with other aspects of the environment such as the economic and social environment within which we work, and those courses that attempt a complete survey of the 'whole' of environmental studies. It was agreed that topping up is the easier task, for the solid base of understanding exists, and it is usually clear what must be added. The complete training was seen to pose greater problems, and it was for this reason that later in the day the Swedish proposals were looked at in some detail.

One point of some significance here was that the Swedish delegate responsible for this course was present in the Group, and he was able to clarify many points about the aim and content of the course. This, as always, kept the discussion to the real points at issue and kept the discussants from straying far from the real problems that have to be faced. Some participants

echoed complaints that have already been heard within Sweden
that the course understresses the biological side of the environment. It was pointed out that to reach a compromise which
allows the teaching of all relevant topics within a restricted
time-scale leaves every subject feeling short of time to make
its points fully. As an aside, the Group took up some aspects
of this problem by considering how it was possible to identify
topics within existing fields which might be left out of the curriculum in order to leave time for full consideration of environmental matters. It was also pointed out that the course has to
leave out the important problem of non-renewable resources.

Agreement was reached that there was room for a change
of balance within the course to suit local circumstances, and
also that it would be appropriate to choose ecosystems that were
related to local circumstances in choosing illustrative examples.
Given this flexibility, the Group felt happy to recommend the
course, not as an unalterable framework, but as a good example
of a One-Year course at that level. One side issue that came up
was not specifically related to this course. This is how far it is
possible, or desirable, to allow freedom of choice within an
environmental education. There is here a conflict between a
need to give the student some freedom of choice, and the need
to cover adequately most of a very broad field. The choice was
agreed to be a difficult one, and was left unresolved, but it may
be noted that, once selected, the Swedish course allows no student choice of curriculum. Yet another related problem here
is the contrast between those larger countries with freedom of
choice between university courses, and those with much less
choice to offer the intending student.

At one stage in the afternoon, and not when the sun was
highest in the sky, the Group found itself discussing games. This
referred to the technique of using game theory and simulation
games to act out environmental situations outside the real world.
The idea was novel to many, but a number of cases were described. Where the involvement is emotional, there can of course
be dangers. At advanced level, the effort of preparation may
outweigh the educational gain. But there are advantages in the
approach and it is possible to acquire ready-made games in a
number of fields if it is thought worthwhile experimenting with
this technique. Certainly the Group was happy to add it to the
list of pedagogic techniques in its second resolution. There was
also some detailed discussion of examples of projects in the
teaching of environmental science, notably those involving participation in the problems of the local community. To this extent
it is difficult to improve on the realities of a real world solution,

297

despite the political complications of such involvement, and the difficulties of planning and teaching in a live situation.

Appendix 2

A SHORT REPORT ON ENVIRONMENTAL EDUCATION AT THE SWEDISH UNIVERSITIES AND INSTITUTES OF HIGHER EDUCATION

By Mr. Ulf FORNSTEDT
Secretary of Department
The Office of the Chancellor of the Swedish Universities

I. <u>INTRODUCTION</u>

1. BACKGROUND

Environmental education has of course been pursued at the universities and institutes of higher learning for many years. During the latter part of the 1960's some universities started short integrated undergraduate courses in environmental studies. These courses were sporadically distributed and were not included in the permanent study programs at the universities. When attention was drawn to environmental problems in public and political debates, an organized integrated environmental education was also called for. Very often the students themselves were urging on in this context.

In 1969 the Office of the Chancellor of the Swedish Universities (OCSU) initiated short introductory courses in environmental education at the universities. At the same time a committee was appointed to plan for a one-year course.

The OCSU requested in its budget proposals an improvement of the biological field of research in order to, among other things, be able to meet with the demands for research within the field of environmental problems.

2. GENERAL PRINCIPLES

Upon looking over the needs of environmental education the OCSU found - after having discussed the matter with specialists, teachers and students - that education at different levels and for different groups of students was needed. The committee appointed by the OCSU for the planning of this one-year course expresses this idea as follows :

"University and environmental education at the post-secondary school level can be divided essentially into four lines :

301

a) Knowledge, whose application can influence environment, must be brought about together with knowledge on how this is done. Concerning subjects and courses already available the contents must therefore be related to the aspects of environment control and to a larger extent than today.

b) The demand for an introductory course on environmental problems can be met with an interdisciplinary course which gives 10 points. Courses of this kind have been offered for some years. These courses are intended for students of different faculties and for those who are employed.

c) The need for research and the supply of highly qualified specialists within the different branches of environment will not be met with within the basic education. The training of researchers within branches will therefore be as necessary in the future as it is today. The training of researchers with special reference to environmental matters, which is pursued within some fields of study today, must be enlarged and strengthened as soon as possible.

d) Many persons with different vocational training deal directly with environmental problems in their professions, without being specialists of environment. A common advanced training will be required for them. This training should convey general knowledge about human environment, how man influences it and what effect this has on his possibilities to survive. The course should correspond to this demand for environmental education. "

II. CURRENT UNIVERSITY COURSES

1. SHORT INTRODUCTORY COURSES

As of spring semester 1970 every Swedish university arranges introductory environmental courses. These include ten weeks' full-time studies but are to some extent given in the evenings so that the actual time of study is twice as long. The objective of this education is : to teach basic knowledge and give a brief outline on environmental problems, to serve as a basis for a broader and more objective moulding of public opinion, and to give the student a basic training of his ability to critically use the knowledge concerning the environmental problems in their social context.

302

The courses are intended for students at universities and institutes of higher learning and for those who in their professions are concerned with environmental problems or who would like to be enlightened on these matters in general. Admission to the courses is free for all those who are 25 years of age and who have been working for five years. So far more than 1 600 students have completed these courses.

The main contents of the courses are described in Appendix 1.

2.   ONE-YEAR COURSES

The committee appointed by the OCSU made its report in 1969 and after it had been sent to the various institutions the first one-year course in environmental studies with 48 enrolled could start at the University of Lund during the spring semester of 1971. Since education within this field of study has just started, one does not yet know how the courses will work out. The committee based its proposal for a curriculum of studies on the following principles :

Disposition of the course of study

Knowledge of human environment intersects most sciences and therefore demands an interdisciplinary way of looking at things. This implies that all necessary knowledge cannot possibly be held by one person. Everyone who through his work has contact with environmental problems must have a good understanding of the field. The aim of the environmental studies program is to impart knowledge to make such an understanding possible.

Training of specialists

A broad outlook can never replace thorough knowledge of every branch of the field. Research training or some other lengthy work within a branch of the field is needed for this specialized knowledge. The course of study in question can neither provide nor replace this knowledge.

The objective of environmental education

In our current society a large number of resolutions are passed in which the decision-makers for the present are not aware of the risks their decisions are having upon the environment. That's why as many decision-makers as possible in different positions must complete their education with training in the field of environmental education.

Environmental education will - because of its very special nature - never alone enable the student to be qualified for any profession. The aim of this education must therefore be to provide the students with knowledge which will help them to perform their profession in a way which is in accordance with the demands of environment. The course of study will also enable the student to communicate with environmental experts.

Future employers

Public and local administrations, organizations and private enterprise are in need of persons whose vocational training has been completed with environmental education. There are a large number of posts, for which from society's point of view it would be reasonable to demand that vocational training be completed with environmental education. The environmental studies course will, of course, broaden the vocational training but the latter will be the basis for the securement of employment. An important field where many students will find employment is within the educational system. Students wishing to continue their studies for a Ph. D. degree to acquire specialized knowledge within some field of environmental education should be offered a possibility to - before this education starts, or, as a part of it - broaden their knowledge by studying environmental problems.

Qualifications

Since the objective of the course of environmental studies is, among other things, to supplement earlier acquired vocational training it should be taken as the last phase of this training. In so doing it can start at different levels during that phase. By finishing his education at a later stage of his studies, the student will be able to put the knowledge he has already acquired in relation to the whole.

Organization

The students' varying backgrounds make alternative courses necessary so that to some degree the knowledge differences can be levelled out. The alternative courses initiate the study course and consist of 12 points altogether. The remaining 28 points apply to the main education.

Alternative courses

The alternative courses are constructed like a module system in which the different parts give light on some important matters

on which the following part must be built. There are four courses which each are worth 6 points. The student is supposed to
choose at least two of these. The courses which the student
chooses depends on his earlier vocational training.

The main course

After the introductory alternative courses there are courses
which together give 28 points. The education is here the same
for all students. Co-operation and contact among the students
with different backgrounds makes it possible for them to exchange
knowledge and experiences among them and makes the contents
of the course more intense. One way of studying is through teamwork and seminars.

Laboratory work, demonstrations and field work

Laboratory work and demontrations are necessary in order
to give the students a realistic idea of the different environmental problems and methods to tackle them. The theoretical
education is supplemented not only by laboratory work and demonstrations but also by field work and field trips (connected
with these studies).

Practice

A real understanding of the acquired knowledge is first obtained
through the students' application of this knowledge.
The students' various frames of reference and knowledge give
possibilities for them to penetrate these problems. At the same
time as the studies are pursued the student also performs a
practical exercise which is accounted for at the seminars.

The OCSU supports these principles. On the basis of the committee's proposal for a curriculum and other points of view which
were delivered, the education has begun in accordance with a
curriculum, the contents and organisation of which are to be
found in Appendix 2.

3. COURSES AT INSTITUTES OF TECHNOLOGY AND OTHER INSTITUTES OF HIGHER LEARNING

Just as at the universities, environmental studies have been
pursued within different fields of study at different institutes of
higher learning. During the past years the institutes of higher
learning have taken various steps in creating an integrated environmental education. For instance, Chalmers Institute of

Technology has given a series of lectures on environmental problems of the metropolitan cities. Work is going on now to introduce short courses of environmental studies at the institutes of technology, colleges of agriculture, forestry and veterinary medicine. These institutes and colleges are all alike in having their teaching very well controlled which makes it more difficult to introduce comprehensive courses that do not specifically belong to their special field of study and that can be included in the different degrees. Environmental education will, however, expand during the next few years at these institutes and colleges. It should be noted that the students of the institutes and colleges mentioned above are entitled to enroll in these courses in environmental studies offered at the universities.

4.   ORGANIZATION AND PLACEMENT

a) All the courses of study within environmental education at the universities and institutes of higher learning are arranged at the existing departments. Different departments at different universities may arrange the same course of study, depending upon where the initiative originates and where appropriate teachers can be found. The teachers are recruited from different departments and faculties and co-operate in planning the integrated education. At the University of Lund a special environmental studies program has been started which is supervised by the University Council. On the Board of Directors are included teachers and students from different departments and faculties. This education is arranged independently of faculties and departments. The teaching is, however, confined to the departments.

b) The ten weeks' course as well as the one-year course may be included in the basic degree and are formally equally valuable to other courses at the university.

Since the government sponsors the environmental education no fees are charged and the students are entitled to study.Finally, it should be said that the above mentioned courses have been started as experiments. Discussions about them will continue and changes can be undertaken when the first results are presented.

Appendix 1

CURRICULUM FOR 10 WEEK INTRODUCTORY COURSE
ON POLLUTION AND NATURAL RESOURCE PLANNING

SOCIETY AND ENVIRONMENT	2 p
SOIL, DIFFERENT KINDS OF WASTES	2 p
WATER POLLUTION	2 p
AIR POLLUTION AND NOISE	2 p
INTRODUCTION	2 p

10 p ←

25 YEARS OF AGE, 5 YEARS WORKING

307

CURRICULUM FOR ONE-YEAR COURSE
ON ENVIRONMENTAL MANAGEMENT
AND NATURAL RESOURCE PLANNING

40 p

SOCIETY AND ENVIRONMENT (legislation, regional planning, nature conservancy, etc.)	5 p
ENVIRONMENTAL HYGIENE (biocides, toxicology, noise, etc.)	5 p
GENERAL ENVIRONMENTAL MANAGEMENT (air, water, soil)	8 p
AGRICULTURE, FORESTRY AND TECHNOLOGY AND THEIR EFFECTS ON NATURE	4 p
ECOLOGY AND GEOSCIENCE II	6 p

PLANNING AND ECONOMIC GEOGRAPHY	ECOLOGY AND GEOSCIENCE I	6 p
BASIC LAW AND ECONOMICS	BASIC CHEMISTRY, MEDICINE AND PHYSIOLOGY	6 p

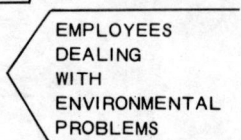

SCIENCE STUDENTS

SOCIAL SCIENCE STUDENTS

EMPLOYEES DEALING WITH ENVIRONMENTAL PROBLEMS

Appendix 3

LIST OF PARTICIPANTS
AT THE WORKSHOP OF TOURS

I. NATIONAL DELEGATES

AUSTRIA

Dr. H. TRAWL
Délégation permanente auprès de
l'OCDE
3 rue Albéric-Magnard
75016 - Paris

BELGIUM

Prof. P. DUVIGNEAUD
Laboratoire de Botanique Systé-
matique et d'Ecologie
Université Libre de Bruxelles
28 Avenue Héger
1050 - Bruxelles

Prof. J. HUBLE
Laboratoire d'Ecologie Animale
Université de Gand
Ledegankstraat, 35
B - 9000 Gand

CANADA

Dr. R. HURTUBISE
Vice-Recteur
Université du Québec à Montréal
1180 rue Bleury
Montréal

DENMARK

Prof. J. HEDEGAARD
Laboratory for Microbiology
Danmarks Polyteckniske Laereans-
talt Lundtoftevej n° 100
Bygn 221
DK Lyngby 2800 - Copenhague

Prof. S.E. JØRGENSEN
Civilingeniør M. SC.
Langkaer Vaenge 9
3500 Vaerløse
Copenhague

Prof. A. MUNK
Dr. Philosophy
Royal Danish School of Educational
Studies
Emdrupvej 101
2400 Copenhague N. W.

Amanuensis S. STRUWE
University of Copenhagen
Øster Farimagsgade 2 D
1353 Copenhague K

FINLAND

Prof. P. MIKOLA
Professor of Forest Biology
Dept. of Silviculture
University of Helsinki
Unioninkatu 40
Helsinki 17

Dr. P. SEISKARI
Member of the Secretariat of
the Environment Council
University of Helsinki
Helsinki

FRANCE

Mr. H. ASTIER
Directeur du 3ème Cycle d'Aménagement du Territoire et d'Ur-
banisme, Institut d'études Politiques
de Paris,
Chargé de Mission au Secrétariat
Général du Haut Comité de
l'environnement
4, rue de l'Abbaye
75006 - Paris

310

Mr. R. BENOIT
Directeur de l'U.E.R.
"Aménagement, Géographie,
Informatique", Centre d'Etudes
Supérieures de l'Aménagement
Université de Tours
Parc Grand'Mont
37 - Tours

GERMANY

Prof. Dr. EGLE
Botanisches Institut der
Johann Wolfgang Goethe - Universität
Siesmayerstrasse, 70
Frankfurt/Main

GREECE

Prof. C. CONOPHAGOS
Ecole Polytechnique d'Athènes
42, rue Patission
Athènes

Madame E. EVANGELIDOU-TSOLI
Docteur en Chimie
Ministère de la Coordination
3-5, rue Ippocratous
Athènes

IRELAND

The Rev. J.J. MOORE, S.J.
Lecturer in Botany
University College Dublin
Dublin, 4

Mr. K. NOWLAN
Lecturer in Urban Planning
University College Dublin
Dublin

ITALY

Prof. G. BACCI
Directeur de l'Institut de Zoologie
de l'Université de Turin
Turin

NETHERLANDS	Prof. Dr. D. J. KUENEN General Director of the Research Institute for Nature Management Professor of Environmental Biology University of Leiden Wolfhezerweg 91 Wolfheze
	Prof. Dr. R.L. ZIELHUIS University of Amsterdam Coronel Laboratory for Occupational Medecine and Environmental Health Eerste Constantijn Huygensstraat 20 Amsterdam
NORWAY	Prof. F.R. FØRSUND Institute of Economics Blindern University of Oslo Oslo 3
	Prof. S. SKJESETH The Agricultural College of Norway 1430 Aas
SPAIN	Dr. Arch. ANTONIO F. ALBA Catedra de Elementos de Composicion Escuela de Arquitectura Avenida Juan de Herrera Ciudad Universitaria Madrid
SWEDEN	Mr. Ulf FORNSTEDT Head of Section The Office of the Chancellor of the Swedish Universities Box 163 34 S - 103 26 Stockholm 16
	Prof. Nils MALMER University of Lund Department of Plant Ecology Ostra Vallgatan 14 S 223 61 Lund

Prof. STIG NORDQVIST
Nordiska-Institutet
för Samhällsplanering
Skeppsholmen
11149 Stockholm

SWITZERLAND   Dr. T. CONRAD
                   Chef de Section
                   Institut fédéral pour l'aménagement,
                   l'épuration et la protection de l'eau
                   Uberlandstrasse 133
                   8600 Dübendorf
                   Zürich

TURKEY   Dr. S.C. ÖZOĞLU
                   Executive Secretary of the Group on
                   the Education of Young Scientists in
                   Turkish Scientific and Technical
                   Research Council
                   (Tubitak)
                   Türkiye Bilimsel ve Teknik Araş-
                   tirma Kurumu
                   Bayindir Sokak n° 33
                   Ankara

II. EXPERTS

CANADA   Prof. G. FRANCIS
                   Chairman
                   Department of Man-Environment
                   Studies Division of Environmental
                   Studies, University of Waterloo
                   Waterloo
                   Ontario

DENMARK   Prof. Dr. B.O. HOLMA
                   Institute of Hygiene
                   University of Copenhagen
                   Blegdamsvej 21
                   2100 Copenhagen

FRANCE

Prof. J.M. ABILLON
Maître-Assistant
Université de Paris VII
4, rue de la Fontaine
91 - Gif-sur-Yvette

Prof. R. BUVET
Faculté des Sciences
Université de Paris VI
Laboratoire énergétique électro-
chimique
10, rue Vauquelin
75005 - Paris

Prof. M.H. BOISOT
Maître de Conférence
Ecole Nationale des Ponts et
Chaussées
10, rue de Marignan
75008 - Paris

Prof. F. BOURLIERE
Professeur Agrégé à la Faculté
de Médecine de Paris, Président
du Programme Biologique International
45, rue des Saints-Pères
Paris

Madame J. de FELICE
Université de Paris VII
"Etude du Milieu"
31, rue de Turin
75008 - Paris

Mr. A. GILBERT
Etudiant au Centre d'Etudes
Supérieures de l'Aménagement
Université de Tours
Parc Grandmont
37 - Tours

Prof. V. LABEYRIE
Directeur du Laboratoire d'Ecologie
Expérimentale
Centre d'Etudes Supérieures de
l'Aménagement
Université de Tours
Parc Grandmont
37 - Tours

Prof. A. ROUSSEL
Professeur Agrégé à la Faculté
de Médecine de Paris
Directeur Adjoint de l'INSERM
44, Chemin de Ronde
78 - Le Vésinet

GERMANY

Dr. Erich HODL
Institut für Makro-Und Struktur-
planung, Technische Hochschule
Darmstadt Institute for Social and
Economic Planning
61 Darmstadt, Schloss

Prof. Dr. H. MISLIN
Director
Institut für Physiologische Zoologie
Mainz Universität
Postfach 3980
6500 Mainz

NORWAY

Dr. Olaf I. RØNNING
Professeur d'Ecologie
Universitetet I Trondheim, NLHT
Botanisk Institutt
7000 Trondheim

SPAIN

Prof. SILVA DELGADO
Architect
Professor of the Institute of
Local Administration
Zurbaran 19, 6°
Madrid, 4

UNITED KINGDOM

Mr. R.A. BECHER
Assistant Director
The Nuffield Foundation,
Nuffield Lodge, Regent's Park
London, N.W.1.

Prof. K.M. CLAYTON
Dean of the School of
Environmental Sciences
University of East Anglia
Norwich NOR 88C

Prof. P.J. NEWBOULD
Professor of Biology
The New University of Ulster
Coleraine
Co. Londonderry
Northern Ireland

UNITED STATES

Prof. E.W. WEIDNER
Chancellor
University of Wisconsin - Green Bay
2309 Bay Settlement Road
Green Bay
Wisconsin 54301

Prof. K.E. SCHAEFER
Director of the Department of
Physiology
Groton
Connecticut. 06040

III. OBSERVERS

E.E.C.

Mr. M. CARPENTIER
Chef de Division
Direction Générale des Affaires
Industrielles, Technologiques
et Scientifiques
61, rue des Belles-Feuilles
75016 - Paris

Conseil of Europe	Miss P. GIONGO Division de l'Enseignement Supérieur et de la Recherche Conseil de l'Europe Place Lenôtre 67 - Strasbourg
UNESCO	Mr. F.E. ECKARDT Spécialiste du Programme Ecologie et Conservation UNESCO Place de Fontenoy 75007 - Paris
W.H.O.	Prof. S. JANKOVIC 1211 Genève 27

IV. SECRETARIAT   P. DUGUET, CERI

V. FRENCH OFFICIALS ATTENDING THE CLOSING SESSION
OF THE WORKSHOP

- Ministry of Environment :

M.R. POUJADE, Minister,
MM. BARRE and SERVAT, Technical advisers,

- Academic representatives :

M. G. ANTOINE, Recteur de l'Académie d'Orléans-Tours,
M. J. BODY, Président de l'Université de Tours.

- Local Authorities :

M. J. PENEL, Préfet d'Indre et Loire,
M. J. ROYER, Député-Maire de Tours,
M. M. TROCHU, Adjoint au Député-Maire de Tours.

- M. F. VALERY : Ambassador, Head of the French Delegation to the OECD

- OECD :

M. G. ELDIN, Deputy Secretary-General,
M. J.R. GASS, Director of CERI.

Appendix 4

LIST OF BACKGROUND PAPERS

(available by request from OECD-CERI, 2, rue André Pascal
75016 - Paris. France)

CERI/HE/CP/71.02   M.H. Boisot (France) - A tentative operational approach to the problems of the environment

CERI/HE/CP/71.03   O.I. Rønning (Norway) - Some Thoughts about Curricula and Organisation of Environmental Education

CERI/HE/CP/71.04   P.J. Newbould (U.K.) - The Teaching of Environmental Studies at University Level

CERI/HE/CP/71.05   H. Mislin (Germany) - Protection of the Environment and Nature Conservation

CERI/HE/CP/71.06   G.R. Francis (Canada) - Objectives and Approaches to Environmental Education : Some first reflections from a beginning experiment

CERI/HE/CP.71.07   K.M. Clayton (U.K.) - Environmental Science at the University of East Anglia

CERI/HE/CP/71.08   E.W. Weidner (U.S.A.) - Environmental Education : Implications for Institutional Structure

319

CERI/HE/CP/71.09   V. Labeyrie (France) - Objectives,
                       content organisation of resource -
                       development and resource - mana-
                       gement education

CERI/HE/CP/71.13   K.E. Schaefer (U.S.A.) - Critical
                       Analysis of the Eight Working Papers

CERI/HE/CP/70.29   M.H. Boisot (France) - Discipline,
                       interdisciplinarity, and interdisci-
                       plinarity programme

CERI/HE/CP/70.26   E.W. Weidner (U.S.A.) - The Uni-
                       versity of Wisconsin-Green Bay :
                       an example of a university oriented
                       towards Environmental Problems

CERI/HE/CP/70.22   J.L. Michaud and M. Paoletti
                       (France) - Example of a theoretical
                       mode of an Interdisciplinary Uni-
                       versity oriented towards environ-
                       mental problems

OECD SALES AGENTS
DEPOSITAIRES DES PUBLICATIONS DE L'OCDE

ARGENTINE
Libreria de las Naciones
Alsina 500, BUENOS AIRES.

AUSTRALIA – AUSTRALIE
B.C.N. Agencies Pty, Ltd.,
178 Collins Street, MELBOURNE 3000.

AUSTRIA – AUTRICHE
Gerold and Co., Graben 31, WIEN 1.
Sub-Agent: GRAZ: Buchhandlung Jos. A. Kien-
reich, Sackstrasse 6.

BELGIUM – BELGIQUE
Librairie des Sciences
Coudenberg 76-78
B 1000 BRUXELLES 1.

BRAZIL — BRESIL
Mestre Jou S.A., Rua Guaipá 518,
Caixa Postal 24090, 05000 SAO PAULO 10.
Rua Senador Dantas 19 s/205-6, RIO DE
JANEIRO GB.

CANADA
Information Canada
OTTAWA.

DENMARK – DANEMARK
Munksgaards Boghandel
Nørregade 6
1165 KØBENHAVN K.

FINLAND – FINLANDE
Akateeminen Kirjakauppa
Keskuskatu 1
00100 HELSINKI 10.

FORMOSA – FORMOSE
Books and Scientific Supplies Services, Ltd.
P.O.B. 83, TAIPEI,
TAIWAN.

FRANCE
Bureau des Publications de l'OCDE
2 rue André-Pascal, 75775 PARIS CEDEX 16
Principaux sous dépositaires :
PARIS : Presses Universitaires de France,
49 bd Saint-Michel, 75005 Paris.
Sciences Politiques (Lib.)
30 rue Saint-Guillaume, 75007 Paris.
13100 AIX-EN-PROVENCE : Librairie de l'Université.
38000 GRENOBLE : Arthaud.
67000 STRASBOURG : Berger-Levrault.
31000 TOULOUSE : Privat.

GERMANY – ALLEMAGNE
Deutscher Bundes-Verlag G.m.b.H.
Postfach 9380, 53 BONN.
Sub-Agent : HAMBURG : Reuter-Klöckner ;
und in den massgebenden Buchhandlungen
Deutschlands.

GREECE – GRECE
Librairie Kauffmann, 28 rue du Stade,
ATHENES 132.
Librairie Internationale Jean Mihalopoulos et Fils
75 rue Hermou, B.P. 73, THESSALONIKI.

ICELAND – ISLANDE
Snaebjörn Jónsson and Co., h.f.,
Hafnarstræti 4 and 9
P.O.B. 1131
REYKJAVIK

INDIA – INDE
Oxford Book and Stationery Co.:
NEW DELHI, Scindia House.
CALCUTTA, 17 Park Street.

IRELAND – IRLANDE
Eason and Son, 40 Lower O'Connell Street,
P.O.B. 42, DUBLIN 1.

ISRAEL
Emanuel Brown :
35 Allenby Road, TEL AVIV
also at
9 Shlomzion Hamalka Street, JERUSALEM.
48 Nahlath Benjamin Street, TEL AVIV.

ITALY – ITALIE
Libreria Commissionaria Sansoni :
Via Lamarmora 45, 50121 FIRENZE.
Via Bartolini 29, 20155 MILANO.
Sous-dépositaires :
Editrice e Libreria Herder,
Piazza Montecitorio 120, 00186 ROMA.
Libreria Hoepli, Via Hoepli 5, 20121 MILANO.
Libreria Lattes, Via Garibaldi 3, 10122 TORINO.
La diffusione delle edizioni OCDE è inoltre assicu-
rata dalle migliori librerie nelle città più importanti.

JAPAN – JAPON
OECD Publications Centre,
Akasaka Park Building,
2-3-4 Akasaka,
Minato-ku
TOKYO 107 (Tel.(03)586 20 16)
Maruzen Company Ltd.,
6 Tori-Nichome Nihonbashi, TOKYO 103,
P.O.B. 5050, Tokyo International 100-31.

LEBANON – LIBAN
Documenta Scientifica/Redico
Edison Building, Bliss Street,
P.O.Box 5641
BEIRUT

THE NETHERLANDS – PAYS-BAS
W.P. Van Stockum
Buitenhof 36, DEN HAAG.

NEW ZEALAND – NOUVELLE-ZELANDE
The Publications Officer
Government Printing Office
Mulgrave Street (Private Bag)
WELLINGTON
and Government Bookshops at
AUCKLAND (P.O.B. 5344)
CHRISTCHURCH (P.O.B. 1721)
HAMILTON (P.O.B. 857)
DUNEDIN (P.O.B. 1104).

NORWAY – NORVEGE
Johan Grundt Tanums Bokhandel,
Karl Johansgate 41/43, OSLO 1.

PAKISTAN
Mirza Book Agency, 65 Shahrah Quaid-E-Azam,
LAHORE 3.

PORTUGAL
Livraria Portugal,
Rua do Carmo 70-74
LISBOA 2

SPAIN – ESPAGNE
Libreria Mundi Prensa
Castelló, 37
MADRID-1

SWEDEN – SUEDE
Fritzes Kungl. Hovbokhandel,
Fredsgatan 2,
11152 STOCKHOLM 16.

SWITZERLAND – SUISSE
Librairie Payot, 6 rue Grenus,.1211 GENEVE 11
et à LAUSANNE, NEUCHATEL, VEVEY,
MONTREUX, BERNE, BALE, ZURICH.

TURKEY – TURQUIE
Librairie Hachette,
469 Istiklal Caddesi,
Beyoglu
ISTANBUL et
14 E Ziya Gökalp Caddesi
ANKARA

UNITED KINGDOM – ROYAUME-UNI
H.M. Stationery Office, P.O.B. 569, LONDON
SE1 9 NH
or
49 High Holborn
LONDON WC1V 6HB (personal callers)
Branches at: EDINBURGH, BIRMINGHAM,
BRISTOL, MANCHESTER, CARDIFF,
BELFAST.

UNITED STATES OF AMERICA
OECD Publications Center, Suite 1207,
1750 Pennsylvania Ave, N.W.
WASHINGTON, D.C. 20006. Tel.: (202)298-8755.

VENEZUELA
Libreria del Este, Avda. F. Miranda 52,
Edificio Galipan, Aptdo. 60 337, CARACAS 106.

YUGOSLAVIA – YOUGOSLAVIE
Jugoslovenska Knjiga, Terazije 27, P.O.B. 36,
BEOGRAD.

Les commandes provenant de pays où l'OCDE n'a pas encore désigné de dépositaire
peuvent être adressées à :
OCDE, Bureau des Publications, 2 rue André-Pascal, 75775 Paris CEDEX 16
Orders and inquiries from countries where sales agents have not yet been appointed may be sent to
OECD, Publications Office, 2 rue André-Pascal, 75775 Paris CEDEX 16